Jonathan Swift

The Prose Works Of Jonathan Swift D.D.

Vol IV

Jonathan Swift

The Prose Works Of Jonathan Swift D.D.
Vol IV

ISBN/EAN: 9783741103575

Manufactured in Europe, USA, Canada, Australia, Japa

Cover: Foto ©Andreas Hilbeck / pixelio.de

Manufactured and distributed by brebook publishing software
(www.brebook.com)

Jonathan Swift

The Prose Works Of Jonathan Swift D.D.

Jonathan Swift

THE PROSE WORKS

OF

JONATHAN SWIFT, D.D.

EDITED BY

TEMPLE SCOTT

WITH A BIOGRAPHICAL INTRODUCTION BY

THE RT. HON. W. E. H. LECKY, M.P.

VOL. IV

LONDON

GEORGE BELL AND SONS

1898

CHISWICK PRESS:—CHARLES WHITTINGHAM AND CO.
TOOKS COURT, CHANCERY LANE, LONDON.

SWIFT'S
WRITINGS ON RELIGION
AND THE CHURCH

VOL. II

EDITED BY

TEMPLE SCOTT.

LONDON
GEORGE BELL AND SONS
1898

CONTENTS.

NOTE.

THE portrait which forms the frontispiece to this volume is taken, by permission, from the painting in the possession of the Earl of Howth, K.P.

A LETTER

FROM A MEMBER OF THE HOUSE OF COMMONS IN IRELAND TO
A MEMBER OF THE HOUSE OF COMMONS IN ENGLAND

CONCERNING THE

SACRAMENTAL TEST.

WRITTEN IN THE YEAR 1708.

NOTE.

IN the "foreword" to the reprint of this tract in the "Miscellanies" of 1711, Swift remarks: "I have been assured that the suspicion which the supposed author lay under for writing this letter absolutely ruined him with the late ministry." The "late ministry" was the Whig ministry of which Godolphin was the Premier. To this ministry the repeal of the Test Act was a matter of much concern. To test the effect of such a repeal it was determined to try it in Ireland first. There the Presbyterians had distinguished themselves by their loyalty to William and the Protestant succession. These, therefore, offered a good excuse for the introduction of such a measure, particularly when, in 1708, an invasion was rumoured, they were the first to send in loyal addresses to the Queen. Swift likened this method to "that of a discreet physician, who first gives a new medicine to a dog, before he prescribes it to a human creature." Further, the Speaker of the Irish House had come over to England to agitate for the repeal. On this matter Swift wrote to Archbishop King, under date April 15th (the letter was first published by Mr. John Forster in his "Life of Swift," p. 246), as follows: "Some days ago my Lord Somers entered with me into discourse about the Test clause, and desired my opinion upon it, which I gave him truly, though with all the gentleness I could; because, as I am inclined and obliged to value the friendship he professes for me, so he is a person whose favour I would engage in the affairs of the First Fruits. . . . If it became me to give ill names to ill things and persons, I should be at a loss to find bad enough for the villainy and baseness of a certain lawyer of Ireland [Speaker Brodrick, afterwards Lord Midleton], who is in a station the least of all others excusable for such proceedings, and yet has been going about most industriously to all his acquaintance of both houses towards the end of the session to show the necessity of taking off the Test clause in Ireland by an act here, wherein you may be sure he had his brother's assistance. If such a project should be resumed next session, and I in England, unless your grace send me your absolute commands to the contrary, which I should be sorry to receive, I could hardly forbear publishing some paper in opposition to it, or leaving one behind me, if there should be occasion." In August of the same year the agitation for the repeal was renewed, and in December Swift published his "Letter on the Sacramental Test," writing as if from Dublin and as a member of the Irish House of Commons. When he writes to King in the following month he makes a mild attempt to convince the Archbishop that the pamphlet was not of his authorship. "The author has gone out of his way to reflect on me as a person likely to write for repealing the test, which I am sure is very unfair treatment. This is all I am likely to get by the company I keep. I am used like a sober man with a drunken face, have the scandal of the vice without the satisfaction." But King was not deceived. In his reply to Swift he simply remarks : "You need not be concerned : I will engage you will lose nothing by that paper." Swift, however, lost more than the Archbishop thought; for "that paper" led to his severance from the Whigs, and, in after life, to much contumely cast on his character for being a political renegade. Because "he was not Whig enough;" because he would not forsake his Church for his party, critics and biographers have thought fit to make little of him, and to compare him to his discredit with contemporaries whose intellects he held in the palm of his hand, and to whom he might have stood as a moral exemplar.

Swift refers to this tract in his "Memoirs relating to the change in the Queen's Ministry," as follows :—"It was everybody's opinion, that the Earl of Wharton would endeavour, when he went to Ireland, to take off the test, as a step to have it taken off here : upon which I drew up and printed a pamphlet, by way of a letter from a member of parliament here, shewing the danger to the Church by such an intent. Although I took all care to be private, yet the Lieutenant's chaplain, and some others guessed me to be the author, and told his Excellency their suspicions; whereupon I saw him no more until I went to Ireland."

The tract is one of the most favourable specimens of Swift's controversial method and trenchant satire. The style is excellent—forcible and pithy; while the arguments are like most of Swift's arguments, aptly to the point with yet a potentiality of application which fits them for the most general statement of the principles under discussion. Scott considers the pamphlet "as having materially contributed to the loss of the bill for repeal of the Test Act during the Earl of Pembroke's viceroyalty."

In the same year Swift wrote "A Letter to a Member of Parliament in Ireland on choosing a new Speaker there." This short tract bears also on the question of the Test; but it is not included in this volume, since it was intended as an electioneering pamphlet.

I have been unable to obtain access to a copy of the first edition of the "Letter on the Sacramental Test." The text here given is that of the "Miscellanies" of 1711, collated with that given in the "Miscellanies," 1728, and with those printed by Faulkner, Hawkesworth, and Scott.

[T. S.]

A LETTER CONCERNING THE SACRAMENTAL TEST.

ADVERTISEMENT.[1]

THE following letter is supposed by some judicious persons to be of the same author, and, if their conjectures be right, it will be of no disadvantage to him to have it revived, considering the time when it was writ, the persons then at the helm, and the designs in agitation, against which this paper so boldly appeared. I have been assured that the suspicion which the supposed author lay under for writing this letter, absolutely ruined him with the late ministry. I have taken leave to omit about a page which was purely personal, and of no use to the subject.

Dublin, Dec. 4, 1708.

SIR,

I received your letter, wherein you tell me of the strange representations made of us on your side of the water. The instance you are pleased to mention is that of the Presbyterian missionary, who, according to your phrase, hath been lately persecuted at Drogheda for his religion : But it is easy to observe, how mighty industrious some people have been for three or four years past, to hand about stories of the hardships, the merits, the number, and the power of the Presbyterians in Ireland, to raise formidable ideas of the dangers of Popery there, and to transmit all for England, improved by great additions, and with special care to have

---

[1] This " Advertisement " is taken from " Miscellanies in Prose and Verse," printed for John Morphew, 1711. On page 314 of that volume it forms a "foreword" to "A Letter concerning the Sacra-

them inserted with comments in those infamous weekly papers that infest your coffee-houses. So, when the clause enacting a Sacramental Test was put in execution, it was given out in England, that half the justices of peace through this kingdom had laid down their commissions; whereas upon examination, the whole number was found to amount only to a dozen or thirteen, and those generally of the lowest rate in fortune and understanding, and some of them super-annuated. So, when the Earl of Pembroke was in Ireland and the Parliament sitting, a formal story was very gravely carried to his Excellency by some zealous members, of a priest newly arrived from abroad to the north-west parts of Ireland, who had publicly preached to his people, to fall a-murdering the Protestants ; which, though invented to serve an end they were then upon, and are still driving at, it was presently handed over, and printed with shrewd remarks by your worthy scribblers. In like manner, the account of that person who was lately expelled our university for reflecting on the memory of King William, what a dust it raised, and how foully it was related, is fresh enough in memory.[1] Neither

mental Test." It is omitted from the reprint in the " Miscellanies " of 1728. The page which Swift says he has taken leave to omit can-not be identified. Probably this was another of Swift's manœuvres for concealing the identity of the author. The "Advertisement" of George Faulkner to his edition of Swift's Works (vol. iv., 1735) is as follows :

" In the second volume of Doctor Swift's and Mr. Pope's 'Miscel-lanies,' I found the following treatise, which had been printed in London, with some other of the Dean's works, many years before, but at first came out by itself in the year 1708, as the date shews : And it was at a juncture when the Dissenters were endeavouring to repeal the Sacramental Test, as by common fame, and some pamphlets published to the same purpose, they seem to be now again attempting, with great hope of success. I have, therefore, taken the liberty to make an extract out of that discourse, omitting only some passages which relate to certain persons, and are of no consequence to the argument. But the author's weight of reasoning seems at present to have more weight than it had in those times, when the discourse first appeared.

"The author, in this letter, personates a Member of Parliament here [Dublin], to a Member of Parliament in England.

" The Speaker mentioned in this letter was Allen Broderick, after-wards Chancellor and Lord Middleton ; and the prelate was Dr. Lyndsay, afterwards Lord Primate." [T. S.]

[1] The Provost and Fellows of Trinity College, Dublin, had lately expelled Edward Forbes for the cause mentioned in the text. [S.]

would people be convinced till the university was at the pains of publishing a Latin paper to justify themselves. And, to mention no more, this story of the persecution at Drogheda, how it hath been spread and aggravated, what consequences have been drawn from it, and what reproaches fixed on those who have least deserved them, we are already informed. Now if the end of all this proceeding were a secret and mystery, I should not undertake to give it an interpretation, but sufficient care hath been taken to give it sufficient explanation.[1] First, by addresses artificially (if not illegally) procured, to shew the miserable state of the dissenters in Ireland by reason of the Sacramental Test, and to desire the Queen's intercession that it might be repealed. Then it is manifest that our Speaker, when he was last year in England, solicited, in person, several members of both Houses, to have it repealed by an act there, though it be a matter purely national, that cannot possibly interfere with the trade and interest of England, and though he himself appeared formerly the most zealous of all men against the injustice of binding a nation by laws to which they do not consent. And lastly, those weekly libellers, whenever they get a tale by the end relating to Ireland, without ever troubling their thoughts about the truth, always end it with an application against the Sacramental Test, and the absolute necessity there is of repealing it in both kingdoms. I know it may be reckoned a weakness to say anything of such trifles as are below a serious man's notice; much less would I disparage the understanding of any party to think they would choose the vilest and most ignorant among mankind, to employ them for assertors of a cause. I shall only say, that the scandalous liberty those wretches take would hardly be allowed, if it were not mingled with opinions that *some men* would be glad to advance. Besides, how insipid soever those papers are, they seem to be levelled to the understandings of a great number; they are grown a necessary part in coffee-house furniture, and some time or other may happen to be read by customers of all ranks, for curiosity and amusement; because they lie always in the way. One of these authors (the fellow that was

---

[1] Faulkner prints: "But sufficient care hath been taken to explain it." [T. S.]

pilloried I have forgot his name)[1] is indeed so grave, sen-
tentious, dogmatical a rogue, that there is no enduring him;
the *Observator*[2] is much the brisker of the two, and I think
farther gone of late in lies and impudence, than his Presbyterian brother.   The reason why I mention him, is to have
an occasion of letting you know, that you have not dealt so
gallantly with us, as we did with you in a parallel case: Last
year, a paper was brought here from England, called, "A
Dialogue between the Archbishop of Canterbury and Mr.
Higgins," which we ordered to be burnt by the common
hangman, as it well deserved; though we have no more to
do with his Grace of Canterbury[3] than you have with the
Archbishop of Dublin[4]; nor can you love and reverence
your prelate more than we do ours, whom you tamely suffer
to be abused openly, and by name, by that paltry rascal of
an *Observator;* and lately upon an affair wherein he had no
concern; I mean the business of the missionary at Drogheda,
wherein our excellent primate was engaged, and did nothing

---

[1] Daniel Defoe (1663?-1731), the son of a Cripplegate butcher.
Entered business as a hosier, but failed. In 1695 he was appointed one
of the commissioners for duties on glass. Wrote "The True Born
Englishman" (1701); "The Shortest Way with the Dissenters," for
which he was pilloried, fined, and imprisoned; and numerous other
works, including "Robinson Crusoe;" "Life of Captain Singleton;"
"History of Duncan Campbell;" "Life of Moll Flanders;" "Roxana;"
"Life of Colonel Jack;" "Journal of the Plague;" "History of the
Devil;" and "Religious Courtship." He edited a paper called "The
Review," to which Swift here refers, and against which Charles Leslie
wrote his "Rehearsals." [T. S.]

[2] John Tutchin, a virulent writer of the reign of James II. For a
political work in defence of Monmouth he was sentenced by Judge
Jefferies to be whipped through several market towns. He wrote the
"Observator" (begun April, 1702), and suffered at the hands of the
Tories for his writings. He died in great poverty in 1708, at the age of
forty-seven. He was also the author of a play entitled, "The Unfor-
tunate Shepherd." Pope refers to these punishments meted out to
Defoe and Tutchin, in the second book of the "Dunciad":

> "Earless on high, stood unabashed De Foe,
> And Tutchin flagrant from the scourge below." [T. S.]

[3] Dr. Thomas Tenison (1636-1715), born at Cottenham, Cambridge-
shire. For his attacks on the Roman Catholics he was in 1691 created
Bishop of Lincoln. He was made Archbishop of Canterbury in 1694.
He wrote a "Discourse of Idolatry," an answer to Hobbes, and published several sermons. [T. S.]

[4] Dr. William King. See vol. iii., p. 241, note. [T. S.]

but according to law and discretion. But because the Lord Archbishop of Dublin hath been upon several occasions of late years, misrepresented in England, I would willingly set you right in his character. For his great sufferings and eminent services he was by the late King promoted to the see of Derry. About the same time, he wrote a book to justify the Revolution, wherein was an account of King James's proceedings in Ireland, and the late Archbishop Tillotson recommended it to the King as the most serviceable treatise that could have been published at such a juncture.[1] And as his Grace set out upon those principles, he has proceeded so ever since, as a loyal subject to the Queen, entirely for the succession in the Protestant line, and for ever excluding the Pretender; and though a firm friend to the Church, yet with indulgence toward dissenters, as appears from his conduct at Derry, where he was settled for many years among the most virulent of the sect; yet upon his removal to Dublin, they parted from him with tears in their eyes, and universal acknowledgments of his wisdom and goodness. For the rest, it must be owned, he does not busy himself by entering deep into any party, but rather spends his time in acts of hospitality and charity, in building of churches, repairing his palace, in introducing and preferring the worthiest persons he can find, without other regards; in short, in the practice of all virtues that can become a public or private life. This and more, if possible, is due to so excellent a person, who may be justly reckoned among the greatest and most learned prelates of his age, however his character may be defiled by such mean and dirty hands as those of the *Observator* or such as employ him.[2]

I now come to answer the other part of your letter, and shall give you my opinion freely about repealing the Sacra-

[1] Dr. King was twice imprisoned in the castle of Dublin after the landing of King James in Ireland in 1699, and narrowly escaped assassination. The title of the work alluded to is: "The State of the Protestants in Ireland under the late King James's Government, in which their carriage towards him is justified, and the absolute necessity of their endeavouring to be freed from his Government, and of submitting to their present Majesties, is demonstrated." [S.]

[2] The portion of this paragraph beginning with "The reason why I mention him," to the end, "such as employ him," is omitted by Faulkner. [T. S.]

mental Test; only whereas you desire my thoughts as a
friend, and not as I am a member of parliament, I must
assure you they are exactly the same in both capacities.

I must begin by telling you, we are generally surprised at
your wonderful kindness to us on this occasion, it being so
very industrious to teach us to see our interest in a point
where we are so unable to see it ourselves.   This hath given
us some suspicion ; and though in my own particular, I am
hugely bent to believe, that whenever you concern yourselves
in our affairs, it is certainly for our good, yet I have the misfortune to be something singular in this belief, and therefore
I never attempt to justify it, but content myself to possess
my own opinion in private, for fear of encountering men of
more wit or words than I have to spare.

We at this distance, who see nothing of the spring of
actions, are forced by mere conjecture to assign two reasons
for your desiring us to repeal the Sacramental Test : One is,
because you are said to imagine it will be one step towards
the like good work in England : The other more immediate,
that it will open a way for rewarding several persons who
have well deserved upon a great occasion, but who are now
unqualified through that impediment.

I do not frequently quote poets, especially English, but I
remember there is in some of Mr Cowley's love verses, a
strain that I thought extraordinary at fifteen, and have often
since imagined it to be spoken by Ireland :

> " Forbid it Heaven my life should be
> Weigh'd with her least conveniency : "

In short, whatever advantage you propose to yourselves
by repealing the Sacramental Test, speak it out plainly, 'tis
the best argument you can use, for we value your interest
much more than our own : If your little finger be sore, and
you think a poultice made of our vitals will give it any ease,
speak the word and it shall be done ; the interest of our whole
kingdom is at any time ready to strike to that of your poorest
fishing towns ; it is hard you will not accept our services,
unless we believe at the same time that you are only consulting our profit, and giving us marks of your love.   If
there be a fire at some distance, and I immediately blow up
my house before there be occasion, because you are a man

of quality, and apprehend some danger to a corner of your stable; yet why should you require me to attend next morning at your levee with my humble thanks for the favour you have done me?

If we might be allowed to judge for ourselves, we had abundance of benefit by the Sacramental Test, and foresee a number of mischiefs would be the consequence of repealing it, and we conceive the objections made against it by the dissenters are of no manner of force : They tell us of their merits in the late war in Ireland, and how cheerfully they engaged for the safety of the nation ; that had they thought they had been fighting only other people's quarrels, perhaps it might have cooled their zeal ; and that for the future, they shall sit down quietly and let us do our work ourselves ; nay, that it is necessary they should do so, since they cannot take up arms under the penalty of high treason.

Now supposing them to have done their duty, as I believe they did, and not to trouble them about the *fly on the wheel;* I thought Liberty, Property and Religion had been the three subjects of the quarrel, and have not all those been amply secured to them? Had they not at that time a mental reservation for power and employments? And must these two articles be added henceforward in our national quarrels? It is grown a mighty conceit among some men to melt down the phrase of a *Church Established by law* into that of the *Religion of the Magistrate;* of which appellation it is easier to find the reason than the sense: If by the magistrate they mean the prince, the expression includes a falsehood; for when King James was prince,[1] the Established Church was the same it is now. If by the same word they mean the Legislature, we desire no more. Be that as it will, we of this kingdom believe the Church of Ireland to be the National Church, and the only one established by law, and are willing by the same law to give a toleration to dissenters: But if once we repeal our Sacramental Test, and grant a toleration, or suspend the execution of the penal laws, I do not see how we can be said to have any Established Church remaining ; or rather why there will not be as many established churches, as there are sects of dissenters. No, say they, yours will still be the

---

[1] The words from "the expression" to "was prince" are omitted by Faulkner in his edition. [T. S.]

National Church, because your bishops and clergy are
maintained by the public; but, that, I suppose, will be of no
long duration, and it would be very unjust it should, because, to speak in Tindal's phrase,[1] it is not reasonable that
revenues should be annexed to one opinion more than
another, when all are equally lawful, and 'tis the same author's
maxim, that no freeborn subject ought to pay for maintaining
speculations he does not believe. *But why should any man,
upon account of opinions he cannot help, be deprived of the
opportunity of serving his Queen and country?* Their zeal is
commendable, and when employments go a begging for
want of hands, they shall be sure to have the refusal, only
upon condition they will not pretend to them upon maxims
which equally include atheists, Turks, Jews, infidels, and
heretics, or which is still more dangerous, even Papists
themselves; the former you allow, the other you deny,
because these last own a foreign power, and therefore must
be shut out.   But there is no great weight in this; for their
religion can suit with free states, with limited or absolute
monarchies, as well as a better, and the Pope's power in
France is but a shadow; so that upon this foot there need
be no great danger to the constitution by admitting Papists
to employments.   I will help you to enough of them who
shall be ready to allow the Pope as little power here as you
please; and the bare opinion of his being vicar of Christ
is but a speculative point, for which no man it seems ought
to be deprived of the capacity of serving his country.

But, if you please, I will tell you the great objection we
have against repealing this same Sacramental Test.   It is,
that we are verily persuaded the consequence will be an
entire alteration of religion among us in a no great compass
of years.   And, pray observe, how we reason here in Ireland
upon this matter.

We observe the Scots in our northern parts, to be a brave,
industrious people, extremely devoted to their religion, and
full of an undisturbed affection towards each other.   Numbers
of that noble nation, invited by the fertilities of the soil, are
glad to exchange their barren hills of Loquabar, by a voyage
of three hours, for our fruitful vales of Down and Antrim, so

---

[1] See vol. iii., p. 9, note.   [T. S.]

productive of that grain, which, at little trouble and less expense finds diet and lodging for themselves and their cattle.[1] These people by their extreme parsimony, wonderful dexterity in dealing, and firm adherence to one another, soon grow into wealth from the smallest beginnings, never are rooted out where they once fix, and increase daily by new supplies; besides when they are the superior number in any tract of ground, they are not over patient of mixture; but such, whom they cannot assimilate, soon find it their interest to remove. I have done all in my power on some land of my own to preserve two or three English fellows in their neighbourhood, but found it impossible, though one of them thought he had sufficiently made his court by turning Presbyterian. Add to all this, that they bring along with them from Scotland a most formidable notion of our Church, which they look upon at least three degrees worse than Popery; and it is natural it should be so, since they come over full fraught with that spirit which taught them to abolish Episcopacy at home.

Then we proceed farther, and observe, that the gentlemen of employments here, make a very considerable number in the House of Commons, and have no other merit but that of doing their duty in their several stations; therefore when the Test is repealed, it will be highly reasonable they should give place to those who have much greater services to plead. The commissions of the revenue are soon disposed of, and the collectors and other officers throughout this kingdom, are generally appointed by the commissioners, which give them a mighty influence in every country. As much may be said of the great officers in the law; and when this door is open to let dissenters into the commissions of the peace, to make them High Sheriffs, Mayors of Corporations, and officers of the army and militia; I do not see how it can be otherwise, considering their industry and our supineness, but that they may in a very few years grow to a majority in the House of Commons, and consequently make themselves the national religion, and have a fair pretence to demand the revenues of the Church for their teachers. I know it will be objected,

---

[1] From this passage, perhaps, Johnson derived the famous definition of oats, in his Dictionary, as the food of horses in England, and of men in Scotland. [S.]

that if all this should happen as I describe, yet the Presbyterian religion could never be made the national by act of
Parliament, because our bishops are so great a number in
the House of Lords, and without a majority there, the Church
could not be abolished.   But I have two very good ex-
pedients for that, which I shall leave you to guess, and I
dare swear our Speaker here has often thought on, especially
having endeavoured at one of them so lately.   That this
design is not so foreign from some people's thoughts, I must
let you know that an honest bellwether [1] of our house (you
have him now in England, I wish you could keep him there)
had the impudence some years ago, in Parliament time, to
shake my Lord Bishop of Kilaloe [2] by his lawn sleeve, and
tell him in a threatening manner, "that he hoped to live to
see the day when there should not be one of his order in the
kingdom."

These last lines perhaps you think a digression; therefore
to return : I have told you the consequences we fully reckon
upon from repealing the Sacramental Test, which although
the greatest number of such as are for doing it, are actually
in no manner of pain about it, and many of them care not
threepence whether there be any Church, or no; yet because
they pretend to argue from conscience as well as policy and
interest, I thought it proper to understand and answer them
accordingly.

Now, sir, in answer to your question, whether if an attempt
should be made here for repealing the Sacramental Test, it
would be likely to succeed?   The number of professed dissenters in this Parliament was, as I remember, something
under a dozen, and I cannot call to mind above thirty others
who were expected to fall in with them.   This is certain, that
the Presbyterian party having with great industry mustered
up their forces, did endeavour one day upon occasion of a
hint in my Lord Pembroke's speech, to introduce a debate
about repealing the Test clause, when there appeared at
least four to one odds against them ; and the ablest of those
who were reckoned the most staunch and thorough-paced
Whigs upon all other occasions, fell off with an abhorrence
at the first mention of this.

[1] Supposed to be Mr. Broderick. [F.]
[2] Dr. Lindsay, afterwards Lord Primate. [S.]

I must desire you to take notice, that the terms of Whig and Tory, do not properly express the different interests in our parliament. I remember when I was last in England, I told the King, that the highest Tories we had with us would make tolerable Whigs there; this was certainly right, and still in the general continues so, unless you have since admitted new characteristics, which did not come within our definition.[1] Whoever bears a true veneration for the glorious memory of King William, as our great deliverer from Popery and slavery; whoever is firmly loyal to our present Queen, with an utter abhorrence and detestation of the Pretender; whoever approves the succession to the Crown in the House of Hanover, and is for preserving the doctrine and discipline of the Church of England, with an indulgence for scrupulous consciences; such a man we think acts upon right principles, and may be justly allowed a Whig: And I believe there are not six members in our House of Commons, who may not fairly come under this description. So that the parties among us are made up, on one side, of moderate Whigs, and on the other, of Presbyterians and their abettors; by which last I mean, such who can equally go to a Church or Conventicle, or such who are indifferent to all religion in general, or lastly such who affect to bear a personal rancour toward the clergy: These last are a set of men not of our own growth, their principles at least have been imported of late years; yet this whole party put together will not, I am confident, amount to above fifty men in Parliament, which can hardly be worked up into a majority of three hundred.

As to the House of Lords, the difficulty there is conceived at least as great as in ours. So many of our temporal peers live in England, that the bishops are generally pretty near a par of the House, and we reckon they will be all to a man against repealing the Test; and yet their lordships are generally thought as good Whigs upon our principles as any in the kingdom. There are indeed a few lay lords who appear to have no great devotion for Episcopacy; and perhaps one or two more with whom certain powerful motives might be used for removing any difficulty whatsoever; but

[1] The passage beginning with " I remember when I was last in England," and ending with "within our definition," is omitted by Faulkner. [T. S.]

these are in no sort of a number to carry any point against
the conjunction of the rest and the whole bench of bishops.

Besides, the whole body of our clergy is utterly against
repealing the Test, though they are entirely devoted to her
Majesty, and hardly one in a hundred who are not very good
Whigs in our acceptation of the word. And I must let you
know, that we of Ireland are not yet come up to other folk's
refinements; for we generally love and esteem our clergy,
and think they deserve it; nay, we are apt to lay some weight
upon their opinion, and would not willingly disoblige them,
at least unless it were upon some greater point of interest than
this. And their judgment in the present affair is the more to
be regarded, because they are the last persons who will be
affected by it: This makes us think them impartial, and that
their concern is only for religion and the interest of the kingdom. Because the act which repeals the Test, will only
qualify a layman for an employment, but not a Presbyterian or
Anabaptist preacher for a church-living. Now I must take
leave to inform you, that several members of our House, and
myself among the rest, knowing some time ago what was
upon the anvil, went to all the clergy we knew of any distinction, and desired their judgment of the matter, wherein
we found a most wonderful agreement; there being but one
divine that we could hear of in the whole kingdom, who
appeared of a contrary sentiment, wherein he afterwards
stood alone in the convocation, very little to his credit,
though, as he hoped, very much to his interest.

I will now consider a little the arguments offered to shew
the advantages, or rather the necessity, of repealing the Test
in Ireland. We are told, the Popish interest is here so
formidable, that all hands should be joined to keep it under;
that the only names of distinction among us ought to be
those of Protestant and Papist, and that this expedient is the
only means to unite all Protestants upon one common
bottom. All which is nothing but misrepresentation and
mistake.

If we were under any real fear of the Papists in this kingdom, it would be hard to think us so stupid, not to be equally
apprehensive with others, since we are likely to be the
greatest, and more immediate sufferers; but on the contrary,
we look upon them to be altogether as inconsiderable as the

women and children. Their lands are almost entirely taken from them, and they are rendered incapable of purchasing any more; and for the little that remains, provision is made by the late act against Popery, that it will daily crumble away: To prevent which, some of the most considerable among them are already turned Protestants, and so in all probability will many more. Then, the Popish priests are all registered, and without permission (which I hope will not be granted) they can have no successors; so that the Protestant Clergy will find it perhaps no difficult matter to bring great numbers over to the Church; and in the meantime, the common people without leaders, without discipline, or natural courage, being little better than "hewers of wood, and drawers of water," are out of all capacity of doing any mischief, if they were ever so well inclined. Neither are they at all likely to join in any considerable numbers with an invader, having found so ill success when they were much more numerous and powerful; when they had a prince of their own religion to head them, had been trained for some years under a Popish deputy, and received such mighty aids from the French king.

As to that argument used for repealing the Test, that it will unite all Protestants against the common enemy, I wonder by what figure those gentlemen speak who are pleased to advance it: Suppose in order to increase the friendship between you and me, a law should pass that I must have half your estate; do you think that would much advance the union between us? Or, suppose I share my fortune equally between my own children, and a stranger whom I take into my protection; will that be a method to unite them? 'Tis an odd way of uniting parties, to deprive a majority of part of their ancient right, by conferring it on a faction who had never any right at all, and therefore cannot be said to suffer any loss or injury if it be refused them. Neither is it very clear, how far some people may stretch the term of common enemy. How many are there of those that call themselves Protestants, who look upon our worship to be idolatrous as well as that of the Papists, and with great charity put Prelacy and Popery together, as terms convertible?

And, therefore, there is one small doubt, I would be willingly satisfied in before I agree to the repealing of the

IV.   C

Test; that is, whether, these same Protestants, when they have by their dexterity made themselves the national religion, and disposed the Church revenues among their pastors or themselves, will be so kind to allow us dissenters, I do not say a share in employments, but a bare toleration by law? The reason of my doubt is, because I have been so very idle as to read above fifty pamphlets, written by as many Presbyterian divines, loudly disclaiming this idol Toleration, some of them calling it (I know not how properly) a rag of Popery, and all agreeing it was to establish iniquity by law. Now, I would be glad to know when and where their successors have renounced this doctrine, and before what witnesses.   Because, methinks I should be loth to see my poor titular bishop *in partibus*, seized on by mistake in the dark for a Jesuit, or be forced myself to keep my chaplain disguised like my butler, and steal to prayers in a back room,. as my grandfather[1] used in those times when the Church of England was malignant.

But this is ripping up old quarrels long forgot; Popery is now the common enemy, against which we must all unite; I have been tired in history with the perpetual folly of those states who call in foreigners to assist them against a common enemy : But the mischief was, those allies would never be brought to allow that the common enemy was quite subdued. And they had reason ; for it proved at last, that one part of the common enemy was those who called them in, and so the allies became at length the masters.

 'Tis agreed among naturalists that a lion is a larger, a stronger, and more dangerous enemy than a cat; yet if a man were to have his choice, either a lion at his foot, bound fast with three or four chains, his teeth drawn out, and his claws pared to the quick, or an angry cat in full liberty at his throat; he would take no long time to determine.

I have been sometimes admiring the wonderful significancy of that word persecution, and what various interpretations it hath acquired even within my memory.   When I

---

[1] This is Thomas Swift, vicar of Goodrich, in Herefordshire, "much distinguished by his courage, as well as his loyalty to King Charles the First, and the sufferings he underwent for that prince, more than any person of his condition in England." See the "Fragment of Autobiography," printed by Scott and Forster in their Lives of Swift. [T. S.]

was a boy, I often heard the Presbyterians complain that they were not permitted to serve God in their own way; they said they did not repine at our employments, but thought that all men who live peaceably ought to have liberty of conscience, and leave to assemble. That impediment being removed at the Revolution, they soon learned to swallow the Sacramental Test and began to take very large steps, wherein all that offered to oppose them, were called men of a persecuting spirit. During the time the Bill against Occasional Conformity was on foot, persecution was every day rung in our ears, and now at last the Sacramental Test itself has the same name. Where then is this matter likely to end, when the obtaining of one request is only used as a step to demand another? A lover is ever complaining of cruelty while anything is denied him, and when the lady ceases to be cruel, she is from the next moment at his mercy: So persecution it seems, is everything that will not leave it in men's power to persecute others.

There is one argument offered against a Sacramental Test, by a sort of men who are content to be styled of the Church of England, who perhaps attend its service in the morning, and go with their wives to a conventicle in the afternoon, confessing they hear very good doctrine in both. These men are much offended that so holy an institution as that of the Lord's Supper should be made subservient to such mercenary purposes as the getting of an employment. Now, it seems, the law, concluding all men to be members of that Church where they receive the Sacrament; and supposing all men to live like Christians (especially those who are to have employments) did imagine they received the Sacrament in course about four times a year, and therefore only desired it might appear by certificate to the public, that such who took an office were members of the Church established, by doing their ordinary duty. However, lest we should offend them, we have often desired they would deal candidly with us; for if the matter stuck only there, we would propose it in parliament, that every man who takes an employment should, instead of receiving the sacrament, be obliged to swear, that he is a member of the Church of Ireland by law established, with Episcopacy, and so forth;

and as they do now in Scotland, *to be true to the Kirk*. But
when we drive them thus far, they always retire to the main
body of the argument, urge the hardship that men should
be deprived the liberty of serving their Queen and country,
on account of their conscience : And, in short, have recourse
to the common style of their half brethren.   Now whether
this be a sincere way of arguing, I will appeal to any other
judgment but theirs.

There is another topic of clamour somewhat parallel to
the foregoing : It seems, by the Test clause, the military
officers are obliged to receive the Sacrament as well as the
civil.   And it is a matter of some patience to hear the dissenters declaiming upon this occasion : They cry they are
disarmed, they are used like Papists; when an enemy
appears at home, or from abroad, they must sit still, and see
their throats cut, or be hanged for high treason if they offer
to defend themselves.   Miserable condition ! Woful dilemma!
It is happy for us all, that the Pretender was not apprized of
this passive Presbyterian principle, else he would have infallibly landed in our northern parts, and found them all sat
down in their formalities, as the Gauls did the Roman
senators, ready to die with honour in their callings.   Sometimes to appease their indignation, we venture to give them
hopes that in such a case the government will perhaps connive, and hardly be so severe to hang them for defending it
against the letter of the law ; to which they readily answer,
that they will not lie at our mercy, but let us fight our battles
ourselves.   Sometimes we offer to get an act, by which upon
all Popish insurrections at home, or Popish invasion from
abroad, the government shall be empowered to grant commissions to all Protestants whatsoever, without that persecuting circumstance of obliging them to say their prayers
when they receive the Sacrament; but they abhor all
thoughts of occasional commissions, they will not do our
drudgery, and we reap the benefit: It is not worth their
while to fight *pro aris et focis*, and they had rather lose their
estates, liberties, religion and lives, than the pleasure of
governing.

But to bring this discourse toward a conclusion : If the
dissenters will be satisfied with such a toleration by law as
hath been granted them in England, I believe the majority

of both Houses will fall readily in with it; farther it will be
hard to persuade this House of Commons, and perhaps
much harder the next. For, to say the truth, we make a
mighty difference here between suffering thistles to grow
among us, and wearing them for posies. We are fully convinced in our consciences, that *we* shall always tolerate
them, but not quite so fully that *they* will always tolerate us,
when it comes to their turn; and *we* are the majority, and
we are in possession.

He who argues in defence of a law in force, not antiquated
or obsolete, but lately enacted, is certainly on the safer side,
and may be allowed to point out the dangers he conceives
to foresee in the abrogation of it.

For if the consequences of repealing this clause, should
at some time or other enable the Presbyterians to work
themselves up into the National Church; instead of uniting
Protestants, it would sow eternal divisions among them.
First, their own sects, which now lie dormant, would be
soon at cuffs again with each other about power and preferment; and the dissenting Episcopals, perhaps discontented to such a degree, as upon some fair unhappy
occasion, would be able to shake the firmest loyalty, which
none can deny theirs to be.

Neither is it very difficult to conjecture from some late
proceedings, at what a rate this faction is likely to drive
wherever it gets the whip and the seat. They have already
set up courts of spiritual judicature in open contempt of
the laws: They send missionaries everywhere, without
being invited, in order to convert the Church of England
folks to Christianity. They are as vigilant as *I know who*,
to attend persons on their death-beds, and for purposes
much alike. And what practices such principles as these
(with many other that might be invidious to mention) may
spawn when they are laid out to the sun, you may determine
at leisure.

Lastly, Whether we are so entirely sure of their loyalty
upon the present foot of government as you may imagine,
their detractors make a question, which however, does, I
think, by no means affect the body of dissenters; but the
instance produced is, of some among their leading teachers
in the north, who having refused the Abjuration Oath, yet

continue their preaching, and have abundance of followers. The particulars are out of my head, but the fact is notorious enough, and I believe has been published ; I think it a pity, it has not been remedied.

Thus, I have fairly given you, Sir, my own opinion, as well as that of a great majority in both Houses here, relating to this weighty affair, upon which I am confident you may securely reckon. I will leave you to make what use of it you please.

I am, with great respect, Sir,

Yours, &c.

THE PRESBYTERIANS' PLEA
OF MERIT.

NOTE.

THE reference casually made by Swift, in his " Letter on the Sacramenal Test," to his grandfather and the "malignant Church," probably points to one of the causes for his persistent dislike towards the Protes'ant dissenters. His attitude displays a profound disgust both for their teaching and their conduct; and he found, very early, occasion to ridicule them, as may be seen in his description of Jack, Martin, and Peter in "A Tale of a Tub" (see vol. i. of this edition). In spite, however, of this attitude, Swift seems to have remained silent on the question of the repeal of the Test Act for a period of more than twenty years. He had published his " Letter from a Member of the House of Commons in Ireland " in 1708; but it was not until 1731 that he again took up his pen against Dissent.

In that year, and in the two subsequent ones, the Presbyterians fought very strenuously for a mitigation of the laws against them; and the literature which has been handed down to us of that fight is by no means insignificant. The tracts which we know to be of Swift's authorship are: "The Presbyterians' Plea of Merit" (1731); "A Narrative of the several Attempts which the Dissenters of Ireland have made for a repeal of the Sacramental Test" (1731); "The Advantages proposed by Repealing the Sacramental Test impartially considered" (1732); "Queries Relating to the Sacramental Test" (1732); "Reasons humbly offered to the Parliament of Ireland for Repealing the Test in favour of Roman Catholics" (1733); "Some Few Thoughts Concerning the Test;" and, according to Sir Walter Scott, "Ten Reasons for Repealing the Test Act."

Monck Mason, in his elaborate note on this particular literature of the period (see " History of St. Patrick's Cathedral," pp. 387, 388, notes), gives a list of sixteen pamphlets, many of which he considers to be so well written that they would have done no discredit to Swift himself. The list is here transcribed for the benefit of the student:

(i.) "Nature and Consequences of the Sacramental Test considered; with Remarks humbly offered for the Repeal of it." 1732.

(ii.) "Remarks on a Pamphlet, entitled, 'The Nature and Consequences of the Sacramental Test Considered.'" Dublin, 1732, 12mo.

(iii.) "The History of the Test Act: in which the Mistakes in some Writings against it are Rectified, and the Importance of it to the Church explained." Printed at London and Dublin: and reprinted by George Faulkner. 1733, 12mo.

(iv.) "Plain Reasons against the Repeal of the Test Act; humbly offered to publick Consideration." Dublin: printed by George Faulkner. 1733, 12mo.

(v.) "The Test Act Examined by the Test of Reason." Dublin, 1733, 12mo.

(vi.) "The Case of the Episcopal Dissenters in Scotland, and that of the Dissenters in Ireland Compared; with Relation to Toleration, and a Capacity for Civil Offices. In a Letter to a Member of Parliament." Dublin, 1733, 8vo.

¶ This tract refers to another entitled: "The Tables Turned against the Presbyterians; or, Reasons against the Sacramental Test, by a General Assembly of Scotland."

(vii.) " The Case of the Test Considered, with respect to Ireland." Dublin, Faulkner, 1733.

(viii.) "The natural Impossibilities of better Uniting Protestants &c. by Repealing the Test." Dublin : Printed by George Faulkner, 1733.

(ix.) "Ten Reasons for Repealing the Test Act."

¶ Scott reprints this as Swift's from the broadside original.

(x-xi.) "A Vindication of the Protestant Dissenters from the Asper- sions Cast upon them in a late Pamphlet, entitled, ' The Presbyterians' Plea of Merit &c.,' with some Remarks on a Paper called ' The Correspondent,' giving a pretended Narrative, &c."

¶ Swift refers to this pamphlet in his " Roman Catholic Reasons for Repealing the Test." It is also noted by the printer of the undated second edition of the London reprint of " The Plea."

(xii.) " The Dispute Adjusted, about the *proper time* of applying for a Repeal of the Corporation and Test Acts : by shewing that *no time is proper*. By the Reverend Father in God, Edmund Lord Bishop of London."

¶ Faulkner, in the second edition of " The Presbyterians' Plea," advertises this tract to appear in 1733. The author of " The Case of the Episcopal Dissenters in Scotland " mentions that it has been " lately re-printed" in Ireland, but that it is "falsely ascribed to the Bishop of London."

(xiii.) "The Test Act considered in a Political Light." 1733. Broadside.

(xiv.) "Queries upon the Demand of the Presbyterians to have the Sacramental Test Repealed at this Session of Parliament." 1733. Broadside.

¶ These Queries differ somewhat from those put by Swift in 1732.

(xv.) "A Letter from a Freeman of a certain Burrough, in the North of Ireland, to his Friend and Representative in Parliament; shewing Reasons why the Test Act should not be Repealed." 1733. Broadside.

(xvi.)   " The Grunter's Request
                  To take Off the Test."
                            [A Poem.] 1733. 12mo.

Scott suggests (" Life of Jonathan Swift," 1824, p. 401) that " probably more occasional tracts " were written by the Dean on the subject of the Test " than have yet been recovered." The curious student may satisfy himself on this matter by reading the above pamphlets. Neither Monck Mason, Dr. Barrett, nor Scott himself, cared to take upon themselves to decide whether any of them were by Swift; nor have any of the Dean's modern biographers thrown any light on the subject. A point to note in this consideration is the fact that Faulkner, in his collected edition of Swift's works, did not include any of these; and, as he himself published many of them, he would certainly have known something of their authorship.

Swift's agitation against the repeal of the Test was so successful that the Irish House of Commons found itself in a majority for the Test. In addition to the prose tracts Swift wrote a stinging poem "On the Words Brother Protestants and Fellow Christians," an expression familiarly used by the advocates for the Repeal of the Test Act. This poem brought him into personal conflict with one Serjeant Bettesworth, who "openly swore, before many hundreds of people, that upon the first opportunity, by the help of ruffians, he would murder or maim the Dean of St. Patrick's." The lines to which the Serjeant took exception were :

> "Thus at the bar the booby Bettesworth,
> Though half-a-crown o'erpays his sweat's worth;
> Who knows in law, nor text, nor margent,
> Calls Singleton his brother serjeant."

The affair ended in the further ridicule of Bettesworth, who complained in the Irish House of Commons that the lampoon had cost him £1,200 a year. A full account of Swift's interview with Bettesworth is given by Swift in a letter to the Duke of Dorset, dated January, 1733-1734; and the "Grub Street Journal" for August 9th, 1734, tells how the inhabitants of the City of Dublin came to Swift's aid. Perhaps Bettesworth finally found consolation in the thought, satirically suggested by Dr. William Dunkin, that, after all, it might be worth the loss of money to be "transmitted to posterity in Dr. Swift's works."

> "For had he not pointed me out, I had slept till
> E'en Doomsday, a poor insignificant reptile ;
> Half lawyer, half actor, pert, dull, and inglorious,
> Obscure, and unheard of—but now I'm notorious :
> Fame has but two gates, a white and a black one;
> The worst they can say is, I got in at the back one :
> If the end be obtained 'tis equal what portal
> I enter, since I'm to be render'd immortal :
> So clysters applied to the anus, 'tis said,
> By skilful physicians, give ease to the head—
> Though my title be spurious, why should I be dastard,
> A man is a man though he should be a bastard.
> Why sure 'tis some comfort that heroes should slay us,
> If I fall, I would fall by the hand of Æneas ;
> And who by the Drapier would not rather damn'd be,
> Than demigoddized by madrigal Namby." [1]

Scott, and all Swift's editors and biographers, state that "The Presbyterians' Plea of Merit" was first published in 1731. What

---

[1] Namby was the nickname for Ambrose Philips.

authority they have for this statement, I have not been able to discover. My own research has, so far, failed to find a copy of it with the date, 1731, on the title-page. The edition upon which the present text is based, is that printed by Faulkner in 1733, of the title-page of which, a facsimile is here given. This, I believe to be the first edition. Scott, following Nichols, states that in the first edition of "The Plea," the "Ode to Humphry French, Esq.," appeared, and that in the second edition, this ode was omitted to make room for the "Narrative of the Several Attempts made for the Repeal of the Test Act." Now in the British Museum, there are two *undated* editions of "The Plea," which bear out this statement; but these, as the title-pages inform us, are London reprints of Dublin editions. Since, however, no one has recorded dated Dublin editions corresponding exactly to these London reprints, the evidence of the reprints counts for very little. Monck Mason, a very accurate authority, usually, says distinctly, "The Plea" was printed in 1731, and a second edition issued in 1733; but one gathers from his note that the only edition in his possession was that of 1733, and this has neither the "Ode" nor the "Narrative"; the last page consisting of an advertisement of the collected editions of Swift's works, which Faulkner was then preparing. The first of the London reprints bears no indication of any particular edition; the second has the words "second edition" on the title-page. In his note to this reprint of the "Narrative," and in his "Life of Swift," Scott refers to a Dublin periodical called "The Correspondent" (in which the "Narrative" was first published) as being printed in 1731. The only edition of this periodical, of which I have either seen or heard, is the copy in the British Museum, and that copy distinctly states: "Printed by James Hoey in Skinner-Row, 1733." If, therefore, this be the first edition of "The Correspondent," the "Narrative" must be ascribed to the year 1733, and the second edition of "The Plea" to the end of the same, or the beginning of the following year. I conclude, therefore, first, that the first edition of "The Plea" is that dated "Dublin, 1733;" second, that the undated London reprint with the "Ode" is of the same year; and, lastly, that the undated second London reprint with the "Narrative," is probably of the year, 1734.

Examining Scott's text of this tract, one is forced to the conclusion that he could not have seen the Dublin edition of 1733; whereas, its almost exact similarity to the London reprint suggests that he used that.

For purposes of the present text all three editions have been collated with one another, and with those given by Faulkner, Hawkesworth and Scott.

[T. S.]

THE
Presbyterians PLEA
OF
MERIT;

In Order to take off the

TEST,

Impartially Examined.

DUBLIN:

Printed and fold by GEORGE FAULKNER, in
Eſſex-ſtreet, oppoſite to the *Bridge*, 1733.

THE PRESBYTERIANS PLEA OF MERIT.

WE have been told in the common newspapers, that all attempts are to be made this session by the Presbyterians, and their abettors, for taking off the Test, as a kind of preparatory step, to make it go down smoother in England. For, if once their light would so shine, the Papists, delighted with the blaze, would all come in, and dance about it. This I take to be a prudent method; like that of a discreet physician, who first gives a new medicine to a dog, before he prescribes it to a human creature.[1]

The Presbyterians have, ever since the Revolution, directed their learned casuists to employ their pens on this subject; by shewing the merits and pretensions upon which they claim this justice; as founded upon the services they did toward the restoration of King Charles the Second; and at the Revolution under the Prince of Orange. Which pleas I take to be the most singular, in their kind, that ever were offered in the face of the sun, against the most glaring light of truth, and against a continuation of public facts, known to all Europe for twenty years together. I shall, therefore, impartially examine the merits and conduct of the Presbyterians, upon those two great events; and the pretensions to favour, which they challenge upon them.

Soon after the Reformation of the Church in England, under Edward the Sixth, upon Queen Mary's succeeding to the crown, who restored Popery, many Protestants fled out of England, to escape the persecution raised against the Church, as her brother had left it established. Some of

---

[1] See note prefixed to the " Letter on the Sacramental Test." [T. S.]

these exiles went to Geneva; which city had received the doctrine of Calvin, and rejected the government of bishops; with many other refinements. These English exiles readily embraced the Geneva system; and having added farther improvements of their own, upon Queen Mary's death returned to England; where they preached up their own opinions; inveighing bitterly against Episcopacy, and all rites and ceremonies, however innocent and ancient in the Church: building upon this foundation; to run as far as possible from Popery, even in the most minute and indifferent circumstances: this faction, under the name of Puritan, became very turbulent, during the whole reign of Queen Elizabeth; and were always discouraged by that wise queen, as well as by her two successors. However, their numbers, as well as their insolence and perverseness, so far increased, that soon after the death of King James the First, many instances of their petulancy and scurrility, are to be seen in their pamphlets, written for some years after; which was a trade they began in the days of Queen Elizabeth: particularly with great rancour against the bishops, the habits, and the ceremonies: Such were that scurrilous libel under the title of Martin Mar-prelate,[1] and several others. And, although the Earl of Clarendon [2] tells us, that, until the year 1640, (as I remember) the kingdom was in a state of perfect peace and happiness, without the least appearance of thought or design toward making any alterations in religion or govern-

[1] According to Mr. Edward Arber the writers of these famous tracts were the Rev. John Penny and Job Throckmorton, Esq. He calls these two writers "the most eminent prose satirists of the Elizabethan age." For a full account of these tracts and the controversy, see Mr. Arber's "Introductory Sketch to the Martin Mar-prelate Controversy, 1588-1590 (1879, English Scholar's Library). The aim of the Mar-prelate writers is thus stated by the able author of that sketch: "To ridicule and affront a proud hierarchy [the bishops] endowed with large legal means of doing mischief, and not wanting in will to exercise these powers to the full. The spell of the unnatural civil power which had been enjoyed by the Papal prelates in this country remained with their Protestant successors until this Controversy broke it: so that from this time onwards the bishops set about to forge a new spell, 'the Divine Right of their temporal position and power,' which hallucination was dissolved by the Long Parliament: from which time a bishop has usually been considered no more than a man" (Preface, pp. 11-12). [T. S.]

[2] Edward Hyde, Earl of Clarendon (1608-1674), the author of the "History of the Great Rebellion." [T. S.]

ment; yet I have found, by often rummaging for old books in Little Britain and Duck-Lane, a great number of pamphlets printed from the year 1530[1] to 1640, full of as bold and impious railing expressions, against the lawful power of the Crown, and the order of bishops, as ever were uttered during the Rebellion, or the whole subsequent tyranny of that fanatic anarchy. However, I find it manifest, that Puritanism did not erect itself into a new, separate species of religion, till some time after the Rebellion began. For, in the latter times of King James the First, and the former part of his son, there were several Puritan bishops, and many Puritan private clergymen; while people went, as their inclinations led them, to hear preachers of each party in the parish churches. For the Puritan clergy had received Episcopal orders as well as the rest. But, soon after the Rebellion broke out, the term Puritan gradually dropped, and that of Presbyterian succeeded; which sect was, in two or three years, established in all its forms, by what they called an Ordinance of the Lords and Commons, without consulting the King; who was then at war against his rebels. And, from this period the Church continued under persecution, till monarchy was restored in the year 1660.

In a year or two after; we began to hear of a new party risen, and growing in the Parliament, as well as the army; under the name of Independent: It spread, indeed somewhat more in the latter; but not equal with the Presbyterians, either in weight or number, till the very time[2] that the King was murdered.

When the King, who was then a prisoner in the Isle of Wight, had made his last concessions for a peace to the Commissioners of the Parliament, who attended him there; upon their return to London, they reported his Majesty's answer to the House. Whereupon, a number of moderate members, who, as Ludlow[3] says, had secured their own

[1] The original edition has 1630. [T. S.]
[2] Faulkner prints: "until some time before the King was murdered." [T. S.]
[3] Edmund Ludlow (1620 ?–1693) lieutenant-general of the Parliamentary army. He was one of the judges of King Charles's trial, and who signed the death-warrant. He died at Vevay, in Switzerland, where

terms with his Majesty, managed with so much art, as to obtain a majority, in a thin house, for passing a vote, that *the King's concessions were a ground for future settlement.* But the great officers of the army, joining with the discontented members, came to a resolution, of excluding all those who had consented to that vote; which they executed in a military way. Ireton told Fairfax the General,[1] a rigid Presbyterian, of this resolution; who thereupon issued his orders for drawing out the army the next morning, and placing guards in Westminster-hall, the Court of Requests, and the lobby; who, in obedience to the General, in conjunction with those members who opposed the vote, would let no member enter the House, except those of their own party. Upon which, the question for bringing the King to justice, was immediately put and carried without opposition, that I can find. Then, an order was made for his trial; the time and place appointed; the judges named; of whom Fairfax himself was one; although by the advice or threats of his wife, he declined sitting among them. However, by fresh orders under his own hand, which I have seen in print, he appointed guards to attend the judges at the trial, and to keep the city in quiet; as he did likewise to prevent any opposition from the people, upon the day of execution.

From what I have already deduced, it appears manifest, that the differences between those two sects, Presbyterian and Independent, did not then amount to half so much as what there is between a Whig and Tory at present among us. The design of utterly extirpating monarchy and episcopacy, was equally the same in both; evidently the consequence of the very same principles, upon which the Presbyterians alone began, continued, and would have ended in the same events; if towards the conclusion, they had not been bearded by that new party, with whom they could not agree about dividing the spoil. However, they held a good share of civil and military employments during the whole time of the usurpation; whose names, and

he had fled on finding that Charles's judges were not included in the Act of Indemnity. His memoirs were printed at Vevay in 1698-1699. 3 vols. 8vo. It is to these Swift refers. [T. S.]

[1] Ireton and Fairfax were two famous generals of the Parliamentary army serving with Cromwell. [T. S.]

actions, and preferments, are frequent in the accounts of those times. For I make no doubt, that all the prudent Presbyterians complied in proper seasons, falling in with the stream; and thereby got that share in employments, which many of them held to the Restoration; and perhaps too many of them after. In the same manner, we find our wisest Tories, in both kingdoms, upon the change of hands and measures at the Queen's death, have endeavoured for several years, by due compliances, to recover the time they had lost by a temporary obstinacy; wherein they have well succeeded, according to their degrees of merit. Of whose names I could here make honourable mention, if I did not fear it might offend their modesty.

As to what is alleged, that some of the Presbyterians declared openly against the King's murder, I allow it to be true. But, from what motives? No other can possibly be assigned, than perfect spite, rage, and envy, to find themselves wormed out of all power by a new infant spawn of Independents, sprung from their own bowels. It is true; the differences in religious tenets between them are very few and trifling; the chief quarrel, as far as I remember, relating to congregational and national assemblies. But, wherever interest or power thinks fit to interfere, it little imports what principles the opposite parties think fit to charge upon each other: for, we see, at this day, that the Tories are more hated by the whole set of zealous Whigs, than the very Papists themselves; and, in effect, as much unqualified for the smallest office: although, both these parties assert themselves to be of the same religion, in all its branches of doctrine and discipline; and profess the same loyalty to the same Protestant King and his heirs.

If the reader would know what became of this Independent party, upon whom all the mischief is charged by their Presbyterian brethren; he may please to observe, that during the whole usurpation, they contended by degrees with their parent sect, and, as I have already said, shared in employments; and gradually, after the Restoration, mingled with the mass of Presbyterians; lying ever since undistinguished in the herd of dissenters.

The Presbyterian merit is of as little weight, when they allege themselves instrumental towards the King's restoration. The kingdom grew tired with those ridiculous models of government : First, by a House of Lords and Commons, without a king; then without bishops; afterwards by a Rump[1] and lords temporal : then by a Rump alone; next by a single person for life, in conjunction with a council : by agitators : by major-generals : by a new kind of repre-sentatives from the three kingdoms : by the keepers of the liberties of England; with other schemes that have slipped out of my memory.   Cromwell was dead; his son Richard, a weak, ignorant wretch, who gave up his monarchy much in the same manner with the two usurping kings of Brentford.[2]   The people harassed with taxes and other oppressions; the King's party, then called the Cavaliers began to recover their spirits.   The few nobility scattered through the kingdom, who lived in a most retired manner, observing the confusion of things, could no longer endure to be ridden by bakers, cobblers, brewers, and the like, at the head of armies; and plundering everywhere like French dragoons : The Rump assembly grew despicable to those who had raised them : The city of London, exhausted by almost twenty years contributing to their own ruin, declared against them.   The Rump, after many deaths and resurrec-tions, was, in the most contemptuous manner, kicked out, and burned in effigy.   The excluded members were let in : a free Parliament called in as legal a manner as the times would allow; and the King restored.

The second claim of Presbyterian merit is founded upon their services against the dangerous designs of King James the Second; while that prince was using all his endeavours to introduce Popery, which he openly professed upon his coming to the crown : To this they add, their eminent services at the Revolution, under the Prince of Orange.

Now, the quantum of Presbyterian merit, during the four years' reign of that weak, bigoted, and ill-advised prince, as well as at the time of the Revolution, will easily be computed, by a recourse to a great number of histories, pamphlets, and public papers, printed in those times, and some afterwards; beside the verbal testimonies of many persons yet alive, who

[1] This name was given to that part of the House of Commons which remained after the moderate men had been expelled by military force. [S.]
[2] In the " Rehearsal."

are old enough to have known and observed the Dissenters' conduct in that critical period.

It is agreed, that upon King Charles the Second's death, soon after his successor had publicly owned himself a Roman Catholic; he began with his first caresses to the Church party; from whom having received very cold discouraging answers; he applied to the Presbyterian leaders and teachers, being advised by the priests and Popish courtiers, that the safest method toward introducing his own religion, would be by taking off the Sacramental Test, and giving a full liberty of conscience to all religions, (I suppose, that professed Christianity.) It seems, that the Presbyterians, in the latter years of King Charles the Second, upon account of certain plots, (allowed by Bishop Burnet to be genuine) had been, for a short time, forbid to hold their conventicles: Whereupon, these charitable Christians, out of perfect resentment against the Church, received the gracious offers of King James with the strongest professions of loyalty, and highest acknowledgments for his favour. I have seen several of their addresses, full of thanks and praises, with bitter insinuations of what they had suffered; putting themselves and the Papists upon the same foot; as fellow-sufferers for conscience; and with the style of, *Our brethren the Roman Catholics.* About this time began the project of closeting, (which has since been practised many times, with more art and success,) where the principal gentlemen of the kingdom were privately catechised by his Majesty, to know whether, if a new parliament were called, they would agree to pass an act for repealing the Sacramental Test, and establishing a general liberty of conscience. But he received so little encouragement, that, despairing of success, he had recourse to his dispensing power, which the judges had determined to be part of his prerogative. By colour of this determination, he preferred several Presbyterians, and many Papists, to civil and military employments. While the king was thus busied, it is well known, that Monsieur Fagel, the Dutch envoy in London, delivered the opinion of the Prince and Princess of Orange, concerning the repeal of the Test; whereof the king had sent an account to their Highnesses, to know how far they approved of it. The substance of their answer, as reported by Fagel, was this, "That their highnesses thought very well of a liberty of conscience; but by no means of giving employments to any other persons, than those who were of the National Church." This opinion was confirmed by several reasons: I cannot be more particular, not having the paper by me, although it hath been printed in many accounts of those times. And thus much every moderate churchman would perhaps submit to: But, to trust any part of the civil power in the hands of those whose interest, inclination, conscience, and former practices have been wholly turned to introduce a different system of religion and government, hath very few examples in any Christian state; nor any at all in Holland, the great patroness of universal toleration.

Upon the first intelligence King James received of an intended invasion by the Prince of Orange; among great numbers of Papists, to increase his troops, he gave commissions to several Presbyterians; some of whom had been officers under the Rump; and particularly he placed one Richards, a noted Presbyterian, at the head of a regiment; who had been governor of Wexford in Cromwell's time, and is often mentioned by Ludlow in his Memoirs. This regiment was raised in England against the Prince of Orange: the colonel made his son a captain, whom I knew, and who was as zealous a Presbyterian as his father. However at the time of the prince's landing, the father easily foreseeing how things would go, went over, like many others to the prince, who continued him in his regiment; but coming over a year or two after to assist in raising the siege of Derry, he behaved himself so like either a coward or a traitor, that his regiment was taken from him.

I will now consider the conduct of the Church party, during the whole reign of that unfortunate king. They were so unanimous against promising to pass an act for repealing the Test, and establishing a general liberty of conscience; that the king durst not trust a parliament; but encouraged by the professions of loyalty given him by his Presbyterian friends, went on with his dispensing power.

The Church clergy, at that time are allowed to have written the best collection of tracts against Popery that ever appeared in England; which are to this day in the highest esteem. But, upon the strictest enquiry, I could never hear of above one or two papers published by the Presbyterians at that time upon the same subject. Seven great prelates (he of Canterbury among the rest) were sent to the Tower, for presenting a petition, wherein they desired to be excused in not obeying an illegal command from the King. The Bishop of London, Dr Compton,[1] was summoned to answer before the Commissioners for Ecclesiastical Affairs, for not suspending Dr Sharp[2] (afterwards Archbishop of York) by the King's command. If the Presbyterians expressed the same zeal upon any occasion, the instances of it are not as I can find, left upon record, or transmitted by tradition. The proceedings against Magdalen College in Oxford, for refusing to comply with the King's mandate for admitting a professed Papist upon their foundation, are a standing proof of the courage and firmness in religion shewn by that learned society, to the ruin of their fortunes. The Presbyterians know very well, that I could produce many more instances of the same kind. But these are enough in so short a paper as I intend at present.

It is indeed very true, that after King William was settled on the English throne, the Presbyterians began to appear, and offer their credentials, and demand favour; and the new King having been originally bred a Calvinist, was desirous enough to make them easy (if that would do it) by a legal toleration; although in his heart he never bore much affection to that sect; nor designed to favour them farther than it stood with the present scheme of politics: as I have long since been assured by the greatest men of Whig principles at that time in England.

[1] Henry Compton (1632-1713), educated at Oxford, was created Bishop of London in 1675. During the Revolution of 1688 he conveyed the Princess Anne from London to Nottingham. After, he crowned her Queen of England. He was the author of a few works of little importance, such as the "Treatise on the Holy Communion." [T. S.]
[2] John Sharp (1644-1714) was educated at Cambridge, and created Archbishop of York in 1691. He gave great offence to James II. by his preaching against Roman Catholicism. This is the same Archbishop Sharp who prevented Swift's appointment to a bishopric, by urging that the author of "A Tale of a Tub" was not a proper person to hold such an office. See note prefixed to "A Tale of a Tub," vol. i., p. xcvi, of this edition of Swift's Works. [T. S.]

It is likewise true, nor will it be denied ; that when the King was possessed of the English crown ; and the remainder of the quarrel was left to be decided in this kingdom ; the Presbyterians wisely chose to join with the Protestant army, rather than with that of King James their old friend, whose affairs were then in a manner desperate.   They were wise enough to know, that this kingdom, divided against itself, could never prevail against the united power of England. They fought *pro aris et focis ;* for their estates and religion ; which latter will never suffer so much by the Church of England as by that of Rome, where they are counted heretics as well as we : ànd consequently they have no other game to play.   But, what merit they can build upon having joined with a Protestant army, under a King they acknowledged, to defend their own liberties and properties against a Popish enemy under an abdicated King ; is, I confess to me absolutely inconceivable ; and I believe will equally be so for ever, to any reasonable man.

When these sectaries were several years ago making the same attempt for abolishing the Test, many groundless reports were industriously and seasonably spread, of an invasion threatened by the Pretender on the north of Ireland.   At which time the Presbyterians in their pamphlets, argued in a menacing manner, that if the Pretender should invade those parts of the kingdom, where the numbers and estates of dissenters chiefly lay ; they would sit still, and let us fight our own battles ; [1] since they were to reap no advantage, whichever side should be victors.   If this were the course they intended to take in such a case ; I should desire to know, how they could contrive safely to stand neuters, otherwise than by a compact with the Pretender and his army, to support their neutrality, and protect them against the forces of the Crown ?   This is a necessary supposition ; because they must otherwise have inevitably been a prey to both.   However, by this frank declaration,

---

[1] See the poem, reprinted by Monck Mason ("History of St. Patrick's," p. 388 note), entitled :

> "The Grunters' request
> To take off the Test,"

in which the poet advises his "lauds" to "faight y'er ain battel." [T. S.]

they sufficiently shewed their good-will; and confirmed the common charge laid at their door; that a Scottish or northern Presbyterian hates our Episcopal Established Church more than Popery itself. And, the reason for this hatred, is natural enough; because it is the Church alone, that stands in the way between them and power, which Popery doth not.

Upon this occasion I am in some doubt, whether the political spreaders of those chimerical invasions, made a judicious choice in fixing the northern parts of Ireland for that romantic enterprize. Nor, can I well understand the wisdom of the Presbyterians in countenancing and confirming those reports. Because it seems to cast a most infamous reflection upon the loyalty and religious principles of their whole body: For if there had been any truth in the matter, the consequence must have been allowed, that the Pretender counted upon more assistance· from his father's friends the Presbyterians, by choosing to land in those very parts, where their number, wealth, and power most prevailed; rather than among those of his own religion. And therefore, in charity to this sect, I rather incline to believe, that those reports of an invasion were formed and spread by the race of small politicians, in order to do a seasonable job.

As to Popery in general, which for a thousand years past hath been introducing and multiplying corruptions both in doctrine and discipline; I look upon it to be the most absurd system of Christianity professed by any nation. But I cannot apprehend this kingdom to be in much danger from it. The estates of Papists are very few; crumbling into small parcels, and daily diminishing. Their common people are sunk in poverty, ignorance, and cowardice, and of as little consequence as women and children. Their nobility and gentry are at least one-half ruined, banished, or converted: They all soundly feel the smart of what they suffered in the last Irish war. Some of them are already retired into foreign countries; others as I am told, intend to follow them; and the rest, I believe, to a man, who still possess any lands, are absolutely determined never to hazard them again for the sake of establishing their superstition. If it hath been thought fit, as some observe, to abate of the

law's rigour against Popery in this kingdom, I am confident
it was done for very wise reasons, considering the situation
of affairs abroad at different times, and the interest of the
Protestant religion in general. And as I do not find the
least fault in this proceeding; so I do not conceive why a
sunk discarded party, who neither expect nor desire anything more than a quiet life; should under the names of
highflyers, Jacobites, and many other vile appellations, be
charged so often in print, and at common tables, with
endeavouring to introduce Popery and the Pretender; while
the Papists abhor them above all other men, on account of
severities against their priests in her late Majesty's reign;
when the now disbanded reprobate party was in power.
This I was convinced of some years ago by a long journey
into the southern parts; where I had the curiosity to send
for many priests of the parishes I passed through; and, to
my great satisfaction found them everywhere abounding in
professions of loyalty to the late King George; for which
they gave me the reasons above-mentioned; at the same
time complaining bitterly of the hardships they suffered
under the Queen's last ministry.

I return from this digression to the modest demands of the
Presbyterians for a repeal of the Sacramental Test, as a reward for their merits at the Restoration and the Revolution;
which merits I have fairly represented as well as my memory
will allow me. If I have committed any mistakes they
must be of little moment. The facts and principal circumstances are what I have obtained and digested, from
reading the histories of those times, written by each party;
and many thousands have done the same as well as I, who
I am sure have in their minds drawn the same conclusions.

This is the faction, and these the men, who are now
resuming their applications, and giving in their bills of
merit to both kingdoms upon two points, which of all others,
they have the least pretensions to offer. I have collected
the facts with all possible impartiality, from the current
histories of those times; and have shewn, although very
briefly, the gradual proceedings of those sectaries under the
denomination of Puritans, Presbyterians, and Independents,
for about the space of an hundred and eighty years, from the
beginning of Queen Elizabeth to this present time. But,

notwithstanding all that can be said, these very schismatics
(for such they are in temporals as well as spirituals) are now
again expecting, soliciting, and demanding, (not without
insinuating threats, according to their custom) that the
Parliament should fix them upon an equal foot with the
Church established. I would fain know to what branch of
the legislature they can have the forehead to apply. Not to
my lords the bishops; who must have often read, how the
predecessors of this very faction, acting upon the same
principles, drove the whole bench out of the house; who
were then, and hitherto continue one of the three estates.
Not to the temporal peers, the second of the three estates;
who must have heard, that, immediately after those rebellious fanatics had murdered their king, they voted a House
of Lords to be useless and dangerous, and would let them
sit no longer, otherwise than when elected as commoners:
Not to the House of Commons; who must have heard,
that in those fanatic times the Presbyterian and Independent
commanders in the army, by military power, expelled all the
moderate men out of the house, and left a Rump to govern
the nation. Lastly, not to the Crown, which those very
saints destined to rule the earth, trampled under their feet,
and then in cold blood murdered the blessed wearer.

But, the session now approaching, and a clan of dissenting
teachers being come up to town from their northern head-
quarters, accompanied by many of their elders and agents,
and supported by a general contribution, to solicit their
establishment, with a capacity of holding all military as well
as civil employments; I think it high time, that this paper
should see the light. However, I cannot conclude without
freely confessing, that if the Presbyterians should obtain
their ends, I could not be sorry to find them mistaken in
the point which they have most at heart by the repeal of the
Test; I mean the benefit of employments. For, after all,
what assurance can a Scottish northern dissenter, born on
Irish ground, have, that he shall be treated with as much
favour as a true Scot born beyond the Tweed?

I am ready enough to believe that all I have said will
avail but little. I have the common excuse of other men,
when I think myself bound by all religious and civil ties, to
discharge my conscience, and to warn my countrymen upon

this important occasion.   It is true, the advocates for this
scheme promise a new world, after this blessed work shall
be completed: that all animosities and faction must
immediately drop; that the only distinction in this kingdom
will then be of Papist and Protestant.   For, as to Whig and
Tory, High Church and Low Church, Jacobite and Hanoverian, Court and Country party, English and Irish interests,
Dissenters and Conformists, New Light and Old Light,
Anabaptist and Independent, Quaker and Muggletonian,
they will all meet and jumble together into a perfect harmony,
at the sessions and assizes, on the bench and in the
revenues; and upon the whole, in all civil and military
trust, not excepting the great councils of the nation.   For it
is wisely argued thus, that a kingdom being no more than a
larger knot of friends met together, it is against the rules of
good manners to shut any person out of the company,
except the Papists; who profess themselves of another
club.

I am at a loss to know what arts the Presbyterian sect
intends to use, in convincing the world of their loyalty to
kingly government; which long before the prevalence, or
even the birth of their independent rivals, as soon as the
King's forces were overcome, declared their principles to be
against monarchy, as well as Episcopacy and the House
of Lords, even till the King was restored: At which event,
although they were forced to submit to the present power,
yet I have not heard that they did ever, to this day, renounce
any one principle by which their predecessors then acted; yet
this they have been challenged to do, or at least to shew that
others have done it for them, by a certain doctor,[1] who, as I
am told, has much employed his pen in the like disputes.
I own, they will be ready enough to insinuate themselves
into any government: But, if they mean to be honest and
upright, they will and must endeavour by all means, which
they shall think lawful, to introduce and establish their own
scheme of religion, as nearest approaching to the word of
God, by casting out all superstitious ceremonies, ecclesiastical
titles, habits, distinctions, and superiorities, as rags of
Popery; in order to a thorough reformation; and, as in

[1] Dr. Tisdal, in a tract entitled, "The Case of the Sacramental Test
stated and argued."   Tisdal died 4th June, 1736."   [T. S.]

charity bound, to promote the salvation of their countrymen : wishing with St. Paul, that the whole kingdom were as they are. But what assurance will they please to give, that when their sect shall become the national established worship, they will treat Us Dissenters as we have treated them? Was this their course of proceeding during the dominion of the saints? Were not all the remainders of the Episcopal Church in those days, especially the clergy, under a persecution for above a dozen years, equal to that of the primitive Christians under heathen emperors? That this proceeding was suitable to their principles, is known enough ; for many of their preachers then writ books expressly against allowing any liberty of conscience, in a religion different from their own; producing many arguments to prove that opinion ; and among the rest one frequently insisted on ; that allowing such a liberty would be to establish iniquity by a law: Many of these writings are yet to be seen ;[1] and I hear, have been quoted by the doctor above mentioned.

As to their great objection of prostituting that holy institution, the blessed Sacrament, by way of a test before admittance into any employment ; I ask, whether they would not be content to receive it after their own manner, for the office of a judge, for that of a commissioner in the revenue, for a regiment of horse, or to be a lord justice? I believe they would scruple it as little, as a long grace before and after dinner ; which they can say without bending a knee ; for, as I have been told, their manner of taking bread and wine in their conventicles, is performed with little more solemnity than at their common meals. And, therefore, since they look upon our practice in receiving the elements, to be idolatrous ; they neither can, nor ought, in conscience, to allow us that liberty, otherwise than by connivance, and a bare toleration, like what is permitted to the Papists. But, lest we should offend them, I am ready to change this test for another ; although, I am afraid, that sanctified reason is, by no means, the point where the difficulty pinches ; and only offered by pretended churchmen, as if they could be content with our believing, that the impiety and profanation

[1] See many hundred quotations to prove this, in the treatise called "Scotch Presbyterian Eloquence." [Note in Faulkner's edition, 1738.]

of making the Sacrament a test, were the only objection.   I
therefore propose, that before the present law be repealed,
another may be enacted ; that no man shall receive any employment, before he swears himself to be a true member of
the Church of Ireland, in doctrine and discipline, &c., and,
that he will never frequent, or communicate with any other
form of worship.   It shall likewise be further enacted, that
whoever offends, &c., shall be fined five hundred pounds,
imprisoned for a year and a day, and rendered incapable of
all public trust for ever.   Otherwise, I do insist that those
pious, indulgent, external professors of our national religion,
shall either give up that fallacious hypocritical reason for
taking off the Test; or freely confess, that they desire to
have a gate wide open for every sect, without any test at all,
except that of swearing loyalty to the King : Which, however, considering their principles, with regard to monarchy
yet unrenounced, might, if they would please to look deep
enough into their own hearts, prove a more bitter test than
any other that the law hath yet invented.

For, from the first time that these sectaries appeared in
the world, it hath been always found, by their whole proceeding, that they professed an utter hatred to kingly
government.   I can recollect, at present, three civil establish-
ments, where Calvinists, and some other reformers who rejected Episcopacy, possess the supreme power ; and, these
are all republics ; I mean Holland, Geneva, and the reformed
Swiss cantons.   I do not say this in diminution, or disgrace
to commonwealths ; wherein, I confess, I have much altered
many opinions under which I was educated, having been led by
some observation, long experience, and a thorough detestation for the corruptions of mankind : Insomuch, that I am
now justly liable to the censure of Hobbes, who complains,
that the youth of England imbibe ill opinions, from reading
the histories of Ancient Greece and Rome, those renowned
scenes of liberty and every virtue.

But, as to monarchs ; who must be supposed well to study
and understand their own interest ; they will best consider,
whether those people, who in all their actions, preachings,
and writings, have openly declared themselves against regal
power, are to be safely placed in an equal degree of favour
and trust with those who have been always found the true

and only friends to the English establishment. From which consideration, I could have added one more article to my new test, if I had thought it worth my time.

I have been assured by some persons who were present, that several of these dissenting teachers, upon their first arrival hither to solicit the repeal of the Test, were pleased to express their gratitude, by publicly drinking the healths of certain eminent patrons, whom they pretend to have found among us; if this be true, and that the Test must be delivered up by the very commanders appointed to defend it, the affair is already, in effect, at an end. What secret reasons those patrons may have given for such a return of brotherly love, I shall not inquire: "For, O my soul come not thou into their secret, unto their assembly mine honour be not thou united. For in their anger they slew a man, and in their self-will they digged down a wall. Cursed be their anger, for it was fierce, and their wrath, for it was cruel; I will divide them in Jacob, and scatter them in Israel."

A NARRATIVE

OF THE SEVERAL ATTEMPTS, WHICH THE DISSENTERS OF
IRELAND HAVE MADE, FOR A REPEAL OF THE
SACRAMENTAL TEST.

NOTE.

THIS tract occupies Nos. iii. and iv. of a periodical paper called "The Correspondent," originally printed at Dublin "by James Hoey in Skinner-Row, 1733." The text here given is that of the original "Correspondent"; that given by Scott and Nichols is evidently taken from the London reprint. It will be seen that the matter as it was originally printed contains much more than was afterwards reprinted. I have indicated in footnotes where Scott's omissions occur. The title of the periodical runs: "The Correspondent, No. iii. [No. iv.] Humbly inscribed to the Conforming Nobility and Gentry of Ireland." Nos. i. and ii. dealt with "Old and New Light Presbyterians"; but these are not by Swift. In Nichols's edition this pamphlet appears in the second volume of the "Supplement to Dr. Swift's Works," 1779, p. 307. See note to the previous pamphlet, where the question of the date of the first publication of this tract is discussed. It may be, as Monck Mason suggests ("History of St. Patrick's," p. 389, note h), that a separate and second edition of this "Narrative" was likewise printed, of the same size as "The Presbyterians' Plea," and bound up, occasionally with that pamphlet; but such an edition I have never seen. The only reprint of the time examined, is that by A. Dodd, of Temple Bar, affixed to the second London edition of "The Presbyterians' Plea of Merit," and the date of which may be put down to 1734.

[T. S.]

A NARRATIVE OF THE SEVERAL ATTEMPTS, WHICH THE DISSENTERS OF IRELAND HAVE MADE, FOR A REPEAL OF THE SACRAMENTAL TEST.

MY intention is in this and some following "Correspondents," to vindicate the Test Act, from the insolent aspersions which are thrown upon it, and to answer objections, which are raised against it, particularly by an anonymous author, in a paper entitled, "The Nature and Consequence of the Sacramental Test considered," &c., printed *anno* 1731, upon the opening of the last session of parliament, and now republished.

As a proper introduction to this, I must take leave to put the conformists in mind, of what (upon recollection) they may very well remember, and which in some measure they have been formerly apprised of, and that is in[1] a narrative of the several attempts, which the Dissenters of Ireland have made, for a repeal of the Sacramental Test.

When the oath of supremacy was repealed which had been the Church's great security since the second of Queen Elizabeth, against both Papists and Presbyterians, who equally refused it, I presume it is no secret now to tell the

---

[1] From the beginning of this paragraph to the word "in" is omitted in the editions issued by Scott and Nichols. The words "A Narrative . . . . Sacramental Test" are used by Scott as part of the sub-title of the tract; but he adds the date, 1731. This is a mistake, since "The Correspondent" appeared in 1733; and if it did appear in the second edition of "The Plea," that edition was published either in the same or in the following year. [T. S.]

reader, that the repeal of that oath opened a sluice and let in such a current of dissenters into some of our corporations, as bore down all before them.

Although the Sacramental Test had been for a considerable time in force in England, yet that law did not reach Ireland, where the Church was more oppressed by dissenters ; and where her most sanguine friends were glad to compound, to preserve what legal security she had left, rather than to attempt any new, or even to recover what she had lost : And in truth they had no reason to expect it, at a time when the dissenters had the interest to have a motion made and debated in parliament, that there might be a temporary repeal of all the penal laws against them, and when they were so flushed with the conquest they had made in some corporations, as to reject all overtures of a toleration ; and to that end, had employed Mr. Boyse [1] to write against it with the utmost contempt, calling it "a. stone instead of bread ; a serpent instead of a fish."

When the Church was in this situation, the clause of the Sacramental Test was happily sent over from England, tacked to the Popery Bill, which alarmed the whole body of the dissenters to that degree, that their managers began to ply with the greatest artifice, and industry, to prevent its passing into a law.   But (to the honour of that parliament be it spoken), the whole body of both Lords and Commons (some few excepted) passed the clause with great readiness, and defended it afterwards with as great resolution.

The immediate consequence of this law was the recovery of several corporations, which the conformists had given to the dissenters, and the preservation of others, to which the "enterprising people" had made very bold and quick approaches.

It was hoped that this signal defeat would have discouraged the dissenters from any further attempts against a law, which had so unanimously passed both houses : But

---

[1] In his note Scott calls him "Samuel" Boyse, but he is distinctly mentioned further on in the tract as "Jo: Boyse."   The Rev. Joseph Boyse was a native of Leeds, who had settled in Dublin in 1683 as joint-pastor with Dr. Daniel Williams.   He died in poverty in 1728 ; and in the same year his works were published in two folio volumes.   His son, Samuel Boyse, the poet, died in 1749.   [T. S.]

the contrary soon appeared. For, upon meeting of the Parliament, held by the Earl of Pembroke,[1] they quickly reassumed their wonted courage and confidence, and made no doubt, but they should either procure an absolute repeal thereof, or get it so far relaxed, as that they might be admitted to offices of military trust : To this, they apprehended themselves encouraged by a paragraph in his Excellency's speech to both Houses (which they applied to themselves) which was, " That the Queen would be glad of any expedient, for strengthening the interests of her Protestant subjects of Ireland."

The advocates for the dissenters immediately took hold of this handle, and in order to prepare the way for this expedient, insisted boldly upon their merit and loyalty, charged the Church with persecution, and extolled their signal behaviour in the late Revolution, to that degree, as if by their signal prowess, they had saved the nation.

But all this, was only to prepare the way for the grand engine, which was forming to beat down this law ; and that was their expedient addresses.

The first of this kind was, from a provincial synod of the northern dissenters, beginning with high encomiums upon themselves, and as high demands from the public, "for their untainted loyalty in all turns of government," which they said, was " the natural consequence of their known principles " ; expressions, which, had they been applied to them by their adversaries, must have been understood as spoken ironically, and indeed to have been the greatest sarcasm imaginable upon them ; especially, when we consider the insolent treatment given to her Majesty in the very same address ; for immediately after they pass this compliment upon themselves, they tell her Majesty, they deeply regret the Sacramental Test ; and frankly declared, that neither the gentlemen, nor people of their persuasion, could (they must mean *would*) serve her, whatever exigencies might arise, unless that law was repealed.

The managers for the kirk, following this precedent, endeavoured to obtain addresses to the same purpose from

---

[1] It will be remembered that the earl's viceroyalty commenced April 7th, 1707. It was in his train that Swift came to England in that year. [T. S.]

the corporations, and though they proved unsuccessful in most, they procured them from several of our most considerable conforming corporations; and that too at a critical juncture, when numbers of Scotch Presbyterians, who had deserved well in the affair of the Union, and could not be rewarded in England (where the Test Act was in force) stood ready to overrun our preferments as soon as the Test should be repealed in Ireland.

But after all when it came to a decisive trial in the House of Commons, the dissenters were defeated.

When the managers found the House of Commons could not be brought into that scheme of an expedient, to be offered by them; their refinement upon this, was, to move for an address, "That the House would accept of an expedient from her Majesty," but this also was rejected; for by this project, the managers would have led the Queen into this dilemma, either to disoblige the whole body of the dissenters, by refusing to name the expedient, or else to give up the conformists to the insults and encroachments of the dissenters, by the repeal of that law, which was declared by the House of Lords, to be the great security of the Established Church, and of the English interest of Ireland.

The next attempt they made against the Test was during the government of Lord Wharton.[1]

The dissenters seemed more resolute now than ever, to have the Test repealed, especially when his Excellency had declared from the throne, "that they were neither to be persecuted nor molested." For they who had all along called the Test Act a persecution, might reasonably conclude that grievance would be removed; when they were told by the chief governor, that they were not to be even "molested." But to their great confusion, they were soon undeceived, when they found upon trial, that the House of Commons, would not bear the least motion towards it.

---

[1] Wharton was appointed Lord Lieutenant on November 25th, 1708. This Wharton is the Thomas, Lord Wharton, against whom Swift wrote one of his bitterest and most personal attacks. He was the eldest son of Philip, Lord Wharton, and was created a marquis by George I. He died April 12th, 1715. The ballad of "Lillibullero" is attributed to him. [T. S.]

Their movements to repeal the Test Act being stopped this way; the managers were obliged to take several other ways to come at it: And at the time, that some pretended to soothe, others seemed to threaten even the legislature, with a view, (as must be presumed) that those, whom they could not cajole, might be frightened into it.[1]

There happened about the time, when the project of the expedient was on foot, an excellent occasion, to express their resentments against this law, and that was, when great numbers of them refused the oath of allegiance, and to oppose the Pretender; insisting upon a repeal of the Test Act, as the condition of their arming in defence of their Queen and country.

The government was not reduced to such straits, as to submit to that condition; and the Test stood firm, in spite of both the dissenters and the Pretender, until the latter was driven from our coasts: And then, one would have thought the hopes of the former, would have vanished with him.

But it proved quite contrary: For those sons of the earth, rebounding with fresh vigour from their falls, recovered new strength and spirit from every defeat, and the next attempt was bolder (considering the circumstances they were in) than any they had made before.

The case was this: The House of Lords of Ireland had accused them to the Queen of several illegal practices, which highly concerned the safety of our constitution, both in church and state: The particulars of which charge, were summed up in a representation from the Lords to this effect:

"That they (the dissenters) had opposed and persecuted the conformists, in those parts where their power prevailed, had invaded their congregations, propagated their schism in places where it had not the least footing formerly; that they were protected from a legal prosecution by a *noli prosequi* in the case of Drogheda."

"That they refused to take conforming apprentices, and confined trade among themselves, exclusive of the conformists."

[1] Scott omits the words from "with a view" to the end of the paragraph. [T. S.]

"That in their illegal assemblies they had prosecuted and censured their people for being married according to law."

"That they have thrown public and scandalous reflections upon the Episcopal order, and upon our laws, particularly the Sacramental Test, and had misapplied the royal bounty of £1,200 *per annum*, in propagating their schism, and undermining the Church : And had exercised an illegal jurisdiction in their Presbyteries and Synods," &c.

To this representation of the Lords, the dissenters remonstrate in an address to the Queen, or rather an appeal to their own people, in which, although it is evident, they were conscious of those crimes whereof they stood accused, as appears by the evasions they make to this high charge. Yet even under these circumstances (such was their modesty) they pressed for a repeal of the Test Act, by the modest appellation of a grievance and odious mark of infamy, &c. Of which more hereafter. There is one particular in another address which I cannot omit. The House of Lords in their representation, had accused one dissenting teacher in particular (well known to Mr. Boyse). The charge was in these words :

"Nor has the legislature itself escaped the censure of a bold author of theirs, who has published in print, that the Sacramental Test is only an engine to advance a state faction, and to debase religion, to serve base and unworthy purposes."

To this, Mr. Boyse answers, in an address to the Queen, in the year 1712, subscribed only by himself, and five more dissenting teachers, in these words.

"As to this part of their Lordships' complaint, we beg leave to lay before your Majesty the words of that author, which are these.

" ' Nor can we altogether excuse those, who turn the holy Eucharist into an engine, to advance a state faction, and endeavour to confine the communion table of our Lord, by their arbitrary enclosures to a party ; religion is thereby debased to serve mean and unworthy purposes.' We humbly conceive that the author in that passage, makes no mention of the legislature at all, &c., and we cannot omit on this occasion, to regret it, as the great unhappiness of this kingdom, that dissenters should now be disabled from concurring in the defence of it, in any future exigency and danger, and should have the same infamy put upon them with the Irish Papists.

"We therefore humbly hope, that your Majesty shall consider, how little real grounds there are for those complaints made by their Lordships."

What a mixture of impudence and prevarication is this! That one dissenting teacher accused to his prince of having censured the legislature, should presume, backed only by five more of the same quality and profession, to transcribe the guilty paragraph, and (to secure his meaning from all possibility of being mistaken,) annex another to it; wherein, they rail at that very law, for which he in so audacious a manner censured the Queen and Parliament, and at the same time should expect to be acquitted by her Majesty, because he had not mentioned the word "legislature": 'Tis true the word legislature is not expressed in that paragraph; but let Mr. Boyse [1] say, what other power but the legislature, could in this sense, "turn the holy Eucharist into an engine to advance a state faction, or confine offices of trust, or the communion table of our Lord, by their arbitrary enclosures, to a party." It is plain he can from his principles intend no others, but the legislators of the Sacramental Test; though at the same time I freely own, that this is a vile description of them : For neither have they by this law, made the Sacramental Test an engine to advance, but rather to depress a state faction, nor have they made any arbitrary enclosures, of the communion table of our Lord, since as many as please, may receive the Sacrament with us in our churches; and those who will not, may freely, as before, receive it in their separate congregations: Nor in the last place, is religion hereby debased, to serve

---

[1] Scott remarks that "Mr. Boyse is here and in other places, spoken of as alive, which was the case, I presume, when the tract first appeared in 'The Correspondent.'" The tract, however, was printed in the periodical in 1733, and Boyse died in 1728. It may be that when Swift first wrote "The Narrative," Mr. Boyse was alive; in that case its date must be put down to an earlier year than either 1733 or even 1731. Or it may be that the style of so referring to Boyse was used for an argumentative effect, to appeal to any reader who was in sympathy with Boyse's opinions. [T. S.]

mean and unworthy purposes; nor is it any more than all lawgivers do, by enjoining an oath of allegiance, and making that a religious test. For an oath is an act of religious worship as well as the Eucharist.

Upon the whole, is not this an instance of prodigious boldness in Mr. Boyse, backed with only five dissenting teachers, thus to recriminate upon the Irish House of Lords (as they were pleased to call them in the title of their printed address,) and almost to insist with her Majesty, upon the repeal of a law, which she had stamped with her royal authority, but a few years before?

The[1] next instance, of the resolution of the dissenters, against this law, was the attempt made during the government of the Duke of Shrewsbury.[2]

This attack was by the whole compacted body, of their teachers and elders, with a formidable engine, called a "representation of grievances," in which, after they had reviled the Test Act, with the same odious appellations, and insisted upon the same insolent arguments, for the repeal thereof, which they had formerly urged to the Queen: They expressed themselves to his Grace in these words:

"We beg leave to say, that those persons must be inexcusable, and chargeable, with all the bad consequences that may follow, who in such a kingdom as this, disable, disgrace, and divide Protestants; a thing that ought not to be done at any time, or in any place, much less than in this," &c.

Is it possible to conceive any thing more provoking than this humble supplication of these remonstrators? Does not this sound like a demand of the repeal of the Test, at the peril of those, who dare refuse it? Is it not an application with a hat in one hand, and a sword in the other, and that too, in the style of a King of Ulster, to a King of Connaught,—"Repeal the Test, or if you don't   "

But to proceed in this narrative: Notwithstanding the defeat of the dissenters in England, in their late attempt against the Test, their brethren in Ireland, are so far from

_____
[1] From this paragraph to the end is taken from "The Correspondent," No. iv.   The text as given by Scott is considerably altered from that which appeared in the periodical. [T. S.]

[2] From September, 1713, until the Queen's death in 1714. [T. S.]

being discouraged, that they seem now to conceive greater hopes of having it repealed here, than ever.[1] What grounds they have for these hopes, was a secret to us, and I presume, to themselves ; however private whispers begin now to grow into general rumours, and their managers proceed with great art and assiduity, from feeling of pulses, to telling of noses.

In order to prepare necessaries, and furnish topics for this attempt, there was a paper printed upon the opening of last session, and now republished ; entitled, "The Nature and Consequences of the Sacramental Test considered, with reasons humbly offered for the Repeal thereof."[2]

It is not my intention, to follow this author, through all the mazes and windings of his reasoning upon this subject, which (in truth) seem such incoherent shreds, that it is impossible to tie them together; and therefore, what I purpose is, to answer such objections to the Test, as are advanced either by this author, or any other which have any appearance of reason, or plausibility.

I know it is not prudent to despise an adversary, nor fair to prepossess readers, before I show this bold and insolent writer, in his proper figure and dress ; and therefore, however I may take him to be a feeble advocate for the repeal of the Test, in point of reasoning, yet I freely allow him to be a most resolute champion in point of courage, who has, with such intrepidity, attacked, not only the first enactors of this law, but all such, who shall continue it, by giving their negatives to a repeal. I will in this "Correspondent" only transcribe a few quotations from this author, to shew the gallantry of this aggressor.

Page the 19th[3] he says : "the truth is the imposition of the Test, and continuing it in such a state of the kingdom, appears (at first sight,) so great an absurdity in politics, as can never be accounted for."

Who are these absurd politicians? Who first passed, and secondly continue the Sacramental Test, in all the pre-

[1] From this word to the end of this paragraph is omitted by Scott. [T. S.]

[2] This pamphlet was reprinted in London in 1732. See note prefixed to "The Presbyterians' Plea of Merit." [T. S.]

[3] Page 23 in edition London, 1732. [T. S.]

ceding attempts of the Dissenters to repeal it? Are they not the majority of both Houses of Parliament?[1]

But to strengthen his reflections, page 26,[2] he gives the whole legislature to understand, that continuing the Test, does not become the wisdom, and justice of the legislature, under the pretence of its being for the advantage of the state, when it is really prejudicial to it; and further tells us, it infringes on the indisputable rights of the dissenters.

Page, the 57th,[3] he says, "The gentlemen of the House of Commons, who framed the bill, to prevent the farther growth of Popery, instead of approving the Test clause which was inserted, publicly declared their dislike to it, and their resolution to take the first opportunity of repealing it, though at that time they unwillingly passed it, rather than lose a bill they were so fond of. This resolution has not been as yet fulfilled, for what reasons, our worthy patriots themselves know best."

I should be glad this author would inform us, who, and how many of those members joined in this resolution, to repeal the Test; or where that resolution is to be found, which he mentions twice in the same paragraph; surely not in the books of the House of Commons!

If not, suppose some few gentlemen in the House of Commons, and to be sure very few they were, who publicly declared their dislike to it, or entered into any resolution; this, I think, he should have explained, and not insinuated so gross a reflection on a great majority of the House of Commons, who first passed this law, and have ever since opposed all attempts to repeal it; these are the gentleman whom, in sarcasm and irony, he is pleased to call the "worthy," that is, the unworthy patriots themselves.

But to mention no more, he concludes his notable piece, with these remarkable words, pages 62-63.[4]

"Thus it appears, with regard to the Protestant succession,

---

[1] Omitted by Scott in his edition, 1824. [T. S.]
[2] Pp. 32-33 in London reprint. Scott places passages here in quotation marks, the original in "The Correspondent" has no such marks, nor are the passages quoted verbatim from the pamphlet referred to. [T. S.]
[3] P. 71 in London reprint. [T. S.]
[4] P. 79 of London reprint. [T. S.]

which has now happily taken place, how reasonable it is to repeal the Sacramental Test, and that granting that favour to the Dissenters," which, by the way, cannot be granted but by parliament; " can be disagreeable to none, who have a just sense of the many blessings we enjoy, by the Protestant succession, in his Majesty's royal family."

I will not trouble the reader with any more quotations, to the same purpose, out of this libel, for so I must now call it, but take leave to make some general observations on those paragraphs I have mentioned.[1]

I conceive, it will be readily allowed, that in all applications, either from any body of men, or from any particular subject to the legislature, or any branch thereof, we are to take the highest encomiums as purely complimental; if there be the least insinuation of disrespect or reflection therein, in such cases I say, you are to take the compliments in the lowest sense, but all the reflections in the highest sense the expressions can bear; inasmuch as, the first may be presumed matter of form, the latter must be matter of resentment.[2]

Now, if we apply this observation, to what this bold adventurer has said, with respect to the legislators, of the Sacramental Test; Does he not directly and plainly charge them with injustice, imprudence, gross absurdity and Jacobitism? Let the most prejudiced reader that is not pre-determined against conviction, say, whether this libeller of the parliament, has not drawn up a high charge against the makers and continuers of this law.

It is readily allowed, that this has been the old style of these champions, who have attacked the Test, as in the instances before mentioned, with this difference, that he descends lower in his charge, and has been more particular than any of his brethren.[3]

Notwithstanding my resentment, which to be sure, he does not value, I would be sorry he should bring upon himself the resentment of those he has been so free with, and I cannot help advising him, to take all possible care, and use

---

[1] This paragraph is omitted by Scott. [T. S.]
[2] This paragraph is much curtailed by Scott, who combines it with the next paragraph of the present text. [T. S.]
[3] This paragraph is omitted by Scott. [T. S.]

all effectual means, to conjure the printer, corrector, and publisher of this libel to secrecy; that however the author may be suspected, he may not be discovered.   Upon the whole, is not this author, justly to be reputed a defamer, till he produces instances wherein the conforming nobility and gentry of Ireland, have shown their disaffection to the succession of the illustrious House of Hanover?

Did they ever refuse the oath of abjuration, or support any conforming nonjuring teachers in their congregations? Did ever any conforming gentlemen, or common people, refuse to be arrayed, when the militia was raised, upon the invasion of the Pretender?   Did any of them ever shew the least reluctance, or make any exception against their officers, whether they were Dissenters or Churchmen?

It may be said, that from these insinuations, I would have it understood, that the dissenters encouraged some of their teachers, who refused the oath of abjuration; and that eve nin the article of danger, when the Pretender made his attempt in Scotland, our northern Presbyterians shewed great reluctance in taking arms, upon the array of militia.

I freely own it is my intention; and I must affirm both facts to be true, however they have the assurance to deny it.

What can be more notorious, than the protection, countenance, and support, which was continued to Riddall, McBride, and McCrackan,[1] who absolutely refused the oath of abjuration; and yet were continued to teach in their congregations, after they returned from Scotland, when a prosecution was directed, and a council in criminal causes, was sent down to the county of Antrim to prosecute them.

---

[1] Riddall, McBride, and McCrackan were three Presbyterian clergymen who refused to take the oath of abjuring the Pretender.   Of Riddall and McCrackan little is known; but John McBride (1651?-1718) (according to the writer in the "Dictionary of National Biography") was born in Ulster, and graduated at Glasgow.   He was a strong advocate of the Hanoverian succession, but avoided the oath of abjuration, in 1703, by retiring to Glasgow.   He returned to Belfast in 1713, and died there.   His humorous excuse for non-abjuration is recorded by the writer of the article in the Dictionary, and is worth repeating: "Once upon a time there was a bearn, that cou'd not be persuaded to bann the de'el because he did not know but he might soon come into his clutches."   [T. S.]

With respect to the parliament; did ever any House of Commons shew greater alacrity in raising money, and equipping ships, in defence of the King, than the last House did upon the expected invasion of the Pretender? And did ever any parliament give money with greater unanimity, for the support of the Crown, than the present has done, whatever the wants of their private families might be? And must a very great majority of those persons, be branded with the infamous aspersion of disaffection to the illustrious House of Hanover, should they refuse to give their voices for the repeal of the Test?

I am fully persuaded that this author, and his fellowlabourers, do not believe one word of this heavy charge ; but their present circumstances are such, that they must run all hazards.

In many places their congregations are sub-divided, and have chosen an *Old* and *New Light* teacher, and consequently those stipends must support two, which were enjoyed by one before.[1]

A great number of the nonconforming gentlemen daily leave them, though they have not made any convert to their persuasion, among the conforming gentlemen of fortune ; many who were nonconformists themselves, and many men whose parents were elders, or rigid nonconformists, are now constant communicants, and justices of peace in their several counties ; insomuch, that it is highly probable, should the Test continue twenty years longer, there would not be a gentleman left to solicit a repeal.

I shall hereafter take occasion to shew, how inconsiderable they are, for their numbers and fortunes, who can be served or obliged by this repeal, which number is daily lessening.

The dissenting teachers are sufficiently aware, that the general conformity of the gentlemen, will be followed, by the conformity of numbers of the people ; and should it not be so, that they will be but poorly supported by them ; that by the continuance of the Test, "their craft will be in danger to be set at nought," and in all probability, will end in a general conformity of the Presbyterians to the Established Church.

---

[1] This paragraph is omitted by Scott. [T. S.]

So that, they have the strongest reasons in the world, to press for the repeal of the Test; but those reasons, must have equal force for the continuance of it, with all that wish the peace of the Church and State, and would not have us torn in pieces, with endless and causeless divisions.

There is one short passage more, I had like to have omitted, which our author leaves as a sting in the tail of his libel; his words are these, page 59th.[1]

"The truth is, no one party of a religious denomination, in Britain or Ireland, were so united, as they, (the dissenters) indeed, no one, but they, in an inviolable attachment to the Protestant succession." To detect the folly of this assertion, I subjoin the following letter from a person of known integrity, and inviolably attached to the Protestant succession, as any dissenter in the kingdom, I mean Mr. Warreng of Warrengstown, then a member of parliament, and commissioner of array, in the county of Down, upon the expected invasion of the Pretender.

This letter was writ in a short time after the array, of the militia, for the truth of which I refer to Mr. Warreng himself.

"SIR,
    "That I may fulfil your desire, by giving you an account, how the dissenters in my neighbourhood behaved themselves, when we were threatened with an invasion of the Pretender. Be pleased to know, that upon an alarm given of his being landed near Derry, none were more zealous and ready in setting watch and keeping guard, than they, to prevent such disorders, as might happen at that time, by ill-designing persons, passing through, and disturbing the peace of the country.

"But when the government thought fit, to have the kingdom arrayed, and sent commissioners into these parts, some time after it appeared, that the dissenters had, by that time, been otherwise instructed, for several who were so forward before, behaved themselves after a very different manner, some refusing, and others with reluctancy, appearing upon the array, to be enlisted, and serve in the militia.

---

[1] P. 74 in London reprint. [T. S.]

" This behaviour surprised me so much, that I took occasion to discourse several of them, over whom, I thought I had as much influence, as any other person, and found them upon the common argument, of having their hands tied up by a late act of parliament, &c. *Whereupon, I took some pains to shew the act to them, and wherein they were mistaken.* I further pressed their concurrence with us, in procuring the common peace and security of our country, and though they seemed convinced by what I said, yet I was given to understand, their behaviour was according to the sentiments of some persons, whom they thought themselves obliged to observe, or be directed by, &c."

QUÆRIES

WROTE BY

DR. J. SWIFT, IN THE YEAR 1732.

[RELATING TO THE SACRAMENTAL TEST.]

Very proper to be read (at this Time) by every Member of the
Established Church.

NOTE.

THE text of this tract is based on that of the original broadside, collated with those given by Faulkner and Scott. In 1733 was also published a broadside with the title: "Queries upon the Demand of the Presbyterians to have the Sacramental Test repealed at this Session of Parliament." These queries seem to be based on those by Swift, though they are not quite the same.

[T. S.]

QUÆRIES WROTE BY DR. J. SWIFT, IN THE YEAR 1732.

QUERY.

WHETHER hatred and violence between parties in a state be not more inflamed by different views of interest, than by the greater or lesser differences between them, either in religion or government?

Whether it be any part of the question, at this time, which of the two religions is worse, Popery, or Fanaticism; or not rather, which of the two, (having both the same good will) is in the hopefullest condition to ruin the Church?

Whether the sectaries, whenever they come to prevail, will not ruin the Church as infallibly and effectually as the Papists?

Whether the prevailing sectaries could allow liberty of conscience to Dissenters, without belying all their former practice, and almost all their former writings?

Whether many hundred thousand Scotch Presbyterians, are not full as virulent against the Episcopal Church, as they are against the Papists; or, as they would have us think, the Papists are against them?

Whether the Dutch, who are most distinguished for allowing liberty of conscience, do ever admit any persons, who profess a different scheme of worship from their own, into civil employments; although they *may* be forced by the nature of their goverment, to receive mercenary troops of all religions?

Whether the Dissenters ever pretended, until of late years, to desire more than a bare toleration?

Whether, if it be true, what a sorry pamphleteer asserts, who lately writ for repealing the Test, that the Dissenters in

this kingdom are equally numerous with the Churchmen :
It would not be a necessary point of prudence, by all proper
and lawful means to prevent their further increase ?

The great argument given by those whom they call *Low*
Church men, to justify the large tolerations allowed to Dissenters, hath been ; that by such indulgencies, the rancour
of those sectaries would gradually wear off, many of them
would come over to us, and their parties, in a little time,
crumble to nothing.

QUERY. If what the above pamphleteer asserts, that
the sectaries, are in equal numbers with conformists, it doth
not clearly follow, that those repeated tolerations, have oper-
ated directly contrary to what those *Low* Church politicians
pretended to foresee and expect.

Whether any clergyman, however dignified or distinguished,
if he think his own profession most agreeable to Holy Scriptures, and the primitive Church, can really wish in his heart,
that all sectaries should be upon an equal foot with the
Churchmen, in the point of civil power and employments ?

Whether Episcopacy, which is held by the Church to be a
divine and apostolic institution, be not a fundamental point
of religion, particularly in that essential one of conferring
holy orders ?

Whether, by necessary consequences, the several expedi-
ents among the sectaries to constitute their teachers, are not
absolutely null and void ?

Whether the sectaries will ever agree to accept ordination
only from bishops ?

Whether the bishops and clergy will be content to give up
Episcopacy, as a point indifferent, without which the Church
can well subsist ?

Whether that great tenderness towards sectaries, which
now so much prevails, be chiefly owing to the fears of Popery,
or to that spirit of atheism, deism, scepticism, and universal
immorality, which all good men so much lament ?

Granting Popery to have many more errors in religion than
any one branch of the sectaries ; let us examine the actions
of both, as they have each affected the peace of these kingdoms, with allowance for the short time which the sectaries
had to act in, who are in a manner *but of yesterday*. The
Papists in the time of King James II. used all endeavours

to establish their superstition; wherein they failed, by the united power of English Church protestants, with the Prince of Orange's assistance. But it cannot be asserted, that these bigotted Papists had the least design to depose or murder their King, much less to abolish kingly government; nor was it their interest or inclination to attempt either.

On the other side the Puritans, who had almost from the beginning of Queen Elizabeth's reign, been a perpetual thorn in the Church's side, joining with the Scotch enthusiasts, in the time of King Charles the First, were the principal cause of the Irish rebellion and massacre, by distressing that Prince, and making it impossible for him to send over timely succours. And, after that pious Prince had satisfied his Parliament in every single point to be complained of; the same sectaries by poisoning the minds and affections of the people, with the most false and wicked representations of their King, were able, in the compass of a few years, to embroil the three nations in a bloody rebellion, at the expense of many thousand lives; to turn the kingly power into anarchy; or murder their Prince in the face of the world, and (in their own style) to destroy the Church *root and branch*.

The account therefore stands thus. The Papists aimed at one pernicious act, which was to destroy the Protestant religion; wherein, by God's mercy, and the assistance of our glorious King William, they absolutely failed. The sectaries attempted the three most infernal actions, that could possibly enter into the hearts of men, forsaken by God; which were, the murder of a most pious King, the destruction of our monarchy, and the extirpation of the Church; and succeeded in them all.

Upon which, I put the following queries. Whether any of those sectaries have ever yet in a solemn public manner, renounced any one of those principles upon which their predecessors then acted?

Whether, considering the cruel persecutions of the Episcopal Church, during the course of that horrid rebellion and the consequences of it, until the happy Restoration; is it not manifest, that the persecuting spirit lieth so equally divided between the Papists and the sectaries, that a feather would turn the balance on either side?

And, therefore, lastly, Whether any person of common

understanding, who professeth himself a member of the Church established, although, perhaps, with little inward regard to any religion (which is too often the case) if he loveth the peace and welfare of his country; can, after cool thinking, rejoice to see a power placed again in the hands of so restless, so ambitious, and so merciless a faction, to act over all the same parts a second time?

Whether the candour of that expression, so frequent of late in sermons and pamphlets, of the "strength and number of the Papists in Ireland," can be justified? For as to their number, however great, it is always magnified in proportion to the zeal, or politics, of the speaker and writer; but it is a gross imposition upon common reason, to terrify us with their strength. For Popery, under the circumstances it lieth in this kingdom; although it be offensive, and inconvenient enough, from the consequences it hath to increase the rapine, sloth and ignorance, as well as poverty of the natives; is not properly dangerous in that sense, as some would have us take it; because it is universally hated by every party of a different religious profession. It is the contempt of the wise: The best topic for clamours of designing men: But the real terror only of fools. The landed Popish interest in England, far exceedeth that among us, even in proportion to the wealth and extent of each kingdom. The little that remaineth here, is daily dropping into Protestant hands, by purchase or descent; and that affected complaint of counterfeit converts, will fall with the cause of it in half a generation; unless it be raised or kept alive, as a continual fund of merit and eloquence. The Papists are wholly disarmed. They have neither courage, leaders, money, or inclinations to rebel. They want every advantage which they formerly possessed, to follow that trade; and wherein, even with those advantages, they always miscarried. They appear very easy, and satisfied under that connivance which they enjoyed during the whole last reign; nor ever scrupled to reproach another party, under which they pretend to have suffered so much severity.

Upon these considerations I must confess to have suspended much of my pity towards the great dreaders of Popery; many of whom appear to be hale, strong, active young men; who, as I am told, eat, drink, and sleep heartily; and are very cheerful (as they have exceeding good reason) upon all other subjects. However, I cannot too much commend the generous concern, which, our neighbours and others, who come from the same neighbourhood, are so kind to express for us upon this account; although the former be further removed from the dangers of Popery, by twenty leagues of salt water: But this, I fear, is a digression.

When an artificial report was raised here many years ago, of an intended invasion by the Pretender, (which blew over after it had done its office) the Dissenters argued in their talk, and in their pamphlets, after this manner, applying themselves to those of the Church. "Gentlemen, if the Pretender had landed, as the law now standeth, we durst not assist you; and therefore, unless you take off the Test, whenever you shall happen to be invaded in earnest, if we are desired to take up arms in your defence, our answer shall be, Pray, gentlemen, fight your own battles,[1] we will lie by quietly; conquer your enemies by yourselves, if you can; we will not do your drudgery." This way of reasoning I have heard from several of their chiefs and abettors, in an hundred conversations; and have read it in twenty pamphlets: And, I am confident, it will be offered again, if the project should fail to take off the Test.

Upon which piece of oratory and reasoning I form the following query. Whether, in case of an invasion from the Pretender (which is not quite so probable as from the Grand Signior) the Dissenters can, with prudence and safety, offer the same plea; except they shall have made a previous stipulation with the invaders? And, Whether the full freedom of their religion and trade, their lives, properties, wives and children, are not, and have not always been reckoned sufficient motives for repelling invasions, especially in our sectaries, who call themselves the truest Protestants, by virtue of their pretended or real fierceness against Popery?

Whether omitting or neglecting to celebrate the day of

---

[1] See note, p. 40, referring to the poem:

"The Grunters' request
To take off the Test." [T. S.]

the martyrdom of the blessed King Charles the First, en-joined by Act of Parliament, can be justly reckoned a par-ticular and distinguishing mark of good affection to the present government?

Whether in those churches, where the said day is ob-served, it will fully answer the intent of the said Act; if the preacher shall commend, excuse, palliate, or extenuate the murder of that royal Martyr; and lay the guilt of that horrid rebellion, with all its consequences, the following usurpations, the entire destruction of the Church, the cruel and continual persecutions of those who could be discovered to profess its doctrines, with the ensuing Babel of fanaticism, to the account of that blessed King; who, by granting the Petition of Right, and passing every bill that could be asked for the security of the subject, had, by the confession even of those wicked men, before the war began, left them nothing more to demand?

Whether such a preacher as I have named, (whereof there have been more than *one*, not many years past, even in the presence of viceroys) who takes that course as a means for promotion; may not be thought to step a little out of the common road, in a monarchy where the de-scendants of that most blessed Martyr have reigned to this day?

I ground the reason of making these queries, on the title of the act; to which I refer the reader.

THE ADVANTAGES

PROPOSED BY REPEALING THE SACRA-MENTAL TEST,

IMPARTIALLY CONSIDERED.

BY THE REV. DR. SWIFT, DEAN OF ST. PATRICK'S.

Dublin, Printed; London, Re-printed for J. Roberts at the Oxford Arms in Warwick Lane. 1732. (Price Six-pence.)

NOTE.

THE text here given is that of the London reprint of the original edition, which has been collated with that given by Faulkner (vol. iv., 1735). In 1790 the tract was reprinted by J. Walters, and it is evidently from this reprint that Scott obtained his text; for the two agree in almost every particular.

[T. S.]

THE ADVANTAGES PROPOSED BY RE-
PEALING THE SACRAMENTAL
TEST, IMPARTIALLY
CONSIDERED.

W HOEVER writes impartially upon this subject, must do it not only as a mere secular man, but as one who is altogether indifferent to any particular system of Christianity. And, I think, in whatever country that religion predominates, there is one certain form of worship and ceremony, which is looked upon as the established, and consequently only the priests of that particular form, are maintained at the public charge, and all civil employments are bestowed among those who comply (at least outwardly) with the same establishment.

This method is strictly observed, even by our neighbours the Dutch, who are confessed to allow the fullest liberty to conscience of any Christian state ; and yet are never known to admit any persons into religious or civil offices, who do not conform to the legal worship. As to their military men, they are indeed not so scrupulous, being, by the nature of their government, under a necessity of hiring foreign troops of whatever religious denomination, upon every great emergency, and maintaining no small number in time of peace.

This caution therefore of making one established faith, seems to be universal, and founded upon the strongest reasons; the mistaken, or affected zeal of obstinacy, and enthusiasm, having produced such a number of horrible, destructive events, throughout all Christendom. For, whoever begins to think the national worship is wrong, in any important article of practice or belief, will, if he be serious, naturally have a zeal to make as many proselytes as he can, and a nation may possibly have an hundred different sects with their leaders; every one of which hath an equal right to plead; they must "obey God rather than man," must "cry aloud and spare not," must "lift up their voice like a trumpet."

This was the very case of England, during the fanatic times. And against all this, there seems to be no defence, but that of supporting one established form of doctrine and discipline; leaving the rest to a bare liberty of conscience, but without any maintenance or encouragement from the public.

Wherever this national religion grows so corrupt, or is thought to do so by a very great majority of learned [1] people, joined to the governing party, whether prince or senate, or both, it ought to be changed, provided the work might be done without blood or tumults.[2] Yet, whenever such a change shall be made, some other establishment must succeed (although for the worse), allowing all deviations that would break the union to be only tolerated. In this sense, those who affirm, that every law, which is contrary to the law of God, is void in itself, seem to be mistaken. For, many laws in Popish kingdoms and states, many more among the Turks, and perhaps not a few in other countries, are directly against the divine laws; and yet, God knows, are very far from being void in the executive parts.

Thus, for instance, if the three estates of Parliament in England (whereof the lords spiritual [3] are one) should agree, and obtain the royal assent to abolish Episcopacy, together with the liturgy, and the whole frame of the English church, as "burthensome, dangerous, and contrary to Holy Scripture"; and that Presbytery, Anabaptism, Quakerism, Independency,[4] or any other subdivided sect among us, should be established in its place; without question, all peaceable subjects ought passively to submit, and the predominant sect must become the religion established, the public maintaining no other teachers, nor admitting any persons of a different religious profession, into civil offices; at least, if their intention be to preserve the nation in peace.

[1] Scott has "landed." [T. S.]
[2] Scott has "confusion." [T. S.]
[3] Scott inserts here the words: "who represent the Church." [T. S.]
[4] Scott inserts here "Muggletonianism, Brownism, Familism. [T. S.]

Supposing then, that the present system of religion were abolished ; and Presbytery, which stands much the fairest, with its synods and classes, and all its forms and ceremonies, essential or circumstantial, were erected into the national worship : Their teachers, and no others, could have any legal claim to be supported at the public charge, whether by stipends or tithes ; and only the rest of the same faith to be capable of civil employments.

If there be any true reasoning in what I have laid down, it should seem, that the project now in agitation for repealing the Test Act, and yet leaving the name of an establishment to the present national church, is altogether inconsistent, and may admit of consequences, which those, who are the most indifferent to any religion at all, are possibly not aware of.

I presume, whenever the Test shall be repealed, which obliges all men, who enter into office under the Crown, to receive the sacrament according to the rites of the Church of Ireland, the way to employments will immediately be left open to all dissenters, (except Papists) whose consciences can suffer them to take the common oaths in such cases prescribed, after which they are qualified to fill any lay station in this kingdom, from that of chief governor, to an exciseman.

Thus of the three judges on each bench, the first may be a Presbyterian, the second a Free-will Baptist, and the third a Churchman; the Lord Chancellor may be an Independent ; the revenues may be managed by seven commissioners of as many different sects ; and the like of all other employments.   Not to mention the strong probability, that the lawfulness of taking oaths may be *revealed* to the Quakers, who then will stand upon as good a foot for preferment, as any other loyal subject.   It is easy[1] to imagine, under such a motley administration of affairs, what a clashing there will be of interests and inclinations, what pullings and haulings backwards and forwards, what a zeal and bias in each religionist, to advance his own tribe, and depress the others. For, I suppose nothing will be readier granted, than that how indifferent soever most men are in faith and morals, yet whether out of artifice, natural complexion, or love of contradiction, none are more obstinate in maintaining their

---

[1] Scott has "obvious." [T. S.]

own opinions, and worrying all who differ from them, than those who publicly shew the least sense, either of religion or common honesty.

As to the latter, Bishop Burnet tells us, that the Presbyterians, in the fanatic times, professed themselves to be above morality; which, as we find in some of their writings, was numbered among the "beggarly elements"; and accordingly at this day, no scruples of conscience with regard to conformity, are in any trade or calling, inconsistent with the greatest fraud, oppression, perjury, or any other vice.

This brings to my memory a passage in Montaigne, of a common prostitute, who, in the storming of a town, when a soldier came up to her chamber, and offered violence to her chastity, rather chose to venture her neck, by leaping out of the window, than suffer a rape; yet still continued her trade of lewdness, whilst she had any customers left.[1]

I confess, that in my private judgment, an unlimited permission of all sects whatsoever (except Papists) to enjoy employments, would be less pernicious to the public, than a fair struggle between two contenders; because in the former case, such a jumble of principles, might possibly have the effect of contrary poisons mingled together, which a strong constitution might perhaps be able for some time to survive.

But however, I shall take the other, and more probable supposition, that this battle for employments, is to be fought only between the Presbyterians, and those of the church *yet* established. I shall not enter into the merits of either side, by examining which of the two is the better spiritual economy, or which is most suited to the civil constitution: But the question turns upon this point: When the Presbyterians shall have got their share of employments (which must be one full half, or else they cannot look upon themselves as fairly dealt with) I ask, whether they ought not by their own principles, and by the strictest rules of conscience, to use the utmost of their skill, power, and influence, in order to reduce the whole kingdom to an uniformity in religion, both as to doctrine and discipline, most agreeable to the word of

---

[1] The passage referred to by Swift is to be found in the first chapter of the second book of Florio's translation of Montaigne's "Essays"— "Of the Inconstancie of our Actions." [T. S.]

God. Wherein, if they can succeed without blood (as, under the present disposition of things, it is very possible they may) it is to be hoped they will at last be satisfied : Only I would warn them of a few difficulties. The first is for compromising that important controversy about the *Old Light* and the *New ;* [1] which otherwise may, after this establishment, split them as wide as Papist and Protestant, Whig and Tory, or Churchmen and Dissenters ; and consequently the work will be to begin again. For in religious quarrels, it is of little moment how few or small the differences are, especially when the dispute is only about power. Thus the jealous Presbyterians of the north, are more alienated from the established clergy, than from the Romish priests ; taxing the former with idolatrous worship, as disguised Papists, ceremony-mongers, and many other terms of arts, and this for a very powerful reason, because the clergy stand in their way, which the Popish priests do not. Thus I am assured, that the quarrel between *Old* and *New Light men*, is managed with more rage and rancour, than any other dispute of the highest importance ; and this because it serves to lessen or increase their several congregations, from whom they receive their contributions.

Another difficulty which may embarrass the Presbyterians after their establishment, will be how to adjust their claim of the kirk's independency on the civil power, with the constitution of this monarchy ; a point so delicate, that it hath often filled the heads of great patriots with dangerous notions of the church-clergy, without the least ground of suspicion.

As to the Presbyterians allowing liberty of conscience to those of Episcopal principles, when their own kirk is predominant, their writers are so universally agreed in the negative, as well as their practice during Oliver's reign, that I believe no reasonable Churchman, (who must then be a dissenter) will expect it.

I shall here take notice, that in the division of employments among the Presbyterians, after this approaching repeal of the Test Act, supposing them, in proper time, to have an

[1] See "The Correspondent," Nos. 1 and 2, 1733, and note prefixed to present reprint of "Narrative of Several Attempts for the Repeal of the Sacramental Test." [T. S.]

equal share, I compute the odds will be three or four to one on their side, in any further scheme they may have towards making their religion national.   For I reckon, all those gentlemen sent over from England, whatever religion they profess, or have been educated in, to be of that party: Since it is no mark of prudence, for any persons to oppose the current of a nation, where they are in some sort only sojourners, unless they have it in direction.

If there be any maxim in politics, not to be controlled, it must be the following : That those whose private interest is united with the interest of their country, supposing them to be of equal understanding with the rest of their neighbours, will heartily wish, that the nation should thrive.   Out of these are indubitably excepted all persons who are sent from another kingdom, to be employed in places of profit or power ; because they can possibly bear no affection to the place where they sojourn, even for life ; their sole business being to advance themselves, by following the advice of their principals.   I except, likewise, those persons who are taken into offices, although natives of the land, because they are greater gainers while they keep their offices, than they could possibly be by mending the miserable condition of their country.

I except, Thirdly, all hopers, who, by balancing accounts with themselves, turn the scale on the same side; because the strong expectation of a good certain salary, will outweigh the loss by bad rents, received out of lands in moneyless times.

If my lords, the bishops, who, I hear, are now employed in a scheme for regulating the conduct and maintenance of the inferior clergy, shall in their wisdom and piety, and love of the church, consent to this repeal of the Test, I have not the least doubt, that the whole reverend body will cheerfully submit to their spiritual fathers, of whose paternal tenderness for their welfare, they have already found so many amazing instances.

I am not, therefore, under the least concern about the clergy on this account.   They will (*for some time*) be no great sufferers by this repeal; because I cannot recollect among all our sects, any one that gives latitude enough to take the oaths required at an institution to a church-living ;

and, until that bar shall be removed, the present Episcopal clergy are safe for two years.   Although it may be thought somewhat unequal, that in the northern parts, where there may be three Dissenters to one Churchman, the whole revenue should be engrossed by one who hath so small a part of the cure.

It is true, indeed, that this disadvantage, which the Dissenters at present lie under, of a disability to receive church-preferments, will be easily remedied by the repeal of the Test.   For the dissenting teachers are under no incapacity of accepting civil and military employments, wherein they agree perfectly with the Popish clergy, among whom great cardinals and prelates have been commanders of armies, chief ministers, knights of many orders, ambassadors, secretaries of state, and in most high offices under the Crown, although they assert the indelible character, which no sectaries among us did ever assume.   But, that many, both Presbyterians and Independents, commanders, as well as private soldiers, were professed preachers in the time of their dominion, is allowed by all.   Cromwell himself was a preacher, and hath left us one of his sermons in print [1] : So was Col. Howard, Sir George Downing,[2] and several others whose names are on record.   I can, therefore, see no reason why a painful Presbyterian teacher, as soon as the Test shall be repealed, may not be privileged, to hold along with his spiritual office and stipend, a commission in the army, or the civil list *in commendam :* For, as I take it, the Church

[1] Scott inserts here the words: "exactly in the same style and manner with those of our modern Presbyterian teachers." [T. S.]

[2] Sir George Downing (1623?-1684) born in England, completed his education at Harvard, Mass., U.S.A. In 1650, we hear of him as scout-master general of Cromwell's army in Scotland. He wrote many of the letters in " Mercurius Politicus." Distinguished himself principally as Cromwell's ambassador in France and Holland. Through Thomas Howard, however, he obtained an opportunity while legate in Holland for the Rump Parliament, for ingratiating himself in Charles II.'s favour. This Howard was brother to the Earl of Suffolk. As a consequence of this favour, Downing was made a baronet at the Restoration ; and although a man of undoubted ability, his character has come down to us by no means free from taint. Many of his despatches are quoted by Clarendon in that writer's great history. Downing also wrote: "A Reply to the Remarks of the Deputies of the States-General upon Sir G. Downing's Memorial," 1665, ; and "Discourses vindicating his Royal Master from a Libel," 1672. [T. S.]

of England is the only body of Christians, which, in effect,
disqualifies those who are employed to preach its doctrine,
from sharing in the civil power, further than as senators;
which, however, was an institution[1] begun in times of Popery,
many hundred years before the Reformation, and woven
with the very institution of this limited monarchy.

There is indeed another method, by which the stipends
of dissenting teachers may be raised, and the farmer much
relieved; if it should be thought proper to reward a people
so deserving, and so loyal by their principles. Every bishop,
upon the vacancy of a church-living, can sequester the profits
for the use of the next incumbent. Upon a lapse of half a
year, the donation falls to the archbishop, and after a full
year to the Crown, during pleasure; therefore it would be
no hardship for any clergyman alive, if, in those parts of
Ireland, where the number of sectaries much exceed that of
the conformists, the profits, when sequestered, might be
applied to the support of the dissenting teacher, who hath
so many souls to take care of, whereby the poor tenants
would be much relieved in these hard times, and in a better
condition to pay their rents.

But there is another difficulty in this matter, against which
a remedy doth not so readily occur. For, supposing the
Test Act repealed, and the Dissenters in consequence fully
qualified for all secular employments, the question may still
be put, whether those of Ireland will be often the persons
on whom they shall be bestowed; because it is imagined,
there may be another *seminary*[2] in view, *more numerous* and
more needy, as well as *more meriting*, and more easily contented with such low offices, as some nearer neighbours
hardly think it worth stirring from their chimney-sides to
obtain. And, I am told, it is the common practice of those
who are skilled in the management of bees, that when they
see a foreign swarm at some distance, approaching with an
intention to plunder their hives, these artists have a trick to
divert them into some neighbouring apiary, there to make
what havoc they please. This I should not have hinted, if
I had not known it already, to have gotten ground in many

---

[1] Scott has, instead of "which, however, was an institution," the
words, "yet this was a privilege." [T. S.]
[2] Scotland.

suspecting heads : For it is the peculiar talent of this nation, to see dangers afar off : To all which I can only say, that our native Presbyterians, must, by pains and industry, raise such a fund of *merit*, as will answer to a birth six degrees more to the north.   If they cannot arrive at this perfection, as several of the established church have compassed by indefatigable pains, I do not well see how their affairs will much mend by repealing the Test ; for, to be qualified by law for [1] an employment, and yet to be disqualified in fact, as it will much increase the mortification, so it will withdraw the pity of many among their well-wishers, and utterly deprive them of that merit, they have so long made of being a loyal, true Protestant people, persecuted only for religion.

If this happen to be their case, they must wait maturity of time, till they can by prudent, gentle steps make their faith become the religion established in the nation, after which, I do not in the least doubt, their taking the most effectual methods to secure their power against those who must then be Dissenters in their turn, whereof, if we may form a future opinion from present times, and the disposition of Dissenters, who love to make a thorough reformation, the number and qualities will be very inconsiderable.

Thus I have with the utmost sincerity, after long thinking, given my judgment upon this arduous affair ; but with the utmost deference and submission to public wisdom and power.

[1] Scott has " to accept."   [T. S.]

REASONS HUMBLY OFFERED TO THE PARLIAMENT OF IRELAND FOR REPEALING THE SACRAMENTAL TEST, &c.

NOTE.

In the 4to edition of Swift's works (1755) is given the following note :

"The author having before examined 'The Presbyterians' Plea of Merit' with respect to their own principles and practices, has in this tract put them in the balance against Papists."

In a reprint of this tract in the second volume of "Political Tracts," 2 vols. 8vo, 1738, London, is the following "Advertisement"—neither Scott, Faulkner, nor Hawkesworth give this. Probably it appeared in the first edition ; but as I have not been able to come across this, I am not certain.

"In the years 1732, and 1733, an attempt was made for repealing the Test Act in Ireland, introductory of a like attempt in England. The various arguments for it were answered in every shape ; but no way more effectually than by examining what pretence the Presbyterians had to share in all the privileges of government, either from their own principles and behaviour, or compared with those of other sectaries. Under the former head they were fully silenced by our author in 'The Presbyterians' Plea of Merit Impartially Examined." They are now put in the balance with Papists, whom though they have sometimes styled their brethren in adversity, yet when placed in competition, they will hate as brethren likewise. But let them here dispute the preference, and then put in their claim to be part of the establishment."

"The arguments pretended to be urged by the Roman Catholics, in this tract," says Monck Mason, "consist partly of true statements and partly of ironical allusions, which are combined together into such a trellis work, as to render it almost unassailable."

The text here given is that from the 4to edition (1755) of Swift's Works, collated with that in the second volume of "Political Tracts" above referred to.

[T. S.]

REASONS

Humbly offered to the PARLIAMENT of IRELAND

For Repealing the

SACRAMENTAL TEST, &c.

IN FAVOUR OF

THE CATHOLICS,

OTHERWISE CALLED ROMAN CATHOLICS, AND BY THEIR ILL-WILLERS PAPISTS.

Drawn partly from Arguments as they are Catholics, and partly from Arguments common to them with their Brethren the Dissenters.

WRITTEN IN THE YEAR 1733.

REASONS HUMBLY OFFERED TO THE PARLIAMENT OF IRELAND FOR REPEALING THE SACRA-MENTAL TEST, &c.

IT is well known, that the first conquerors of this kingdom were English Catholics, subjects to English Catholic kings, from whom, by their valour and success, they obtained large portions of land given them as a reward for their many victories over the Irish: To which merit our brethren the Dissenters of any denomination whatsoever, have not the least pretensions.

It is confessed, that the posterity of those first victorious Catholics were often forced to rise in their own defence, against new colonies from England, who treated them like mere native Irish, with innumerable oppressions ; depriving them of their lands, and driving them by force of arms into the most desolate parts of the kingdom. Till in the next generation, the children of these tyrants were used in the same manner by new English adventurers, which practice continued for many centuries. But it is agreed on all hands, that no insurrections were ever made, except after great oppressions by fresh invaders. Whereas all the rebellions of Puritans, Presbyterians, Independents, and other sectaries, constantly began before any provocations were given, except that they were not suffered to change the government in Church and State, and seize both into their own hands ; which, however, at last they did, with the murder of their King and of many thousands of his best subjects.

The Catholics were always defenders of monarchy, as constituted in these kingdoms. Whereas our brethren the Dissenters were always republicans, both in principle and practice.

It is well known that all the Catholics of these kingdoms, both priests and laity, are true Whigs in the best and most proper sense of the word; bearing as well in their hearts, as in their outward profession, an entire loyalty to the royal house of Hanover in the person and posterity of George II. against the Pretender and all his adherents. To which they think themselves bound in gratitude as well as conscience, by the lenity wherewith they have been treated since the death of Queen Anne, so different from what they suffered in the four last years of that Princess, during the administration of that *wicked* minister, the Earl of Oxford.

The Catholics of this kingdom humbly hope, that they have at least as fair a title as any of their brother Dissenters, to the appellation of Protestants. They have always protested against the selling, dethroning, or murdering their Kings: Against the usurpations and avarice of the court of Rome: Against Deism, Atheism, Socinianism, Quakerism, Muggletonianism, Fanaticism, Brownism, as well as against all Jews, Turks, Infidels, and Heretics. Whereas the title of Protestants assumed by the whole herd of Dissenters (except ourselves) dependeth entirely upon their protesting against archbishops, bishops, deans, and chapters, with their revenues; and the whole hierarchy. Which are the very expressions used in The Solemn League and Covenant,[1] where the word Popery is only mentioned *ad invidiam*; because the Catholics agree with the Episcopal church in those fundamentals.

Although the Catholics cannot deny, that in the great rebellion against King Charles I. more soldiers of their religion were in the Parliament army than in His Majesty's troops; and that many jesuits and friars went about in the disguise of Presbyterian and Independent ministers, to preach up rebellion; as the best historians of those times inform us; yet the bulk of Catholics in both kingdoms preserved their loyalty entire.

---

[1] A solemn league and covenant entered into between the Scots and English fanatics, in the rebellion against King Charles I., 1643, by which they solemnly engaged, among other things, "To endeavour the extirpation of prelacy, that is, church government by archbishops, bishops, deans, archdeacons, and all other episcopal officers, depending on that hierarchy." [H.]

The Catholics have some reason to think it a little hard, when their enemies will not please to distinguish between the rebellious riot committed by that brutal ruffian, Sir Phelim O'Neal [1] with his tumultuous crew of rabble; and the forces raised afterwards by the Catholic lords and gentlemen of the English pale, in defence of the King after the English rebellion began.   It is well known, that His Majesty's affairs were in great distraction some time before, by an invasion of the covenanting, Scottish, kirk rebels, and by the base terms the King was forced to accept, that they might be kept in quiet, at a juncture when he was every hour threatened at home by that fanatic party, which soon after set all in a flame.   And, if the Catholic army in Ireland fought for their King against the forces sent over by the Parliament, then in actual rebellion against him, what person of loyal principles can be so partial to deny, that they did their duty, by joining with the Marquis of Ormonde, and other commanders, who bore their commissions from the King?   For which, great numbers of them lost their lives, and forfeited their estates; a great part of the latter being now possessed by many descendants from those very men who had drawn their swords in the service of that rebellious Parliament which cut off his head, and destroyed monarchy.   And what is more amazing, although the same persons, when the Irish were entirely subdued, continued in power under the Rump; were chief confidants, and faithful subjects to Cromwell, yet being wise enough to foresee a restoration, they seized the forts and

[1] Sir Phelim O'Neill (1604?-1683) one of the most picturesque characters of Irish history.   For his share in the rebellion of 1641 he was expelled from the Irish House of Commons.   The rebellion was an attempt to assist Charles as against the Parliament, and O'Neill forged a commission, purporting to come from the King, authorizing the Irish to rise in his favour.   The Scottish settlers in Ulster, on whom O'Neill relied for aid disappointed him, and he thereupon set to work to reduce all their towns.   The famous siege of Drogheda was one of the many incidents of his campaign.   He joined forces with his kinsman, Owen Roe O'Neill, but a jealous difference on his part urged Sir Phelim to support Ormonde, in 1640, in that general's endeavours for a peace.   Sir Phelim, however, was not included in the benefit of the Articles of Kilkenny, and a price was placed on his head.   He was betrayed by Philip Roe McHugh O'Neill, brought to Dublin, and executed as a traitor. [T. S.]

castles here, out of the hands of their old brethren in rebellion, for the service of the King; just saving the tide, and putting in a stock of merit, sufficient not only to preserve the lands which the Catholics lost by their loyalty; but likewise to preserve their civil and military employments, or be higher advanced.

Those insurrections wherewith the Catholics are charged from the beginning of the seventeenth century to the great English rebellion, were occasioned by many oppressions they lay under. They had no intention to introduce a new religion, but to enjoy the liberty of preserving the old; the very same which their ancestors professed from the time that Christianity was first introduced into this island, which was by Catholics; but whether mingled with corruptions, as some pretend, doth not belong to the question. They had no design to change the government; they never attempted to fight against, to imprison, to betray, to sell, to bring to a trial, or to murder their King. The schismatics acted by a spirit directly contrary; they united in a Solemn League and Covenant, to alter the whole system of spiritual government, established in all Christian nations, and of apostolic institution; concluding the tragedy with the murder of the King in cold blood, and upon mature deliberation; at the same time changing the monarchy into a commonwealth.

The Catholics of Ireland, in the great rebellion, lost their estates for fighting in defence of their King. The schismatics, who cut off the father's head, forced the son to fly for his life, and overturned the whole ancient frame of government, religious and civil; obtained grants of those very estates which the Catholics lost in defence of the ancient constitution, many of which estates are at this day possessed by the posterity of those schismatics: And thus, they gained by their rebellion what the Catholics lost by their loyalty.[1]

We allow the Catholics to be brethren of the Dissenters; some people, indeed, (which we cannot allow) would have them to be our children, because *we* both dissent from the Church established, and both agree in abolishing this persecuting Sacramental Test; by which negative discourage-

---

[1] This paragraph is omitted in edition of 1743, but it is printed in that of 1755. [T. S.]

ment we are both rendered incapable of civil and military employments.   However, we cannot but wonder at the bold familiarity of these schismatics, in calling the members of the National Church their brethren and fellow Protestants. It is true, that all these sects (except the Catholics) are brethren to each other in faction, ignorance, iniquity, perverseness, pride, and (if we except the Quakers) in rebellion. But, how the churchmen can be styled their fellow Protestants, we cannot comprehend.   Because, when the whole Babel of sectaries joined against the Church, the King, and the nobility for twenty years, in a match at football; where the proverb expressly tells us, that *all are fellows;* while the three kingdoms were tossed to and fro, the churches, and cities, and royal palaces shattered to pieces by their balls, their buffets, and their kicks; the victors would allow no more *fellows at football:* But murdered, sequestered, plundered, deprived, banished to the plantations, or enslaved all their opposers who had lost the game.

It is said the world is governed by opinion; and politicians assure us, that all power is founded thereupon. Wherefore, as all human creatures are fond to distraction of their own opinions; and so much the more, as those opinions are absurd, ridiculous, or of little moment; it must follow, that they are equally fond of power.   But no opinions are maintained with so much obstinacy as those in religion, especially by such zealots who never bore the least regard to religion, conscience, honour, justice, truth, mercy, or common morality, farther than in outward appearance; under the mask of hypocrisy, to promote their diabolical designs.   And therefore Bishop Burnet, one of their oracles, tells us honestly, that the *saints* of those fanatic times, pronounced themselves above morality; which they reckoned among "beggarly elements"; but the meaning of those two last words thus applied, we confess to be above our understanding.

Among those kingdoms and states which first embraced the Reformation, England appears to have received it in the most regular way; where it was introduced in a peaceable manner, by the supreme power of a King,[1] and the three

---

[1] Henry VIII. [H.]

estates in Parliament; to which, as the highest legislative authority, all subjects are bound passively to submit. Neither was there much blood shed on so great a change of religion. But a considerable number of lords, and other persons of quality through the kingdom still continued in their old faith, and were, notwithstanding their difference in religion, employed in offices civil as well as military, more or less in every reign, until the Test Act in the time of King Charles II. However, from the time of the Reformation, the number of Catholics gradually and considerably lessened. So that in the reign of King Charles I. England became, in a great degree, a Protestant Kingdom, without taking the sectaries into the number ; the legality whereof, with respect to human laws, the Catholics never disputed: But the Puritans, and other schismatics, without the least pretence to any such authority, by an open rebellion, destroyed that legal Reformation, as we observed before, murdered their King, and changed the monarchy into a republic. It is therefore not to be wondered at, if the Catholics, in such a Babel of religions, chose to adhere to their own faith left to them by their ancestors, rather than seek for a better among a rabble of hypocritical, rebellious, deluding knaves, or deluded enthusiasts.

We repeat once more, that if a national religion be changed by the supreme legislative power, we cannot dispute the human legality of such a change. But we humbly conceive, that if any considerable party of men which differs from an establishment, either old or new, can deserve liberty of conscience, it ought to consist of those who for want of conviction, or of a right understanding the merits of each cause, conceive themselves bound in conscience to adhere to the religion of their ancestors ; because they are of all others least likely to be authors of innovations, either in Church or State.

On t'other side; If the reformation of religion be founded upon rebellion against the King, without whose consent, by the nature of our constitution, no law can pass. If this reformation be introduced by only one of the three estates, I mean the Commons, and not by one half even of those Commons ; and this by the assistance of a rebellious army : Again, if this reformation were carried on by the exclusion of nobles both lay and spiritual (who constitute the two other parts of the three estates) by the murder of their King, and by abolishing the whole system of government; the Catholics cannot see why the successors of those schismatics, who are universally accused by all parties except themselves, and a few infamous abettors, for still retaining the same principles in religion and government, under which their predecessors acted; should pretend to a better share of civil or military trust, profit and power than the Catholics, who during all that period of twenty years, were continually persecuted with utmost severity, merely on account of their loyalty and constant adherence to kingly power.

We now come to those arguments for repealing the Sacramental Test, which equally affect the Catholics, and their brethren the Dissenters.

First, We agree with our fellow Dissenters; that " persecution merely for conscience' sake, is against the genius of the Gospel."[1] And so likewise is "any law for depriving men of their natural and civil rights which they claim as men." We are also ready enough to allow that "the smallest negative discouragements for uniformity's sake are so many persecutions." Because, it cannot be denied, that the scratch of a pin is in some degree a real wound, as much as a stab through the heart. In like manner, an incapacity by law for any man to be made a judge, a colonel, or justice of the peace, "merely on a point of conscience, is a negative discouragement," and consequently a real persecution: For, in this case, the author of the pamphlet quoted in the margin[2] puts a very pertinent and powerful question: That, "If God be the sole lord of the conscience, why should the rights of conscience be subject to human jurisdiction?" Now to apply this to the Catholics: The belief of transubstantiation "is a matter purely of religion and conscience, which doth not affect the political interest of society as such. Therefore, Why should the rights of conscience, whereof God is the sole lord, be subject to human jurisdiction?" And why should God be deprived of this right over a Catholic's conscience any more than over that of any other Dissenter?

[1] *Vid.* Reasons for the Repeal of the Sacramental Test. [Note in edit. 1738.]
[2] *Idem.*

And whereas another author among our brethren the Dissenters, hath very justly complained, that by this persecuting Test Act, great numbers of true Protestants have been forced to leave the kingdom, and fly to the plantations, rather than stay here branded with an incapacity for civil and military employments; we do affirm, that the Catholics can bring many more instances of the same kind; some thousands of their religion have been forced by the Sacramental Test, to retire into other countries, rather than live here under the incapacity of wearing swords, sitting in Parliament, and getting that share of power and profit which belongs to them as fellow Christians, whereof they are deprived "merely upon account of conscience, which would not allow them to take the sacrament after the manner prescribed in the liturgy." Hence it clearly follows in the words of the same author,[1] "That if we Catholics are uncapable of employments, we are punished for our dissent, that is, for our conscience, which wholly turns upon political considerations."

The Catholics are willing to acknowledge the King's supremacy, whenever their brethren the Dissenters shall please to shew them the example.

Further, The Catholics, whenever their religion shall come to be the national established faith, are willing to undergo the same test offered by the author already quoted. His words are these: " To end this debate, by putting it upon a foot which I hope will appear to every impartial person a fair and equitable one; We Catholics propose, with submission to the proper judges, that effectual security be taken against persecution, by obliging all who are admitted into places of power and trust, whatever their religious profession be, in the most solemn manner to disclaim persecuting principles." It is hoped the public will take notice of these words; "Whatever their religious profession be;" which plainly include the Catholics; and for which we return thanks to our dissenting brethren.

And, whereas it is objected by those of the established Church, that if the schismatics and fanatics were once put into a capacity of possessing civil and military employments; they would never be at ease till they had raised their own

---

[1] See " Reasons against the Test." [Note in edit. 1738.]

way of worship into the national religion through all His Majesty's dominions, equal with the true orthodox Scottish kirk ; which when they had once brought to pass, they would no more allow liberty of conscience to Episcopal Dissenters, than they did in the time of the great English rebellion, and in the succeeding fanatic anarchy till the King was restored. There is another very learned schismatical pamphleteer,[1] who in answer to a malignant libel, called, *The Presbyterians' Plea of Merit, &c.*, clearly wipes off this aspersion ; by assuring all Episcopal Protestants of the present Church, upon his own word, and to his own knowledge, that our brethren the Dissenters will never offer at such an attempt. In like manner, the Catholics when legally required, will openly declare upon their words and honours, that, as soon as their negative discouragements and their persecution shall be removed by repealing the Sacramental Test, they will leave it entirely to the merits of the cause, whether the kingdom shall think fit to make their faith the established religion or not.

And again, Whereas our Presbyterian brethren in many of their pamphlets, take much offence, that the great rebellion in England, the murder of the King, with the entire change of religion and government, are perpetually objected against them both in and out of season, by our common enemy, the present conformists : We do declare in the defence of our said brethren, that the reproach aforesaid is *an old worn-out threadbare cant*, which they always disdained to answer : And I very well remember, that, having once told a certain conformist, how much I wondered to hear him and his tribe, dwelling perpetually on so beaten a subject ; he was pleased to divert the discourse with a foolish story, which I cannot forbear telling to his disgrace. He said, there was a clergyman in Yorkshire, who for fifteen years together preached every Sunday against drunkenness : Whereat the parishioners being much offended, complained to the archbishop ; who having sent for the clergyman, and severely reprimanded him, the minister had no better an answer, than by confess-

---

[1] "Vindication of the Protestant Dissenters." This pamphlet has been mentioned in the note prefixed to "The Presbyterians' Plea of Merit." It was written as a reply to that tract, and to the "Narrative." [T. S.]

ing the fact; adding, that all the parish were drunkards; that he desired to reclaim them from one vice before he would begin upon another; and, since they still continued to be as great drunkards as before, he resolved to go on, except his Grace would please to forbid him.

We are very sensible how heavy an accusation lieth upon the Catholics of Ireland; that some years before King Charles II. was restored, when theirs and the King's forces were entirely reduced, and the kingdom declared by the Rump to be settled; after all His Majesty's generals were forced to fly to France, or other countries, the heads of the said Catholics who remained here in an enslaved condition, joined to send an invitation to the Duke of Lorrain; engaging, upon his appearing here with his forces, to deliver up the whole island to his power, and declare him their sovereign; which, after the Restoration, was proved against them by Dean Boyle, since primate, who produced the very original instrument at the board. The Catholics freely acknowledge the fact to be true; and, at the same time appeal to all the world, whether a wiser, a better, a more honourable, or a more justifiable project could have been thought of. They were then reduced to slavery and beggary by the English rebels, many thousands of them murdered, the rest deprived of their estates, and driven to live on a small pittance in the wilds of Connaught; at a time when either the Rump or Cromwell absolutely governed the three kingdoms. And the question will turn upon this, Whether the Catholics, deprived of all their possessions, governed with a rod of iron, and in utter despair of ever seeing the monarchy restored, for the preservation of which they had suffered so much, were to be blamed for calling in a foreign prince of their own religion, who had a considerable army to support them; rather than submit to so infamous an usurper as Cromwell, or such a bloody and ignominious conventicle as the Rump. And I have often heard, not only our friends the Dissenters, but even our common enemy the Conformists, who are conversant in the history of those times, freely confess, that considering the miserable situation the Irish were then in, they could not have thought of a braver or more virtuous attempt; by which they might have been instruments of restoring the lawful monarch, at least to the recovery of England and Scotland, from those betrayers, and sellers, and murderers of his royal father.

To conclude, Whereas the last quoted author complains very heavily and frequently of a *brand* that lies upon them, it is a great mistake : For the first original brand hath been long taken off. Only we confess, the scar will probably remain and be visible for ever to those who know the principles by which they acted, and until those principles shall be openly renounced ; else it must continue to all generations, like the mark set upon Cain, which some authors say descended to all his posterity : Or like the Roman nose and Austrian lip, or like the long bag of flesh hanging down from the gills of the people in Piedmont.   But as for any brands fixed on schismatics for several years past, they have been all made with cold iron ; like thieves, who by the benefit of the clergy are condemned to be only burned in the hand ; but escape the pain and the mark, by being in fee with the jailor. Which advantage the schismatical teachers will never want, who, as we are assured, and of which there is a very fresh instance, have the souls, and bodies, and purses of the people a hundred times more at their mercy, than the Catholic priests could ever pretend to.

Therefore, upon the whole, the Catholics do humbly petition (without the least insinuation of threatening) that upon this favourable juncture their incapacity for civil and military employments may be wholly taken off, for the very same reasons (besides others more cogent) that are now offered by their brethren the Dissenters.

And your petitioners, as in duty bound, shall ever pray, &c.[1]

Dublin, Nov. 1733.

---

[1] In this controversy the author was again victorious, for the Test was not repealed. [H.]

SOME FEW THOUGHTS

CONCERNING THE REPEAL OF THE TEST.[1]

THOSE of either side who have written upon this subject of the Test, in making or answering objections, seem to fail by not pressing sufficiently the chief point upon which the controversy turns. The arguments used by those who write for the Church are very good in their kind, but will have little force under the present corruptions of mankind, because the authors treat this subject *tanquam in republicâ Platonis, et non in fæce Romuli.*

It must be confessed, that, considering how few employments of any consequence fall to the share of those English who are born in this kingdom, and those few very dearly purchased, at the expense of conscience, liberty, and all regard for the public good, they are not worth contending for : And, if nothing but profit were in the case, it would hardly cost me one sigh when I should see those few scraps thrown among every species of fanatics, to scuffle for among themselves.

And this will infallibly be the case, after repealing the Test.

For, every subdivision of sect will, with equal justice, pretend to have a share ; and, as it is usual with sharers, will never think they have enough, while any pretender is left unprovided. I shall not except the Quakers ; because, when the passage is once let open for all sects to partake in public emoluments, it is very probable the lawfulness of taking oaths, and wearing carnal weapons,[2] may be revealed

---

[1] The text is that of the quarto edition (1765) of Swift's Works. [T. S.]

[2] The Quakers were more likely to admit this relaxation of their peculiar tenets, as, upon their first appearance as a sect, they did not by any means profess the principle of non-resistance, which they afterwards adopted. [S.]

to the brotherhood; which thought, I confess, was first put into my head by one of the shrewdest Quakers in this kingdom.[1]

[1] The Quaker hinted at by Dr Swift was Mr George Rooke, a linen-draper. In a letter to Mr Pope, Aug. 30, 1716, Dr Swift says, "There is a young ingenious Quaker in this town, who writes verses to his mistress, not very correct, but in a strain purely what a poetical Quaker should do, commending her look and habit, &c. It gave me a hint, that a set of Quaker pastorals might succeed, if our friend Gay would fancy it; and I think it a fruitful subject : pray hear what he says."— Accordingly Gay wrote "The Espousal, a sober Eclogue, between two of the People called Quakers." [S.]

TEN REASONS FOR REPEALING
THE TEST ACT.[1]

1.

BECAUSE the Presbyterians are people of such great interest in this kingdom, that there are not above ten of their persuasion in the House of Commons, and but one in the House of Lords; though they are not obliged to take the sacrament in the Established Church to qualify them to be members of either House.

2. Because those of the Established Church of this kingdom are so disaffected to the King, that not one of them worth mentioning, except the late Duke of Ormond,[2] has been concerned in the rebellion; and that our Parliament, though there be so few Presbyterians, has, upon all occasions, proved its loyalty to King George, and has readily agreed to and enacted what might support his government.

---

[1] "This Tract is from a rare broadside copy. It appears to be written by the Dean, and the arguments correspond with those he uses elsewhere." So says Scott; but Monck Mason considers this tract no more the work of Swift than several others he mentions. See note prefixed to "The Presbyterians' Plea of Merit." [T. S.]

[2] James Butler, Duke of Ormond (1610-1688), was lieutenant-general of the army of Ireland during the rebellion of 1641. After his defeat of General Preston, in 1643, he was appointed Lord-Lieutenant of Ireland; but retired to France on the fall of the Stuart dynasty. The execution of Charles caused Ormond to land again in Ireland for the purpose of rousing that country in favour of the royal cause; but he forsook it on the landing of Cromwell. At the Restoration he came over with Charles, and was raised, for his services, to the dukedom. He was, however, deprived of his lord-lieutenancy for his friendship for the exiled Clarendon. He had a narrow escape for his life from the plots of Colonel Blood, whom he forgave at the request of the King. In 1682 he was rewarded by being promoted to an English dukedom. [T. S.]

3. Because very few of the Presbyterians have lost an employment worth £20 per annum, for not qualifying themselves according to the Test Act; nor will they accept of a militia commission, though they do of one in the army.

4. Because, if they are not in the militia and other places of trust, the Pretender and his adherents will destroy us; when he has no one to support him but the King of Spain; when King George is at a good understanding with Sweden, Prussia, and Denmark; and when he has made the best alliances in Christendom. When the Emperor, King of Great Britain, the French King, the King of Sardinia, are all in the quadruple alliance against the Spaniard, his upstart cardinal,[1] and the Pretender; when bloody plots against Great Britain and France are blown up; when the Spanish fleet is quite dispersed; when the French army is over-running Spain; and when the rebels in Scotland are cut off.

5. The test clause should be repealed, because it is a defence against the reformation the Presbyterians long since promised the churches of England and Ireland, viz. " We, noblemen, barons, knights, gentlemen, citizens, burgesses, ministers of the Gospel, commons of all sorts in the kingdoms of Scotland, England, and Ireland, &c.[2] each one of us for himself, with our hands lifted up to the most high God, do swear, first, That we shall sincerely, really, and constantly, through the grace of God, endeavour, in our several places and callings, the preservation of the reformed

---

[1] Cardinal Julius Alberoni (1664-1752), born at Parma, obtained the favour, when a humble parish priest, of the Duke of Vendôme, by informing that general of the whereabouts of some corn, which the country folk had hidden. He followed the Duke to Spain, and was successful in bringing about the marriage between the Princess of Parma and Philip V. For this service he was made Prime Minister of Spain, a cardinal, and Archbishop of Valencia. He entered heartily into Philip's designs for recovering Spain's lost territory, and showed even more boldness than his royal master in their execution. His reduction of Sardinia precipitated the alliance between England, France, Holland, and afterwards, Austria. Spain, with Alberoni as its guiding spirit, supported the Jacobite cause to harass England, and conquered Sicily. But at Messina the Spanish fleet was destroyed by the English, and in the north of Spain the forces of Philip were repulsed by the French. In the end, Spain gave way, and Alberoni was dismissed to retire to Rome, and to be safely lodged in the Jesuits' College there. On his release he returned to his native town, but died at Rome. [T. S.]

[2] *Vide* " Confession of Faith," pp. 304, 305.

religion in the Church of Scotland, in doctrine, worship, discipline, and government. Secondly, That we shall in like manner, without respect of persons, endeavour the extirpation of Popery, Prelacy ; that is, church-government by archbishops, their chancellors, and commissaries, deans, deacons, and chapters, archdeacons, and all other ecclesiastical officers depending on that hierarchy.

6. Because the Presbyterian Church-Government may be independent of the state. The Lord Jesus is King and Head of his Church ;[1] hath therein appointed a government, in the hands of church-officers, distinct from the civil magistrate. As magistrates may lawfully call a synod of ministers to consult and advise with about matters of religion ; so, if magistrates be open enemies to the Church, the ministers of Christ of themselves, by virtue of their office, or they with other fit persons, upon delegation from their churches, may meet together in such assemblies.[2]

7. Because they have not the free use of their religion, when they disdain a toleration.

8. Because they have so much charity for Episcopacy, as to account it iniquitous. The address of the General Assembly to the Duke of Queensbury in the late reign says, that to tolerate the Episcopal clergy in Scotland would be to establish iniquity by a law.

9. Because repealing the test clause will probably disoblige ten of his Majesty's good subjects, for one it can oblige.

10. Because, if the test clause be repealed, the Presbyterians may with the better grace get into employments, and the easier worm out those of the Established Church.

---

[1] "Confession of Faith," p. 87.
[2] *Ibid.*, pp. 88, 89.

SERMONS.

THE following Form of Prayer, which Dr Swift constantly used in the pulpit before his sermon, is copied from his own handwriting:

"Almighty and most merciful God! forgive us all our sins. Give us grace heartily to repent them, and to lead new lives. Graft in our hearts a true love and veneration for thy holy name and word. Make thy pastors burning and shining lights, able to convince gainsayers, and to save others and themselves. Bless this congregation here met together in thy name; grant them to hear and receive thy holy word, to the salvation of their own souls. Lastly, we desire to return thee praise and thanksgiving for all thy mercies bestowed upon us; but chiefly for the Fountain of them all, Jesus Christ our Lord, in whose name and words we further call upon thee, saying, 'Our Father,' &c."

NOTE.

THESE twelve sermons are what have been handed down to us of a bundle of thirty-five which Swift, some years before his death, gave to Dr. Sheridan. Swift had no great opinion of them himself, if we may judge from what he said to his friend when he offered him the bundle. "You may have them if you please; they may be of use to you, they never were of any to me." There is not much in any of them of that quality which characterizes the average sermon. For the artifices of rhetoric which are usually employed to move hearers Swift had no small contempt. He aimed to convince the mind by plain statements of common-sense views. He had no faith in a conviction brought about under the stress of emotional excitement. His sermons exactly answer to the advice he gave a young clergyman—"First tell the people what is their duty, and then convince them that it is so." In the note to his reprint of these sermons Sir Walter Scott has very admirably summed up their qualities.

"The Sermons of Swift," says Scott, "have none of that thunder which appals, or that resistless and winning softness which melts, the hearts of an audience. He can never have enjoyed the triumph of uniting hundreds in one ardent sentiment of love, of terror, or of devotion. His reasoning, however powerful, and indeed unanswerable, convinces the understanding, but is never addressed to the heart; and, indeed, from his instructions to a young clergyman, he seems hardly to have considered pathos as a legitimate ingredient in an English sermon. Occasionally, too, Swift's misanthropic habits break out even from the pulpit; nor is he altogether able to suppress his disdain of those fellow mortals, on whose behalf was accomplished the great work of redemption. With such unamiable feelings towards his hearers, the preacher might indeed command their respect, but could never excite their sympathy. It may be feared that his Sermons were less popular from another cause, imputable more to the congregation than to the pastor. Swift spared not the vices of rich or poor; and, disdaining to amuse the imaginations of his audience with discussion of dark points of divinity, or warm them by a flow of sentimental devotion, he rushes at once to the point of moral depravity, and upbraids them with their favourite and predominant vices in a tone of stern reproof, bordering upon reproach. In short, he tears the bandages from their wounds, like the hasty surgeon of a crowded hospital, and applies the incision knife and caustic with salutary, but rough and untamed severity. But, alas! the mind must be already victorious over the worst of its evil propensities, that can profit by this harsh medicine. There is a principle of opposition in our nature, which mans itself with obstinacy even against avowed truth, when it approaches our feelings in a harsh and insulting manner. And Swift was probably sensible, that his discourses, owing to these various causes, did not produce the powerful effects most grateful to the feelings of the preacher, because they reflect back to him those of the audience.

"But although the Sermons of Swift are deficient in eloquence, and were lightly esteemed by their author, they must not be undervalued by the modern reader. They exhibit, in an eminent degree, that powerful grasp of intellect which distinguished the author above all his contemporaries. In no religious discourses can be found more sound good sense, more happy and forcible views of the immediate subject. The reasoning is not only irresistible, but managed in a mode so simple and clear, that its force is obvious to the most ordinary capacity. Upon all subjects of morality, the preacher maintains the character of a rigid and inflexible monitor; neither admitting apology for that which is wrong, nor softening the difficulty of adhering to that which is right; a stern stoicism of doctrine, that may fail in finding many converts, but leads to excellence in the few manly minds who dare to embrace it.

"In treating the doctrinal points of belief, (as in his Sermon upon the Trinity,) Swift systematically refuses to quit the high and pre-eminent ground which the defender of Christianity is entitled to occupy, or to submit to the test of human reason, mysteries which are placed, by their very nature, far beyond our finite capacities. Swift considered, that, in religion, as in profane science, there must be certain ultimate laws which are to be received as fundamental truths, although we are incapable of defining or analysing their nature; and he censures those divines, who, in presumptuous confidence of their own logical powers, enter into controversy upon such mysteries of faith, without considering that they give thereby the most undue advantage to the infidel. Our author wisely and consistently declared reason an incompetent judge of doctrines, of which God had declared the fact, concealing from man the manner. He contended, that he who, upon the whole, receives the Christian religion as of divine inspiration, must be contented to depend upon God's truth, and his holy word, and receive with humble faith the mysteries which are too high for comprehension. Above all, Swift points out, with his usual forcible precision, the mischievous tendency of those investigations which, while they assail one fundamental doctrine of the Christian religion, shake and endanger the whole fabric, destroy the settled faith of thousands, pervert and mislead the genius of the learned and acute, destroy and confound the religious principles of the simple and ignorant."

In 1744, Faulkner printed three sermons as a single volume; these were "On Mutual Subjection," "On Conscience," and "On the Trinity." The other sermons appeared in the various editions issued by Nichols and others. The text here given is that of the volume of 1744, of Hawkesworth and Scott.

[T. S.]

ON MUTUAL SUBJECTION.

I PETER, V. 5.

" —— Yea, all of you be subject one to another."

THE Apostle having in many parts of this epistle given directions to Christians concerning the duty of subjection or obedience to superiors; in the several instances of the subject to his prince, the child to his parent, the servant to his master, the wife to her husband, and the younger to the elder; doth here, in the words of my text, sum up the whole, by advancing a point of doctrine, which at first may appear a little extraordinary: "Yea, all of you," saith he, "be subject one to another." For it should seem, that two persons cannot properly be said to be subject to each other, and that subjection is only due from inferiors to those above them: yet St Paul hath several passages to the same purpose. For he exhorts the Romans, "in honour to prefer one another;"[1] and the Philippians, "that in lowliness of mind they should each esteem other better than themselves;"[2] and the Ephesians, "that they should submit themselves one to another in the fear of the Lord."[3] Here we find these two great apostles recommending to all Christians this duty of mutual subjection. For we may observe by St Peter, that having mentioned the several relations which men bear to each other, as governor and subject, master and servant, and the rest which I have already repeated, he maketh no exception, but sums up the whole with commanding "all to be subject one to another." From whence we may conclude, that this subjection due from all men to all men, is something more than the compliment of course, when our betters

---

[1] Rom. xii. 10.   [2] Philip. ii. 3.   [3] Ephes. v. 21.

are pleased to tell us they are our humble servants, but understand us to be their slaves.

I know very well, that some of those who explain this text, apply it to humility, to the duties of charity, to private exhortations, and to bearing with each other's infirmities: And it is probable, the apostle may have had a regard to all these: But however, many learned men agree, that there is something more understood, and so the words in their plain natural meaning must import; as you will observe yourselves, if you read them with the beginning of the verse, which is thus: "Likewise ye younger submit yourselves unto the elder; yea, all of you be subject one to another." So, that upon the whole, there must be some kind of subjection due from every man to every man, which cannot be made void by any power, pre-eminence, or authority whatsoever. Now, what sort of subjection this is, and how it ought to be paid, shall be the subject of my present discourse.

As God hath contrived all the works of nature to be useful, and in some manner a support to each other, by which the whole frame of the world under his providence is preserved and kept up; so, among mankind, our particular stations are appointed to each of us by God Almighty, wherein we are obliged to act, as far as our power reacheth, toward the good of the whole community. And he who doth not perform that part assigned him, toward advancing the benefit of the whole, in proportion to his opportunities and abilities, is not only a useless, but a very mischievous member of the public: Because he taketh his share of the profit, and yet leaves his share of the burden to be borne by others, which is the true principal cause of most miseries and misfortunes in life. For, a wise man who doth not assist with his counsels, a great man with his protection, a rich man with his bounty and charity, and a poor man with his labour, are perfect nuisances in a commonwealth. Neither is any condition of life more honourable in the sight of God than another; otherwise he would be a respecter of persons, which he assureth us he is not: For he hath proposed the same salvation to all men, and hath only placed them in different ways or stations to work it out. Princes are born with no more advantages of strength or wisdom than other men; and, by an unhappy education, are usually more defective in both than thousands of their subjects. They depend for every necessary of life upon the meanest of their people: Besides, obedience and subjection were never enjoined by God to humour the passions, lusts, and vanities of those who demand them from us; but we are commanded to obey our governors, because disobedience would breed seditions in the state. Thus servants are directed to obey their masters, children their parents, and wives their husbands; not from any respect of persons in God, but because otherwise there would be nothing but confusion in private families. This matter will be clearly explained, by considering the comparison which St Paul maketh between the Church of Christ and the body of man: For the same resemblance will hold, not only to families and kingdoms, but to the whole corporation of mankind. "The eye," saith he,[1] "cannot say unto the hand, I have no need of thee; nor again the head to the feet, I have no need of thee. Nay, much more, those members of the body which seem to be more feeble, are necessary. And whether one member suffer, all the members suffer with it; or one member be honoured, all the members rejoice with it." The case is directly the same among mankind. The prince cannot say to the merchant, I have no need of thee; nor the merchant to the labourer, I have no need of thee. Nay, much more those members, &c. For the poor are generally more necessary members of the commonwealth than the rich: Which clearly shews, that God never intented such possessions for the sake and service of those to whom he lends them: but because he hath assigned every man his particular station to be useful in life; and this for the reason given by the apostle, "that there should be no schism in the body."[2]

From hence may partly be gathered the nature of that subjection which we all owe to one another. God Almighty hath been pleased to put us into an imperfect state, where we have perpetual occasion of each other's assistance. There is none so low, as not to be in a capacity of assisting the highest; nor so high, as not to want the assistance of the lowest.

It plainly appears from what hath been said, that no one

[1] 1 Corin. xii. 21, 23, 26.　　　[2] 1 Corin. xii. 25.

IV.　　　1

human creature is more worthy than another in the sight of God; farther, than according to the goodness or holiness of their lives; and, that power, wealth, and the like outward advantages, are so far from being the marks of God's approving or preferring those on whom they are bestowed, that, on the contrary, he is pleased to suffer them to be almost engrossed by those who have least title to his favour. Now, according to this equality wherein God hath placed all mankind, with relation himself, you will observe, that in all the relations between man and man, there is a mutual dependence, whereby the one cannot subsist without the other. Thus, no man can be a prince without subjects, nor a master without servants, nor a father without children. And this both explains and confirms the doctrine of the text: For, where there is a mutual dependence, there must be a mutual duty, and consequently a mutual subjection. For instance, the subject must only obey his prince, because God commands it, human laws require it, and the safety of the public maketh it necessary: (For the same reasons we must obey all that are in authority, and submit ourselves, not only to the good and gentle, but also to the froward, whether they rule according to our liking or no.) On the other side, in those countries that pretend to freedom, princes are subject to those laws which their people have chosen; they are bound to protect their subjects in liberty, property, and religion; to receive their petitions, and redress their grievances: So, that the best prince is, in the opinion of wise men, only the greatest servant of the nation; not only a servant to the public in general, but in some sort to every man in it. In the like manner, a servant owes obedience, and diligence and faithfulness to his master, from whom, at the same time, he hath a just demand for protection, and maintenance, and gentle treatment. Nay, even the poor beggar hath a just demand of an alms from the rich man, who is guilty of fraud, injustice, and oppression, if he doth not afford relief according to his abilities.

But this subjection we all owe one another is nowhere more necessary than in the common conversations of life; for without it there could be no society among men. If the learned would not sometimes submit to the ignorant, the wise to the simple, the gentle to the froward, the old to the weaknesses of the young, there would be nothing but everlasting variance in the world. This our Saviour himself confirmed by his own example; for he appeared in the form of a servant, and washed his disciples' feet, adding those memorable words: " Ye call me Lord and Master, and ye say well, for so I am. If I then your Lord and Master wash your feet, how much more ought ye to wash one another's feet?" Under which expression of washing the feet, is included all that subjection, assistance, love, and duty, which every good Christian ought to pay his brother, in whatever station God hath placed him. For the greatest prince and the meanest slave, are not, by infinite degrees so distant, as our Saviour and those disciples whose feet he vouchsafed to wash.

And, although this doctrine of subjecting ourselves to one another may seem to grate upon the pride and vanity of mankind, and may therefore be hard to be digested by those who value themselves upon their greatness or their wealth; yet, it is really no more than what most men practise upon other occasions. For, if our neighbour who is our inferior comes to see us, we rise to receive him, we place him above us, and respect him as if he were better than ourselves; and this is thought both decent and necessary, and is usually called good manners. Now the duty required by the apostle, is only that we should enlarge our minds, and that what we thus practice in the common course of life, we should imitate in all our actions and proceedings whatsoever; since our Saviour tells us, that every man is our neighbour, and since we are so ready in the point of civility, to yield to others in our own houses, where only we have any title to govern.

Having thus shewn you what sort of subjection it is which all men owe one to another, and in what manner it ought to be paid, I shall now draw some observations from what hath been said.

And *first*: A thorough practice of this duty of subjecting ourselves to the wants and infirmities of each other, would utterly extinguish in us the vice of pride. For, if God hath pleased to entrust me with a talent, not for my own sake, but for the service of others, and at the same time hath left me full of wants and necessities which others must supply; I can then have no cause to set any extraordinary value upon myself, or to despise my brother, because he hath not the same talents which were lent to me. His being may probably be as useful to the public as mine; and, therefore, by the rules of right reason, I am in no sort preferable to him.

Secondly: It is very manifest, from what hath been said, that no man ought to look upon the advantages of life, such as riches, honour, power, and the like, as his property, but merely as a trust, which God hath deposited with him, to be employed for the use of his brethren; and God will certainly punish the breach of that trust, although the laws of man will not, or rather indeed cannot; because the trust was conferred only by God, who hath not left it to any power on earth to decide infallibly whether a man maketh a good use of his talents or no, or to punish him where he fails. And therefore God seems to have more particularly taken this matter into his own hands, and will most certainly reward or punish us in proportion to our good or ill performance in it. Now, although the advantages which one man possesseth more than another, may in some sense be called his property with respect to other men, yet with respect to God they are, as I said, only a trust: which will plainly appear from hence. If a man doth not use those advantages to the good of the public, or the benefit of his neighbour, it is certain he doth not deserve them; and consequently, that God never intended them for a blessing to him; and on the other side, whoever doth employ his talents as he ought, will find by his own experience, that they were chiefly lent him for the service of others: for to the service of others he will certainly employ them.

Thirdly: If we could all be brought to practise this duty of subjecting ourselves to each other, it would very much contribute to the general happiness of mankind: for this would root out envy and malice from the heart of man; because you cannot envy your neighbour's strength, if he maketh use of it to defend your life, or carry your burden; you cannot envy his wisdom, if he gives you good counsel; nor his riches, if he supplieth you in your wants; nor his greatness, if he employs it to your protection. The miseries of life are not properly owing to the unequal distribution of things; but God Almighty, the great King of Heaven, is treated like the kings of the earth; who, although perhaps intending well themselves, have often most abominable ministers and stewards; and those generally the vilest, to whom they entrust the most talents. But here is the difference, that the princes of this world see by other men's eyes, but God sees all things; and therefore whenever he permits his blessings to be dealt among those who are unworthy, we may certainly conclude that he intends them only as a punishment to an evil world, as well as to the owners. It were well, if those would consider this, whose riches serve them only as a spur to avarice, or as an instrument to their lusts; whose wisdom is only of this world, to put false colours upon things, to call good evil, and evil good, against the conviction of their own consciences; and lastly, who employ their power and favour in acts of oppression or injustice, in misrepresenting persons and things, or in countenancing the wicked to the ruin of the innocent.

Fourthly: The practice of this duty of being subject to one another, would make us rest contented in the several stations of life wherein God hath thought fit to place us; because it would in the best and easiest manner bring us back as it were to that early state of the Gospel when Christians had all things in common. For, if the poor found the rich disposed to supply their wants; if the ignorant found the wise ready to instruct and direct them; or if the weak might always find protection from the mighty; they could none of them with the least pretence of justice lament their own condition.

From all that hath been hitherto said, it appears, that great abilities of any sort, when they are employed as God directs, do but make the owners of them greater and more painful servants to their neighbour, and the public; however, we are by no means to conclude from hence, that they are not really blessings, when they are in the hands of good men. For first, what can be a greater honour than to be chosen one of the stewards and dispensers of God's bounty to mankind? What is there, that can give a generous spirit more pleasure and complacency of mind, than to consider that he is an instrument of doing much good? that great numbers owe to him, under God, their subsistence, their

safety, their health, and the good conduct of their lives ?
The wickedest man upon earth taketh a pleasure in doing
good to those he loveth; and therefore surely a good
Christian, who obeys our Saviour's command of loving all
men, cannot but take delight in doing good even to his
enemies.   God, who giveth all things to all men, can receive
nothing from any ; and those among men, who do the most
good, and receive the fewest returns, do most resemble their
Creator : for which reason, St Paul delivereth it as a saying
of our Saviour, that "it is more blessed to give than to
receive."   By this rule, what must become of those things
which the world valueth as the greatest blessings, riches,
power, and the like, when our Saviour plainly determines,
that the best way to make them blessings, is to part with
them ?   Therefore, although the advantages which one man
hath over another, may be called blessings, yet they are by
no means so in the sense the world usually understands.
Thus, for example, great riches are no blessing in themselves;
because the poor man, with the common necessaries of life
enjoys more health, and hath fewer cares without them :
How then do they become blessings?   No otherwise, than
by being employed in feeding the hungry, clothing the naked,
rewarding worthy men, and in short, doing acts of charity
and generosity.   Thus likewise, power is no blessing in itself,
because private men bear less envy, and trouble, and anguish
without it.   But when it is employed to protect the innocent,
to relieve the oppressed, and to punish the oppressor, then
it becomes a great blessing.   And so lastly even great wisdom
is in the opinion of Solomon not a blessing in itself : For "in
much wisdom is much sorrow ;" and men of common understandings, if they serve God and mind their callings, make
fewer mistakes in the conduct of life than those who have
better heads.   And yet, wisdom is a mighty blessing, when
it is applied to good purposes, to instruct the ignorant, to be
a faithful counsellor either in [public or private, to be a
director to youth, and to many other ends needless here to
mention.

To conclude : God sent us into the world to obey his
commands, by doing as much good as our abilities will
reach, and as little evil as our many infirmities will permit.
Some he hath only trusted with one talent, some with five,

and some with ten. No man is without his talent; and
he that is faithful or negligent in a little, shall be rewarded or punished, as well as he that hath been so in a
great deal.

Consider what hath been said; and the Lord give you a
right understanding in all things. To whom with the Son
and the Holy Ghost, be all honour and glory, now and for
ever.

TESTIMONY OF CONSCIENCE.

2 CORINTHIANS, I. 12. PART OF IT.

" —— For our rejoicing is this, the testimony of our conscience."

THERE is no word more frequently in the mouths of men, than that of conscience, and the meaning of it is in some measure generally understood : However, because it is likewise a word extremely abused by many people, who apply other meanings to it, which God Almighty never intended ; I shall explain it to you in the clearest manner I am able. The word conscience properly signifies, that knowledge which a man hath within himself of his own thoughts and actions. And, because, if a man judgeth fairly of his own actions by comparing them with the law of God, his mind will either approve or condemn him according as he hath done good or evil ; therefore this knowledge or conscience may properly be called both an accuser and a judge. So that whenever our conscience accuseth us, we are certainly guilty ; but we are not always innocent when it doth not accuse us : For very often, through the hardness of our hearts, or the fondness and favour we bear to ourselves, or through ignorance or neglect, we do not suffer our conscience to take any cognizance of several sins we commit. There is another office likewise belonging to conscience, which is that of being our director and guide ; and the wrong use of this hath been the occasion of more evils under the sun, than almost all other causes put together. For, as conscience is nothing else but the knowledge we have of what we are thinking and doing ; so it can guide us no farther than that knowledge reacheth. And therefore God hath placed conscience in us to be our director only in those actions which Scripture and reason plainly tell us to be good or evil. But in cases too difficult or doubtful for us to comprehend or determine, there conscience is not concerned; because it cannot advise in what it doth not understand, nor decide where it is itself in doubt: but, by God's great mercy, those difficult points are never of absolute necessity to our salvation. There is likewise another evil, that men often say, a thing is against their conscience, when really it is not. For instance: Ask any of those who differ from the worship established, why they do not come to church? They will say, they dislike the ceremonies, the prayers, the habits, and the like, and therefore it goes against their conscience: But they are mistaken, their teacher hath put those words into their mouths; for a man's conscience can go no higher than his knowledge; and therefore until he has thoroughly examined by Scripture, and the practice of the ancient church, whether those points are blameable or no, his conscience cannot possibly direct him to condemn them. Hence have likewise arisen those mistakes about what is usually called "Liberty of Conscience"; which, properly speaking, is no more than a liberty of knowing our own thoughts; which liberty no one can take from us. But those words have obtained quite different meanings: Liberty of conscience is now-a-days not only understood to be the liberty of believing what men please, but also of endeavouring to propagate the belief as much as they can, and to overthrow the faith which the laws have already established, to be rewarded by the public for those wicked endeavours: And this is the liberty of conscience which the fanatics are now openly in the face of the world endeavouring at with their utmost application. At the same time it cannot but be observed, that those very persons, who under pretence of a public spirit and tenderness towards their Christian brethren, are so zealous for such a liberty of conscience as this, are of all others the least tender to those who differ from them in the smallest point relating to government; and I wish I could not say, that the Majesty of the living God may be offended with more security than the memory of a dead prince. But the wisdom of the world at present seems to agree with that of the heathen Emperor, who said, if the gods were offended, it was their own concern, and they were able to vindicate themselves.[1]

But although conscience hath been abused to those wicked purposes which I have already related, yet a due regard to the directions it plainly giveth us, as well as to itsaccusations, reproaches, and advices, would be of the greatest use to mankind, both for their present welfare and future happiness.

Therefore, my discourse at this time shall be directed to prove to you, that there is no solid, firm foundation for virtue, but on a conscience which is guided by religion.

In order to this, I shall first shew you the weakness and uncertainty of two false principles, which many people set up in the place of conscience, for a guide to their actions.

The first of these principles is, what the world usually calls *Moral Honesty*. There are some people, who appear very indifferent as to religion, and yet have the repute of being just and fair in their dealings; and these are generally known by the character of good moral men. But now, if you look into the grounds and the motives of such a man's actions, you shall find them to be no other than his own ease and interest. For example: You trust a moral man with your money in the way of trade; you trust another with the defence of your cause at law, and perhaps they both deal justly with you. Why? Not from any regard they have for justice, but because their fortune depends upon their credit, and a stain of open public dishonesty must be to their disadvantage. But let it consist with such a man's interest and safety to wrong you, and then it will be impossible you can have any hold upon him; because there is nothing left to give him a check, or put in the balance against his profit. For, if he hath nothing to govern himself by, but the opinion of the world, as long as he can conceal his injustice from the world, he thinks he is safe.

Besides, it is found by experience, that those men who set up for morality without regard to religion, are generally but virtuous in part; they will be just in their dealings between man and man; but if they find themselves disposed to pride, lust, intemperance, or avarice, they do not think their

---

[1] The saying of Tiberius as given by Tacitus ("Annals," bk. i., c. lxxiii.), *Deorum offensa diis curæ.* [T. S.]

morality concerned to check them in any of these vices, because it is the great rule of such men, that they may lawfully
follow the dictates of nature, wherever their safety, health,
and fortune, are not injured. So, that upon the whole, there
is hardly one vice which a mere moral man may not upon
some occasions allow himself to practise.

The other false principle, which some men set up in the
place of conscience to be their director in life, is what those
who pretend to it, call *Honour*.

This word is often made the sanction of an oath; it is
reckoned a great commendation to be a man of strict
honour; and it is commonly understood, that a man of
honour can never be guilty of a base action. This is usually
the style of military men; of persons with titles; and of
others who pretend to birth and quality.   It is true, indeed,
that in ancient times it was universally understood, that
honour was the reward of virtue; but if such honour as is
now-a-days going will not permit a man to do a base action,
it must be allowed, there are very few such things as base
actions in nature. No man of honour, as that word is
usually understood, did ever pretend that his honour obliged
him to be chaste or temperate; to pay his creditors; to be
useful to his country; to do good to mankind; to endeavour
to be wise, or learned; to regard his word, his promise, or
his oath ; or if he hath any of these virtues, they were never
learned in the catechism of honour; which contains but two
precepts, the punctual payment of debts contracted at play,
and the right understanding the several degrees of an affront,
in order to revenge it by the death of an adversary.

But suppose, this principle of honour, which some men so
much boast of, did really produce more virtues than it ever
pretended to; yet since the very being of that honour
dependeth upon the breath, the opinion, or the fancy of the
people, the virtues derived from it could be of no long or
certain duration.   For example: Suppose a man from a
principle of honour should resolve to be just, or chaste, or
temperate; and yet the censuring world should take a
humour of refusing him those characters; he would then
think the obligation at an end.   Or, on the other side, if he
thought he could gain honour by the falsest and vilest action,
(which is a case that very often happens,) he would then

make no scruple to perform it.   And God knows, it would be an unhappy state, to have the religion, the liberty, or the property of a people lodged in such hands, which however hath been too often the case.

What I have said upon this principle of honour may perhaps be thought of small concernment to most of you who are my hearers : However, a caution was not altogether unnecessary ; since there is nothing by which not only the vulgar, but the honest tradesman hath been so much deceived, as this infamous pretence to honour in too many of their betters.

Having thus shewn you the weakness and uncertainty of those principles which some men set up in the place of conscience to direct them in their actions, I shall now endeavour to prove to you that there is no solid, firm foundation of virtue, but in a conscience directed by the principles of religion.

There is no way of judging how far we may depend upon the actions of men, otherwise than by knowing the motives, and grounds, and causes of them ; and, if the motives of our actions be not resolved and determined into the law of God, they will be precarious and uncertain, and liable to perpetual changes.   I will shew you what I mean, by an example : Suppose a man thinks it his duty to obey his parents, because reason tells him so, because he is obliged by gratitude, and because the laws of his country command him to do so; but, if he stops here, his parents can have no lasting security; for an occasion may happen, wherein it may be extremely his interest to be disobedient, and where the laws of the land can lay no hold upon him : therefore, before such a man can safely be trusted, he must proceed farther, and consider, that his reason is the gift of God ; that God commanded him to be obedient to the laws, and did moreover in a particular manner enjoin him to be dutiful to his parents ; after which, if he lays due weight upon those considerations, he will probably continue in his duty to the end of his life: Because no earthly interest can ever come in competition to balance the danger of offending his Creator, or the happiness of pleasing him.   And of all this his conscience will certainly inform him, if he hath any regard to religion.

Secondly: Fear and hope are the two greatest natural motives of all men's actions : But, neither of these passions will ever put us in the way of virtue, unless they be directed by conscience. For although virtuous men do sometimes accidentally make their way to preferment, yet the world is so corrupted, that no man can reasonably hope to be rewarded in it, merely upon account of his virtue. And consequently, the fear of punishment in this life will preserve men from very few vices, since some of the blackest and basest do often prove the surest steps to favour; such as ingratitude, hypocrisy, treachery, malice, subornation, atheism, and many more which human laws do little concern themselves about. But when conscience placeth before us the hopes of everlasting happiness, and the fears of everlasting misery, as the reward and punishment of our good or evil actions, our reason can find no way to avoid the force of such an argument, otherwise than by running into infidelity.

Lastly : Conscience will direct us to love God, and to put our whole trust and confidence in him. Our love of God will inspire us with a detestation for sin, as what is of all things most contrary to his divine nature ; and if we have an entire confidence in him, *that* will enable us to subdue and despise all the allurements of the world.

It may here be objected, if conscience be so sure a director to us Christians in the conduct of our lives, how comes it to pass, that the ancient heathens, who had no other lights but those of nature and reason, should so far exceed us in all manner of virtue, as plainly appears by many examples they have left on record ?

To which it may be answered ; first, those heathens were extremely strict and exact in the education of their children; whereas among us this care is so much laid aside, that the more God hath blessed any man with estate or quality, just so much the less in proportion is the care he taketh in the education of his children, and particularly of that child which is to inherit his fortune: Of which the effects are visible enough among the great ones of the world. Again, those heathens did in a particular manner instil the principle into their children, of loving their country ; which is so far otherwise now-a-days, that, of the several parties among us, there is none of them that seems to have so much as heard, whether there be such a virtue in the world ; as plainly appears by their practices, and especially when they are placed in those stations where they can only have opportunity of shewing it. Lastly; the most considerable among the heathens did generally believe rewards and punishments in a life to come; which is the great principle for conscience to work upon: Whereas too many of those who would be thought the most considerable among us, do, both by their practices and their discourses, plainly affirm, that they believe nothing at all of the matter.

Wherefore, since it hath manifestly appeared that a religious conscience is the only true solid foundation upon which virtue can be built, give me leave, before I conclude, to let you see how necessary such a conscience is, to conduct us in every station and condition of our lives.

That a religious conscience is necessary in any station, is confessed even by those who tell us, that all religion was invented by cunning men, in order to keep the world in awe. For, if religion, by the confession of its adversaries, be necessary towards the well-governing of mankind; then every wise man in power will be sure not only to choose out for every station under him such persons as are most likely to be kept in awe by religion, but likewise to carry some appearance of it himself, or else he is a very weak politician. And accordingly in any country where great persons affect to be open despisers of religion, their counsels will be found at last to be fully as destructive to the state as to the church.

It was the advice of Jethro to his son-in-law Moses, to "provide able men, such as fear God, men of truth, hating covetousness," and to place such over the people; and Moses, who was as wise a statesman, at least, as any in this age, thought fit to follow that advice. Great abilities, without the fear of God, are most dangerous instruments, when they are trusted with power. The laws of man have thought fit, that those who are called to any office of trust should be bound by an oath to the faithful discharge of it: But, an oath is an appeal to God, and therefore can have no influence except upon those who believe that he is, and that he is a rewarder of those that seek him, and a punisher of those who disobey him: And therefore, we see, the laws themselves are forced to have recourse to conscience in these cases, because their penalties cannot reach the arts of cunning men, who can find ways to be guilty of a thousand injustices without

being discovered, or at least without being punished.   And
the reason why we find so many frauds, abuses, and corruptions, where any trust is conferred, can be no other, than that
there is so little conscience and religion left in the world, or
at least that men in their choice of instruments have private
ends in view, which are very different from the service of the
public.   Besides, it is certain, that men who profess to have
no religion, are full as zealous to bring over proselytes as
any Papist or fanatic can be.   And therefore, if those who
are in station high enough to be of influence or example to
others ; if those (I say) openly profess a contempt or dis-
belief of religion, they will be sure to make all their depend-
ents of their own principles ; and what security can the
public expect from such persons, whenever their interests, or
their lusts, come into competition with their duty ?   It is
very possible for a man who hath the appearance of religion,
and is a great pretender to conscience, to be wicked and a
hypocrite ; but, it is impossible for a man who openly
declares against religion, to give any reasonable security that
he will not be false and cruel, and corrupt, whenever a
temptation offers, which he values more than he does the
power wherewith he was trusted.   And, if such a man doth
not betray his cause and his master, it is only because the
temptation was not properly offered, or the profit was too
small, or the danger was too great.   And hence it is, that
we find so little truth or justice among us, because there are
so very few, who either in the service of the public, or in
common dealings with each other, do ever look farther than
their own advantage, and how to guard themselves against
the laws of the country ; which a man may do by favour, by
secrecy, or by cunning, although he breaks almost every law
of God.

Therefore to conclude : It plainly appears, that unless
men are guided by the advice and judgment of a conscience
founded on religion, they can give no security that they will
be either good subjects, faithful servants of the public, or
honest in their mutual dealings ; since there is no other tie
through which the pride, or lust, or avarice, or ambition of
mankind will not certainly break one time or other.

Consider what has been said, &c.

TRINITY.

" For there are three that bear record in Heaven, the Father, the
Word, and the Holy Ghost ; and these Three are One."

THIS day being set apart to acknowledge our belief in
the Eternal Trinity, I thought it might be proper to
employ my present discourse entirely upon that subject ;
and, I hope, to handle it in such a manner, that the most
ignorant among you may return home better informed of
your duty in this great point, than probably you are at
present.

It must be confessed, that by the weakness and indiscre-
tion of busy (or at best, of well-meaning) people, as well as
by the malice of those who are enemies to all revealed religion, and are not content to possess their own infidelity in
silence, without communicating it to the disturbance of
mankind ; I say, by these means, it must be confessed, that
the doctrine of the Trinity hath suffered very much, and
made Christianity suffer along with it. For these two things
must be granted : First, that men of wicked lives would be
very glad there were no truth in Christianity at all ; and
secondly, if they can pick out any one single article in the
Christian religion which appears not agreeable to their own
corrupted reason, or to the arguments of those bad people,
who follow the trade of seducing others, they presently conclude, that the truth of the whole Gospel must sink along
with that one article ; which is just as wise, as if a man
should say, because he dislikes one law of his country, he

will therefore observe no law at all; and yet, that one law may be very reasonable in itself, although he does not allow it, or does not know the reason of the law-givers.

Thus it hath happened with the great doctrine of the Trinity; which word is indeed not in the Scripture, but was a term of art invented in the earlier times to express the doctrine by a single word, for the sake of brevity and convenience. The doctrine then, as delivered in Holy Scripture, although not exactly in the same words, is very short, and amounts only to this, that the Father, the Son, and the Holy Ghost, are each of them God, and yet there is but one God. For, as to the word Person, when we say there are three Persons; and as to those other explanations in the Athanasian Creed this day read to you (whether compiled by Athanasius or no) they were taken up three hundred years after Christ, to expound this doctrine; and I will tell you upon what occasion. About that time there sprang up a heresy of a people called Arians, from one Arius the leader of them. These denied our Saviour to be God, although they allowed all the rest of the Gospel (wherein they were more sincere than their followers among us). Thus the Christian world was divided into two parts, until at length, by the zeal and courage of St Athanasius, the Arians were condemned in a general council, and a creed formed upon the true faith, as St Athanasius hath settled it. This creed is now read at certain times in our churches, which, although it is useful for edification to those who understand it; yet, since it containeth some nice and philosophical points which few people can comprehend, the bulk of mankind is obliged to believe no more than the Scripture doctrine, as I have delivered it. Because that creed was intended only as an answer to the Arians in their own way, who were very subtle disputers.

But this heresy having revived in the world about a hundred years ago, and continued ever since; not out of a zeal to truth, but to give a loose to wickedness, by throwing off all religion; several divines, in order to answer the cavils of those adversaries to truth and morality, began to find out farther explanations of this doctrine of the Trinity, by rules of philosophy; which have multiplied controversies to such a degree, as to beget scruples that have perplexed the minds

IV.   K

of many sober Christians, who otherwise could never have entertained them.

I must therefore be bold to affirm, that the method taken by many of those learned men to defend the doctrine of the Trinity, hath been founded upon a mistake.

It must be allowed, that every man is bound to follow the rules and directions of that measure of reason which God hath given him; and indeed he cannot do otherwise, if he will be sincere, or act like a man. For instance: If I should be commanded by an angel from heaven to believe it is midnight at noon-day; yet I could not believe him. So, if I were directly told in Scripture that three are one, and one is three, I could not conceive or believe it in the natural common sense of that expression, but must suppose that something dark or mystical was meant, which it pleased God to conceal from me and from all the world. Thus, in the text, "There are Three that bear record," &c. Am I capable of knowing and defining what union and what distinction there may be in the divine nature, which possibly may be hid from the angels themselves? Again, I see it plainly declared in Scripture, that there is but one God; and yet I find our Saviour claiming the prerogative of God in knowing men's thoughts; in saying, "He and his Father are one;" and, "before Abraham was, I am." I read, that the disciples worshipped him; that Thomas said to him, "My Lord and my God." And St John, chap. 1st, "In the beginning was the Word, and the Word was with God, and the Word was God." I read likewise that the Holy Ghost bestowed the gift of tongues, and the power of working miracles; which, if rightly considered, is as great a miracle as any, that a number of illiterate men should of a sudden be qualified to speak all the languages then known in the world; such as could be done by the inspiration of God alone. From these several texts it is plain, that God commands us to believe that there is an union and there is a distinction; but what that union, or what that distinction is, all mankind are equally ignorant, and must continue so, at least till the day of judgment, without some new revelation.

But because I cannot conceive the nature of this union and distinction in the divine nature, am I therefore to reject them as absurd and impossible ; as I would, if any one told me that three men are one, and one man is three ? We are told, that a man and his wife are one flesh ; this I can comprehend the meaning of ; yet, literally taken, it is a thing impossible. But the apostle tell us, " We see but in part, and we know but in part ; " and yet we would comprehend all the secret ways and workings of God.

Therefore I shall again repeat the doctrine of the Trinity, as it is positively affirmed in Scripture : that God is there expressed in three different names, as Father, as Son, and as Holy Ghost : that each of these is God, and that there is but one God. But this union and distinction are a mystery utterly unknown to mankind.

This is enough for any good Christian to believe on this great article, without ever inquiring any farther : And, this can be contrary to no man's reason, although the knowledge of it is hid from him.

But there is another difficulty of great importance among those who quarrel with the doctrine of the Trinity, as well as with several other articles of Christianity ; which is, that our religion abounds in mysteries, and these they are so bold as to revile as cant, imposture, and priestcraft. It is impossible for us to determine for what reasons God thought fit to communicate some things to us in part, and leave some part a mystery. But so it is in fact, and so the Holy Scripture tells us in several places. For instance : the resurrection and change of our bodies are called mysteries by St Paul ; and our Saviour's incarnation is another : The Kingdom of God is called a mystery by our Saviour, to be only known to his disciples ; so is faith, and the word of God by St Paul. I omit many others. So, that to declare against all mysteries without distinction or exception, is to declare against the whole tenor of the New Testament.

There are two conditions that may bring a mystery under suspicion. First, when it is not taught and commanded in Holy Writ ; or, secondly, when the mystery turns to the advantage of those who preach it to others. Now, as to the first, it can never be said, that we preach mysteries without warrant from Holy Scripture, although I confess this of the Trinity may have sometimes been explained by human invention, which might perhaps better have been spared. As

to the second, it will not be possible to charge the Protestant
priesthood with proposing any temporal advantage to themselves by broaching or multiplying, or preaching of mysteries.
Does this mystery of the Trinity, for instance, and the descent
of the Holy Ghost, bring the least profit or power to the
preachers ? No ; it is as great a mystery to themselves as it
is to the meanest of their hearers ; and may be rather a cause
of humiliation, by putting their understanding in that point
upon a level with the most ignorant of their flock.   It is
true indeed, the Roman church hath very much enriched
herself by trading in mysteries, for which they have not the
least authority from Scripture, and were fitted only to
advance their own temporal wealth and grandeur ; such as
transubstantiation, the worshipping of images, indulgences
for sins, purgatory, and masses for the dead ; with many
more : But, it is the perpetual talent of those who have ill-
will to our Church, or a contempt for all religion, taken up
by the wickedness of their lives, to charge us with the errors
and corruptions of Popery, which all Protestants have thrown
off near two hundred years : whereas, those mysteries held
by us have no prospect of power, pomp, or wealth, but have
been ever maintained by the universal body of true believers
from the days of the apostles, and will be so to the resurrection ; neither will the gates of hell prevail against them.
   It may be thought perhaps a strange thing, that God
should require us to believe mysteries, while the reason or
manner of what we are to believe is above our comprehension, and wholly concealed from us : neither doth it appear
at first sight, that the believing or not believing them doth
concern either the glory of God, or contribute to the goodness or wickedness of our lives.   But this is a great and
dangerous mistake.   We see what a mighty weight is laid
upon faith, both in the Old and New Testament.   In the
former we read how the faith of Abraham is praised, who
could believe that God would raise from him a great nation,
at the very time that he was commanded to sacrifice his only
son, and despaired of any other issue.   And this was to him
a great mystery.   Our Saviour is perpetually preaching faith
to his disciples, or reproaching them with the want of it :
and St Paul produceth numerous examples of the wonders
done by faith.   And all this is highly reasonable : For faith

is an entire dependence upon the truth, the power, the justice, and the mercy of God; which dependence will certainly incline us to obey him in all things. So, that the great excellency of faith, consists in the consequence it hath upon our actions: as, if we depend upon the truth and wisdom of a man, we shall certainly be more disposed to follow his advice. Therefore, let no man think that he can lead as good a moral life without faith as with it; for this reason, because he who hath no faith, cannot, by the strength of his own reason or endeavours, so easily resist temptations, as the other who depends upon God's assistance in the overcoming his frailties, and is sure to be rewarded for ever in heaven for his victory over them. " Faith," says the apostle, " is the evidence of things not seen ": he means, that faith is a virtue by which anything commanded us by God to believe appears evident and certain to us, although we do not see, nor can conceive it; because, by faith we entirely depend upon the truth and power of God.

It is an old and true distinction, that things may be above our reason, without being contrary to it. Of this kind are the power, the nature, and the universal presence of God, with innumerable other points. How little do those who quarrel with mysteries, know of the commonest actions of nature! The growth of an animal, of a plant, or of the smallest seed, is a mystery to the wisest among men. If an ignorant person were told that a loadstone would draw iron at a distance, he might say it was a thing contrary to his reason, and could not believe before he saw it with his eyes.

The manner whereby the soul and body are united, and how they are distinguished, is wholly unaccountable to us. We see but one part, and yet we know we consist of two; and this is a mystery we cannot comprehend, any more than that of the Trinity.

From what hath been said, it is manifest that God did never command us to believe, nor his ministers to preach, any doctrine which is contrary to the reason he hath pleased to endow us with; but for his own wise ends has thought fit to conceal from us the nature of the thing he commands; thereby to try our faith and obedience, and increase our dependence upon him.

It is highly probable, that if God should please to reveal unto us this great mystery of the Trinity, or some other mysteries in our holy religion, we should not be able to understand them, unless he would at the same time think fit to bestow on us some new powers or faculties of the mind, which we want at present, and are reserved till the day of resurrection to life eternal. "For now," as the apostle says, "we see through a glass darkly, but then face to face."

Thus, we see, the matter is brought to this issue: We must either believe what God directly commands us in Holy Scripture, or we must wholly reject the Scripture, and the Christian religion which we pretend to profess. But this, I hope, is too desperate a step for any of us to make.

I have already observed, that those who preach up the belief of the Trinity, or of any other mystery, cannot propose any temporal advantage to themselves by so doing. But this is not the case of those who oppose these doctrines. Do *they* lead better moral lives than a good Christian? Are *they* more just in their dealings? more chaste, or temperate, or charitable? Nothing at all of this; but on the contrary, their intent is to overthrow all religion, that they may gratify their vices without any reproach from the world, or their own conscience: and are zealous to bring over as many others as they can to their own opinions; because it is some kind of imaginary comfort to have a multitude on their side.

There is no miracle mentioned in Holy Writ, which, if it were strictly examined, is not as much contrary to common reason, and as much a mystery, as this doctrine of the Trinity; and therefore we may, with equal justice deny the truth of them all. For instance: It is against the laws of nature, that a human body should be able to walk upon the water, as St Peter is recorded to have done; or that a dead carcass should be raised from the grave after three days, when it began to be corrupted; which those who understand anatomy will pronounce to be impossible by the common rules of nature and reason. Yet these miracles, and many others, are positively affirmed in the Gospel; and these we must believe, or give up our holy religion to atheists and infidels.

I shall now make a few inferences and observations upon what has been said.

First: It would be well, if people would not lay so much weight on their own reason in matters of religion, as to think everything impossible and absurd which they cannot conceive. How often do we contradict the right rules of reason in the whole course of our lives! Reason itself is true and just, but the reason of every particular man is weak and wavering, perpetually swayed and turned by his interests, his passions, and his vices. Let any man but consider, when he hath a controversy with another, although his cause be ever so unjust, although the world be against him, how blinded he is by the love of himself, to believe that right is wrong, and wrong is right, when it maketh for his own advantage. Where is then the right use of his reason, which he so much boasts of, and which he would blasphemously set up to control the commands of the Almighty?

Secondly: When men are tempted to deny the mysteries of religion, let them examine and search into their own hearts, whether they have not some favourite sin which is of their party in this dispute, and which is equally contrary to other commands of God in the Gospel. For, why do men love darkness rather than light? The Scripture tells us, " Because their deeds are evil ; " and there can be no other reason assigned. Therefore when men are curious and inquisitive to discover some weak sides in Christianity, and inclined to favour everything that is offered to its disadvantage ; it is plain they wish it were not true, and those wishes can proceed from nothing but an evil conscience ; because, if there be truth in our religion, their condition must be miserable.

And therefore, *Thirdly:* Men should consider, that raising difficulties concerning the mysteries in religion, cannot make them more wise, learned, or virtuous ; better neighbours, or friends, or more serviceable to their country ; but, whatever they pretend, will destroy their inward peace of mind, by perpetual doubts and fears arising in their breasts. And, God forbid we should ever see the times so bad, when dangerous opinions in religion will be a means to get favour and preferment ; although, even in such a case, it would be an ill traffic, to gain the world, and lose our own souls.   So, that upon the whole, it will be impossible to find any real use toward a virtuous or happy life, by denying the mysteries of the Gospel.

Fourthly : Those strong unbelievers, who expect that all mysteries should be squared and fitted to their own reason, might have somewhat to say for themselves, if they could satisfy the general reason of mankind in their opinions : But herein they are miserably defective, absurd, and ridiculous ; they strain at a gnat, and swallow a camel ; they can believe that the world was made by chance ; that God doth not concern himself with things below ; will neither punish vice, nor reward virtue ; that religion was invented by cunning men to keep the world in awe ; with many other opinions equally false and detestable, against the common light of nature as well as reason ; against the universal sentiments of all civilized nations, and offensive to the ears even of a sober heathen.

Lastly : Since the world abounds with pestilent books particularly against this doctrine of the Trinity ; it is fit to inform you, that the authors of them proceed wholly upon a mistake : They would shew how impossible it is that three can be one, and one can be three ; whereas the Scripture saith no such thing, at least in that manner they would make it : but, only, that there is some kind of unity and distinction in the divine nature, which mankind cannot possibly comprehend : thus, the whole doctrine is short and plain, and in itself incapable of any controversy : since God himself hath pronounced the fact, but wholly concealed the manner.   And therefore many divines, who thought fit to answer those wicked books, have been mistaken too, by answering fools in their folly ; and endeavouring to explain a mystery, which God intended to keep secret from us. And, as I would exhort all men to avoid reading those wicked books written against this doctrine, as dangerous and pernicious ; so I think they may omit the answers, as un- necessary.   This I confess will probably affect but few or none among the generality of our congregations, who do not much trouble themselves with books, at least of this kind.   However, many who do not read themselves, are seduced by others that do ; and thus become unbelievers upon trust and at second-hand; and this is too frequent a case: for which reason I have endeavoured to put this doctrine upon a short and sure foot, levelled to the meanest understanding; by which we may, as the apostle directs, be ready always to give an answer to every man that asketh us a reason of the hope that is in us, with meekness and fear.

And, thus I have done with my subject, which probably I should not have chosen, if I had not been invited to it by the occasion of this season, appointed on purpose to cele-brate the mysteries of the Trinity, and the descent of the Holy Ghost, wherein we pray to be kept stedfast in this faith; and what this faith is I have shewn you in the plainest manner I could. For, upon the whole, it is no more than this: God commandeth us, by our dependence upon His truth, and His Holy Word, to believe a fact that we do not understand. And, this is no more than what we do every day in the works of nature, upon the credit of men of learning. Without faith we can do no works acceptable to God; for, if they proceed from any other principle, they will not advance our salvation; and this faith, as I have explained it, we may acquire without giving up our senses, or contradicting our reason. May God of his infinite mercy inspire us with true faith in every article and mystery of our holy religion, so as to dispose us to do what is pleasing in his sight; and this we pray through Jesus Christ, to whom, with the Father and the Holy Ghost, the mysterious, in-comprehensible ONE GOD, be all honour and glory now and for evermore! *Amen.*

BROTHERLY LOVE.[1]

HEB. XIII. I.

" Let brotherly love continue."

IN the early times of the Gospel, the Christians were very
much distinguished from all other bodies of men, by the
great and constant love they bore to each other; which,
although it was done in obedience to the frequent injunc-
tions of our Saviour and his apostles, yet, I confess, there
seemeth to have been likewise a natural reason, that very
much promoted it. For the Christians then were few and
scattered, living under persecution by the heathens round
about them, in whose hands was all the civil and military
power; and there is nothing so apt to unite the minds and
hearts of men, or to beget love and tenderness, as a general
distress. The first dissensions between Christians took their
beginning from the errors and heresies that arose among
them; many of those heresies, sometimes extinguished, and
sometimes reviving, or succeeded by others, remain to this
day; and having been made instruments to the pride,
avarice, or ambition, of ill-designing men, by extinguishing
brotherly love, have been the cause of infinite calamities, as

[1] Notwithstanding the text and title of this sermon, and the many
excellent observations which it contains in illustration of both, there
are several passages in it which the dissenters of the time would hardly
consider as propitiatory towards the continuance of brotherly love.
There are also various allusions to the parties which raged at the time,
and some which appear to have been written in defence of the preacher's
character, then severely arraigned by the Irish Whigs, and held in
abhorrence by the people of Dublin, by whom he was afterwards
idolized. [S.]

well as corruptions of faith and manners, in the Christian world.

The last legacy of Christ was peace and mutual love ; but then he foretold, that he came to send a sword upon the earth : The primitive Christians accepted the legacy, and their successors down to the present age have been largely fulfilling his prophecy. But whatever the practice of mankind hath been, or still continues, there is no duty more incumbent upon those who profess the Gospel, than that of brotherly love ; which, whoever could restore in any degree among men, would be an instrument of more good to human society, than ever was, or will be, done by all the statesmen and politicians in the world.

It is upon this subject of brotherly love, that I intend to discourse at present, and the method I observe shall be as follows :—

I. *First*, I will inquire into the causes of this great want of brotherly love among us.
II. *Secondly*, I will lay open the sad effects and consequences, which our animosities and mutual hatred have produced.
III. *Lastly*, I will use some motives and exhortations, that may persuade you to embrace brotherly love, and continue in it.

I. *First*, I shall enquire into the causes of this great want of brotherly love among us.

This nation of ours hath, for an hundred years past, been infested by two enemies, the Papists and fanatics, who, each in their turns, filled it with blood and slaughter, and, for a time, destroyed both the Church and government. The memory of these events hath put all true Protestants equally upon their guard against both these adversaries, who, by consequence, do equally hate us. The fanatics revile us, as too nearly approaching to Popery; and the Papists condemn us, as bordering too much on fanaticism. The Papists, God be praised, are, by the wisdom of our laws, put out of all visible possibility of hurting us; besides, their religion is so generally abhorred, that they have no advocates or abettors among Protestants to assist them. But the fanatics are to be considered in another light; they have had of late years the power, the luck, or the cunning, to divide us among ourselves; they have endeavoured to represent all those who have been so bold as to oppose their errors and designs, under the character of persons disaffected to the government; and they have so far succeeded, that, now-a-days, if a clergyman happens to preach with any zeal and vehemence against the sin and danger of schism, there will not want too many, in his congregation, ready enough to censure him as hot and high-flying, an inflamer of men's minds, an enemy to moderation, and disloyal to his prince. This hath produced a formed and settled division between those who profess the same doctrine and discipline; while they who call themselves moderate are forced to widen their bottom, by sacrificing their principles and their brethren to the encroachments and insolence of dissenters, who are therefore answerable, as a principal cause of all that hatred and animosity now reigning among us.

Another cause of the great want of brotherly love is the weakness and folly of too many among you of the lower sort, who are made the tools and instruments of your betters to work their designs, wherein you have no concern. Your numbers make you of use, and cunning men take the advantage, by putting words into your mouths, which you do not understand; then they fix good or ill characters to those words, as it best serves their purposes: And thus you are taught to love or hate, you know not what or why; you often suspect your best friends, and nearest neighbours, even your teacher himself, without any reason, if your leaders once taught you to call him by a name, which they tell you signifieth some very bad thing.

A third cause of our great want of brotherly love seemeth to be, that this duty is not so often insisted on from the pulpit, as it ought to be in such times as these; on the contrary, it is to be doubted, whether doctrines are not sometimes delivered by an ungoverned zeal, a desire to be distinguished, or a view of interest, which produce quite different effects; when, upon occasions set apart to return thanks to God for some public blessing, the time is employed in stirring up one part of the congregation against the other, by representations of things and persons, which God, in his mercy, forgive those who are guilty of.

The last cause I shall mention of the want of brotherly love is, that unhappy disposition towards politics among the trading people, which has been industriously instilled into them. In former times, the middle and lower sorts of mankind seldom gained or lost by the factions of the kingdom, and therefore were little concerned in them, further than as matter of talk and amusement; but now the meanest dealer will expect to turn the penny by the merits of his party. He can represent his neighbour as a man of dangerous principles, can bring a railing accusation against him, perhaps a criminal one, and so rob him of his livelihood, and find his own account by that much more than if he had disparaged his neighbour's goods, or defamed him as a cheat. For so it happens, that, instead of enquiring into the skill or honesty of those kind of people, the manner is now to enquire into their party, and to reject or encourage them accordingly; which proceeding hath made our people, in general, such able politicians, that all the artifice, flattery, dissimulation, diligence, and dexterity, in undermining each other, which the satirical wit of men hath charged upon courts; together with all the rage and violence, cruelty and injustice, which have been ever imputed to public assemblies; are with us (so polite are we grown) to be seen among our meanest traders and artificers in the greatest perfection. All which, as it may be matter of some humiliation to the wise and mighty of this world, so the effects thereof may, perhaps, in time, prove very different from what, I hope in charity, were ever foreseen or intended.

II. I will therefore now, in the second place, lay open some of the sad effects and consequences which our animosities and mutual hatred have produced.

And the first ill consequence is, that our want of brotherly love hath almost driven out all sense of religion from among us, which cannot well be otherwise; for since our Saviour laid so much weight upon his disciples loving one another, that he gave it among his last instructions; and since the primitive Christians are allowed to have chiefly propagated the faith by their strict observance of that instruction, it must follow that, in proportion as brotherly love declineth, Christianity will do so too. The little religion there is in

the world, hath been observed to reside chiefly among the
middle and lower sorts of people, who are neither tempted
to pride nor luxury by great riches, nor to desperate courses
by extreme poverty: And truly I, upon that account, have
thought it a happiness, that those who are under my immediate care are generally of that condition; but where
party hath once made entrance, with all its consequences
of hatred, envy, partiality, and virulence, religion cannot
long keep its hold in any state or degree of life whatsoever.
For, if the great men of the world have been censured in
all ages for mingling too little religion with their politics,
what a havoc of principles must they needs make in un-
learned and irregular heads; of which indeed the effects
are already too visible and melancholy all over the
kingdom !

Another ill consequence from our want of brotherly love
is, that it increaseth the insolence of the fanatics; and this
partly ariseth from a mistaken meaning of the word moderation; a word which hath been much abused, and bandied
about for several years past. There are too many people
indifferent enough to all religion; there are many others,
who dislike the clergy, and would have them live in poverty
and dependence; both these sorts are much commended by
the fanatics for moderate men, ready to put an end to our
divisions, and to make a general union among Protestants.
Many ignorant well-meaning people are deceived by these
appearances, strengthened with great pretences to loyalty:
and these occasions the fanatics lay hold on, to revile the
doctrine and discipline of the Church, and even insult and
oppress the clergy wherever their numbers or favourers will
bear them out; insomuch, that one wilful refractory fanatic
hath been able to disturb a whole parish for many years together. But the most moderate and favoured divines dare not
own, that the word moderation, with respect to the dissenters,
can be at all applied to their religion, but is purely personal
or prudential. No good man repineth at the liberty of conscience they enjoy; and, perhaps a very moderate divine
may think better of their loyalty than others do; or, to
speak after the manner of men, may think it necessary, that
all Protestants should be united against the common enemy;
or out of discretion, or other reasons best known to himself,

be tender of mentioning them at all. But still the errors of the dissenters are all fixed and determined, and must, upon demand, be acknowledged by all the divines of our church, whether they be called, in party phrase, high or low, moderate or violent. And further, I believe it would be hard to find many moderate divines, who, if their opinion were asked whether dissenters should be trusted with power, could, according to their consciences, answer in the affirmative; from whence it is plain, that all the stir which the fanatics have made with this word moderation, was only meant to increase our divisions, and widen them so far as to make room for themselves to get in between. And this is the only scheme they ever had (except that of destroying root and branch) for the uniting of Protestants, they so much talk of.

I shall mention but one ill consequence more, which attends our want of brotherly love; that it hath put an end to all hospitality and friendship, all good correspondence and commerce between mankind. There are indeed such things as leagues and confederacies among those of the same party; but surely God never intended that men should be so limited in the choice of their friends: However, so it is in town and country, in every parish and street; the pastor is divided from his flock, the father from his son, and the house often divided against itself. Men's very natures are soured, and their passions inflamed, when they meet in party clubs, and spend their time in nothing else but railing at the opposite side; thus every man alive among us is encompassed with a million of enemies of his own country, among which his oldest acquaintance and friends, and kindred themselves, are often of the number; neither can people of different parties mix together without constraint, suspicion, or jealousy, watching every word they speak, for fear of giving offence, or else falling into rudeness and reproaches, and so leaving themselves open to the malice and corruption of informers, who were never more numerous or expert in their trade. And as a further addition to this evil, those very few, who, by the goodness and generosity of their nature, do in their own hearts despise this narrow principle of confining their friendship and esteem, their charity and good offices, to those of their own party, yet dare not discover their good inclinations, for fear of losing their favour and interest. And others again, whom God had formed with mild and gentle dispositions. think it necessary to put a force upon their own tempers, by acting a noisy, violent, malicious part, as a means to be distinguished. Thus hath party got the better of the very genius and constitution of our people; so that whoever reads the character of the English in former ages, will hardly believe their present posterity to be of the same nation or climate.

III. I shall now, in the last place, make use of some motives and exhortations, that may persuade you to embrace brotherly love, and continue in it. Let me apply myself to you of the lower sort, and desire you will consider, when any of you make use of fair and enticing words to draw in customers, whether you do it for their sakes or your own. And then, for whose sakes do you think it is, that your leaders are so industrious to put into your heads all that party rage and virulence? Is it not to make you the tools and instruments, by which they work out their own designs? Has this spirit of faction been useful to any of you in your worldly concerns, except to those who have traded in whispering, backbiting, or informing, and wanted skill or honesty to thrive by fairer methods? It is no business of yours to inquire, who is at the head of armies, or of councils, unless you had power and skill to choose, neither of which is ever likely to be your case; and therefore to fill your heads with fears, and hatred of persons and things, of which it is impossible you can ever make a right judgment, or to set you at variance with your neighbour, because his thoughts are not the same as yours, is not only in a very gross manner to cheat you of your time and quiet, but likewise to endanger your souls.

Secondly : In order to restore brotherly love, let me earnestly exhort you to stand firm in your religion; I mean, the true religion hitherto established among us, without varying in the least either to Popery on the one side, or to fanaticism on the other; and in a particular manner beware of that word, moderation; and believe it, that your neighbour is not immediately a villain, a Papist, and a traitor, because the fanatics and their adherents will not allow him to be a moderate man.

Nay, it is very probable, that your teacher himself may be a loyal, pious, and able divine, without the least grain of moderation, as the word is too frequently understood. Therefore, to set you right in this matter, I will lay before you the character of a truly moderate man, and then I will give you the description of such a one as falsely pretendeth to that title.

A man truly moderate is steady in the doctrine and discipline of the Church, but with a due Christian charity to all who dissent from it out of a principle of conscience; the freedom of which, he thinketh, ought to be fully allowed, as long as it is not abused, but never trusted with power. He is ready to defend with his life and fortune the Protestant succession, and the Protestant established faith, against all invaders whatsoever. He is for giving the Crown its just prerogative, and the people their just liberties. He hateth no man for differing from him in political opinions; nor doth he think it a maxim infallible, that virtue should always attend upon favour, and vice upon disgrace. These are some few lineaments in the character of a truly moderate man; let us now compare it with the description of one who usually passeth under that title.

A moderate man, in the new meaning of the word, is one to whom all religion is indifferent; who although he denominates himself of the Church, regardeth it no more than a conventicle. He perpetually raileth at the body of the clergy, with exceptions only to a very few, who, he hopeth, and probably upon false grounds, are as ready to betray their rights and properties as himself. He thinketh the power of the people can never be too great, nor that of the prince too little; and yet this very notion he publisheth, as his best argument, to prove him a most loyal subject. Every opinion in government, that differeth in the least from his, tendeth directly to Popery, slavery, and rebellion. Whoever lieth under the frown of power, can, in his judgment, neither have common sense, common honesty, nor religion. Lastly, his devotion consisteth in drinking gibbets, confusion, and damnation;[1] in profanely idolizing the memory of one

---

[1] The subject of these political toasts was the theme of much discussion in Ireland. [S.]

dead prince,[1] and ungratefully trampling upon the ashes of another.[2]

By these marks you will easily distinguish a truly moderate man from those who are commonly, but very falsely, so called; and while persons thus qualified are so numerous and so noisy, so full of zeal and industry to gain proselytes, and spread their opinions among the people, it cannot be wondered at that there should be so little brotherly love left among us.

Lastly: It would probably contribute to restore some degree of brotherly love, if we would but consider, that the matter of those disputes, which inflame us to this degree, doth not, in its own nature, at all concern the generality of mankind. Indeed as to those who have been great gainers or losers by the changes of the world, the case is different; and to preach moderation to the first, and patience to the last, would perhaps be to little purpose: But what is that to the bulk of the people, who are not properly concerned in the quarrel, although evil instruments have drawn them into it? For, if the reasonable men on both sides were to confer opinions, they would find neither religion, loyalty, nor interest, are at all affected in this dispute. Not religion, because the members of the Church, on both sides, profess to agree in every article: Not loyalty to our prince, which is pretended to by one party as much as the other, and therefore can be no subject for debate: Not interest, for trade and industry lie open to all; and, what is further, concerns only those who have expectations from the public: So that the body of the people, if they knew their own good, might yet live amicably together, and leave their betters to quarrel among themselves, who might also probably soon come to a better temper, if they were less seconded and supported by the poor deluded multitude.

I have now done with my text, which I confess to have treated in a manner more suited to the present times, than to the nature of the subject in general. That I have not been more particular in explaining the several parts and properties of this great duty of brotherly love, the apostle to the Thessalonians will plead my excuse.—" Touching

---

[1] King William.   [2] Queen Anne.

brotherly love" (saith he) "ye need not that I write unto you, for ye yourselves are taught of God to love one another."[1] So that nothing remains to add, but our prayers to God, that he would please to restore and continue this duty of brotherly love or charity among us, the very bond of peace and of all virtues.

Nov. 29, 1717.

[1] I Thess. iv. 9.

DIFFICULTY OF KNOWING ONE'S-SELF.[1]

2 KINGS, VIII. PART OF THE 13TH VERSE.

"And Hazael said, But what, is thy servant a dog, that he should do this great thing?"

WE have a very singular instance of the deceitfulness of the heart, represented to us in the person of Hazael; who was sent to the prophet Elisha, to enquire of the Lord concerning his master the King of Syria's recovery. For the man of God, having told him that the king might recover from the disorder he was then labouring under, begun to set and fasten his countenance upon him of a sudden, and to break out into the most violent expressions of sorrow, and a deep concern for it; whereupon, when Hazael, full of shame and confusion, asked, "Why weepeth my lord?" he answered, "Because I know all the evil that thou wilt do unto the children of Israel; their strongholds wilt thou set on fire, and their young men wilt thou slay with the sword, and wilt dash their children, and rip up their women with child." Thus much did the man of God say and know of him, by a

---

[1] Prefixed to the issue in volume ten, "Miscellanies," 1745, is the following:

"ADVERTISEMENT.

"The manuscript title page of the following sermon being lost, and no memorandum writ upon it, as there were upon the others, when and where it was preached, made the editor doubtful whether he should print it as the Dean's, or not. But its being found amongst the same papers; and the hand, though writ somewhat better, bearing a great similitude to the Dean's, made him willing to lay it before the public, that they might judge whether the style and manner also does not render it still more probable to be his." [T. S.]

light darted into his mind from heaven.   But Hazael not knowing himself so well as the other did, was startled and amazed at the relation, and would not believe it possible that a man of his temper could ever run out into such enormous instances of cruelty and inhumanity.   "What!" says he, " is thy servant a dog, that he should do this great thing?"

And yet, for all this, it is highly probable that he was then that man he could not imagine himself to be ; for we find him, on the very next day after his return, in a very treacherous and disloyal manner murdering his own master, and usurping his kingdom ; which was but a prologue to the sad tragedy which he afterwards acted upon the people of Israel.

And now the case is but very little better with most men, than it was with Hazael ; however it comes to pass, they are wonderfully unacquainted with their own temper and disposition, and know very little of what passes within them : For of so many proud, ambitious, revengeful, envying, and ill-natured persons, that are in the world, where is there one of them, who, although he has all the symptoms of the vice appearing upon every occasion, can look with such an impartial eye upon himself, as to believe that the imputation thrown upon him is not altogether groundless and unfair? Who, if he were told by men of a discerning spirit and a strong conjecture, of all the evil and absurd things which that false heart of his would at one time or other betray him into, would not believe as little, and wonder as much, as Hazael did before him?   Thus, for instance ; tell an angry person that he is weak and impotent, and of no consistency of mind ; tell him, that such or such a little accident, which he may then despise and think much below a passion, shall hereafter make him say and do several absurd, indiscreet, and misbecoming things : He may perhaps own that he has a spirit of resentment within him, that will not let him be imposed on, but he fondly imagines that he can lay a becoming restraint upon it when he pleases, although 'tis ever running away with him into some indecency or other.

Therefore, to bring the words of my text to our present occasion, I shall endeavour, in a further prosecution of them, to evince the great necessity of a nice and curious inspection into the several recesses of the heart, being the surest and the

shortest method that a wicked man can take to reform himself: For let us but stop the fountain, and the streams will
spend and waste themselves away in a very little time ; but
if we go about, like children, to raise a bank, and to stop the
current, not taking notice all the while of the spring which
continually feeds it, when the next flood of temptation rises,
and breaks in upon it, then we shall find that we have begun
at the wrong end of our duty, and that we are very little
more the better for it, than if we had sat still, and made no
advances at all.

But, in order to a clearer explanation of the point, I shall
speak to these following particulars :—

First : By endeavouring to prove, from particular instances,
   that man is generally the most ignorant creature in the
   world of himself.
Secondly : By inquiring into the grounds and reasons of his
   ignorance.
Thirdly and *Lastly :* By proposing several advantages that
   do most assuredly attend a due improvement in the knowledge of ourselves.

First, then: To prove that man is generally the most
ignorant creature in the world, of himself.

To pursue the heart of man through all the instances of
life, in all its several windings and turnings, and under that
infinite variety of shapes and appearances which it puts on,
would be a difficult and almost impossible undertaking ; so
that I shall confine myself to such as have a nearer reference
to the present occasion, and do, upon a closer view, shew
themselves through the whole business of repentance.   For
we all know what it is to repent, but whether he repents him
truly of his sins or not, who can know it?

Now the great duty of repentance is chiefly made up of
these two parts, a hearty sorrow for the follies and miscarriages of the time past, and a full purpose and resolution
of amendment for the time to come.   And now, to shew the
falseness of the heart in both these parts of repentance.
And

First : As to a hearty sorrow for the sins and miscarriages
of the time past.   Is there a more usual thing than for a

man to impose upon himself, by putting on a grave and demure countenance, by casting a severe look into his past conduct, and making some few pious and devout reflections upon it, and then to believe that he has repented to an excellent purpose, without ever letting it step forth into practice, and shew itself in a holy conversation? Nay, some persons do carry the deceit a little higher; who if they can but bring themselves to weep for their sins, they are then full of an ill-grounded confidence and security; never considering that all this may prove to be no more than the very garb and outward dress of a contrite heart, which another heart, as hard as the nether millstone, may as well put on. For tears and sighs, however in some persons they may be decent and commendable expressions of a godly sorrow, are neither necessary, nor infallible signs of a true and unfeigned repentance. Not necessary, because sometimes, and in some persons, the inward grief and anguish of the mind may be too big to be expressed by so little a thing as a tear, and then it turneth its edge inward upon the mind; and like those wounds of the body which bleed inwardly, generally proves the most fatal and dangerous to the whole body of sin: Not infallible, because a very small portion of sorrow may make some tender dispositions melt, and break out into tears; or a man may perhaps weep at parting with his sins, as he would bid the last farewell to an old friend.

But there is still a more pleasant cheat in this affair, that when we find a deadness, and a strange kind of unaptness and indisposition to all impressions of religion, and that we cannot be as truly sorry for our sins as we should be, we then pretend to be sorry that we are not more sorry for them; which is not more absurd and irrational, than that a man should pretend to be very angry at a thing, because he did not know how to be angry at all.

But after all, what is wanting in this part of repentance, we expect to make up in the next; and to that purpose we put on a resolution of amendment, which we take to be as firm as a house built upon a rock; so that let the floods arise, and the winds blow, and the streams beat vehemently upon it, nothing shall shake it into ruin or disorder. We doubt not, upon the strength of this resolve, to stand fast and unmoved amid the storm of a temptation; and do firmly believe, at the time we make it, that nothing in the world will ever be able to make us commit those sins over again, which we have so firmly resolved against.

Thus many a time have we come to the Sacrament of the Lord's Supper, with a full purpose of amendment, and with as full a persuasion of putting that same purpose into practice ; and yet have we not all as often broke that good purpose, and falsified that same persuasion, by starting aside, like a broken bow, into those very sins, which we then so solemnly and so confidently declared against ?

Whereas had but any other person entered with us into a vow so solemn, that he had taken the Holy Sacrament upon it, I believe had he but once deceived us by breaking in upon the vow, we should hardly ever after be prevailed upon to trust that man again, though we still continue to trust our own fears, against reason and against experience.

This indeed is a dangerous deceit enough, and will of course betray all those well-meaning persons into sin and folly, who are apt to take religion for a much easier thing than it is. But this is not the only mistake we are apt to run into ; we do not only think sometimes that we can do more than we can do, but sometimes that we are incapable of doing less ; an error of another kind indeed, but not less dangerous, arising from a diffidence and false humility. For how much a wicked man can do in the business of religion, if he would but do his best, is very often more than he can tell.

Thus nothing is more common than to see a wicked man running headlong into sin and folly, against his reason, against his religion, and against his God. Tell him, that what he is going to do will be an infinite disparagement to his understanding, which, at another time, he sets no small value upon ; tell him that it will blacken his reputation, which he had rather die for than lose ; tell him that the pleasure of sin is short and transient, and leaves a vexatious kind of sting behind it, which will very hardly be drawn forth ; tell him that this is one of those things for which God will most surely bring him to judgment, which he pretends to believe with a full assurance and persuasion : And yet for all this, he shuts his eyes against all conviction, and rusheth into the sin like a horse into battle ; as if he had nothing left to do, but, like a silly child to wink hard, and to think to escape a certain and infinite mischief, only by endeavouring not to see it.

And now to shew that the heart has given in a false report of the temptation, we may learn from this, that the same weak man would resist and master the same powerful temptation, upon considerations of infinitely less value than those which religion offers, nay such vile considerations, that the grace of God cannot without blasphemy be supposed to add any manner of force and efficacy to them. Thus for instance, it would be a hard matter to dress up a sin in such soft and tempting circumstances, that a truly covetous man would not resist for a considerable sum of money; when neither the hopes of heaven nor the fears of hell could make an impression upon him before. But can anything be a surer indication of the deceitfulness of the heart, than thus to shew more courage, resolution, and activity, in an ill cause, than it does in a good one? And to exert itself to better purpose, when it is to serve its own pride, or lust, or revenge, or any other passion, than when it is to serve God upon motives of the Gospel, and upon all the arguments that have ever been made use of to bring men over to religion and a good life? And thus having shewn that man is wonderfully apt to deceive and impose upon himself, in passing through the several stages of that great duty, repentance, I proceed now, in the

Second place: To inquire into the grounds and reasons of this ignorance, *and to shew whence it comes to pass that man, the only creature in the world that can reflect and look into himself, should know so little of what passes within him, and be so very much unacquainted even with the standing dispositions and complexion of his own heart.* The prime reason of it is, because we so very seldom converse with ourselves, and take so little notice of what passes within us : For a man can no more know his own heart than he can know his own face, any other way than by reflection : He may as well tell over every feature of the smaller portions of his face without the help of a looking-glass, as he can tell all the inward bents and tendencies of his soul, those standing features and lineaments of the inward man, and know all the various changes that this is liable to from custom, from passion, and from opinion, without a very frequent use of looking within himself.

For our passions and inclinations are not always upon the wing, and always moving toward their respective objects, but retire now and then into the more dark and hidden recesses of the heart, where they lie concealed for a while, until a fresh occasion calls them forth again : So that not every transient, oblique glance upon the mind can bring a man into a thorough knowledge of all its strength and weaknesses ; for a man may sometimes turn the eye of the mind inward upon itself, as he may behold his natural face in a glass, and go away, "and straight forget what manner of man he was." But a man must rather sit down and unravel every action of the past day into all its circumstances and particularities, and observe how every little thing moved and affected him, and what manner of impression it made upon his heart ; this done with that frequency and carefulness which the importance of the duty does require, would in a short time bring him into a nearer and more intimate acquaintance with himself.

But when men instead of this do pass away months and years in a perfect slumber of the mind, without once awaking it, it is no wonder they should be so very ignorant of themselves, and know very little more of what passes within them than the very beasts which perish. But here it may not be amiss to inquire into the reasons why most men have so little conversation with themselves.

And, *first* : Because this reflection is a work and labour of the mind, and cannot be performed without some pain and difficulty : For, before a man can reflect upon himself, and look into his heart with a steady eye, he must contract his sight, and collect all his scattering and roving thoughts into some order and compass, that he may be able to take a clear and distinct view of them ; he must retire from the world for a while, and be unattentive to all impressions of sense ; and how hard and painful a thing must it needs be to a man of passion and infirmity, amid such a crowd of objects that are continually striking upon the sense, and soliciting the affections, not to be moved and interrupted by one or other of them. But,

Secondly : Another reason why we so seldom converse with ourselves, is, because the business of the world takes up all our time, and leaveth us no portion of it to spend upon this great work and labour of the mind.   Thus twelve or fourteen years pass away before we can well discern good from evil ; and of the rest so much goes away in sleep, so much in the proper business of our calling, that we have none to lay out upon the more serious and religious employments.   Every man's life is an imperfect sort of a circle, which he repeats and runs over every day ; he has a set of thoughts, desires, and inclinations, which return upon him in their proper time and order, and will very hardly be laid aside, to make room for anything new and uncommon : So that call upon him when you please, to set about the study of his own heart, and you are sure to find him pre-engaged ; either he has some business to do, or some diversion to take, some acquaintance that he must visit, or some company that he must entertain, or some cross accident has put him out of humour, and unfitted him for such a grave employment. And thus it cometh to pass that a man can never find leisure to look into himself, because he does not set apart some portion of the day for that very purpose, but foolishly defers it from one day to another, till his glass is almost run out, and he is called to give a miserable account of himself in the other world.   But,

Thirdly, Another reason why a man does not more frequently converse with himself, is, because such conversation with his own heart may discover some vice or some infirmity lurking within him, which he is very unwilling to believe himself guilty of.   For can there be a more ungrateful thing to a man, than to find that upon a nearer view he is not that person he took himself to be ?   That he had neither the courage, nor the honesty, nor the piety, nor the humility that he dreamed he had ?   That a very little pain, for instance, putteth him out of patience, and as little pleasure softens and disarms him into ease and wantonness ?   That he has been at more pains, and labour, and cost, to be revenged of an enemy, than to oblige the best friend he has in the world ?   That he cannot bring himself to say his prayers, without a great deal of reluctancy ; and when he does say them, the spirit and fervour of devotion evaporate in a very short time, and he can scarcely hold out a prayer of ten lines, without a number of idle and impertinent, if not vain and wicked thoughts coming into his head ? These are very unwelcome discoveries that a man may make of himself; so that 'tis no wonder that every one who is already flushed with a good opinion of himself, should rather study how to run away from it, than how to converse with his own heart.

But further, if a man were both able and willing to retire into his own heart, and to set apart some portion of the day for that very purpose; yet he is still disabled from passing a fair and impartial judgment upon himself, by several difficulties, arising partly from prejudice and prepossession, partly from the lower appetites and inclinations. And,

First: That the business of prepossession may lead and betray a man into a false judgment of his own heart. For we may observe, that the first opinion we take up of anything, or any person, does generally stick close to us; the nature of the mind being such, that it cannot but desire, and consequently endeavour to have some certain principles to go upon, something fixed and unmoveable, whereon it may rest and support itself. And hence it comes to pass, that some persons are with so much difficulty brought to think well of a man they have once entertained an ill opinion of: and perhaps that too for a very absurd and unwarrantable reason. But how much more difficult then must it be for a man, who takes up a fond opinion of his own heart long before he has either years or sense enough to understand it, either to be persuaded out of it by himself, whom he loveth so well, or by another, whose interest or diversion it may be to make him ashamed of himself! Then,

Secondly: As to the difficulties arising from the inferior appetites and inclinations, let any man look into his own heart, and observe in how different a light, and under what different complexions, any two sins of equal turpitude and malignity do appear to him, if he has but a strong inclination to the one, and none at all to the other. That which he has an inclination to, is always drest up in all the false beauty that a fond and busy imagination can give it; the other appears naked and deformed, and in all the true circumstances of folly and dishonour. Thus stealing is a vice that few gentlemen are inclined to; and they justly think it below the dignity of a man to stoop to so base and low a sin; but no principle of honour, no workings of the mind and conscience, not the still voice of mercy, not the dreadful call of judgment, nor any considerations whatever, can put a stop to that violence and oppression, that pride and ambition, that revelling and wantonness, which we every day meet with in the world.   Nay, it is easy to observe very different thoughts in a man, of the sin that he is most fond of, according to the different ebbs and flows of his inclination to it. For as soon as the appetite is alarmed, and seizeth upon the heart, a little cloud gathereth about the head, and spreads a kind of darkness over the face of the soul, whereby 'tis hindered from taking a clear and distinct view of things; but no sooner is the appetite tired and satiated, but the same cloud passes away like a shadow, and a new light springing up in the mind of a sudden, the man sees much more, both of the folly and of the danger of the sin, than he did before.

And thus having done with the several reasons why man, the only creature in the world that can reflect and look into himself, is so very ignorant of what passes within him, and so much unacquainted with the standing dispositions and complexions of his own heart : I proceed now, in the

Third and *Last* place, to lay down several advantages, that do *most assuredly* attend a due improvement in the knowledge of ourselves.   And,

First : One great advantage is, that it tends very much to mortify and humble a man into a modest and low opinion of himself.   For let a man take a nice and curious inspection into all the several regions of the heart, and observe every thing irregular and amiss within him : for instance, how narrow and short-sighted a thing is the understanding; upon how little reason do we we take up an opinion, and upon how much less sometimes do we lay it down again, how weak and false ground do we often walk upon with the biggest confidence and assurance, and how tremulous and doubtful are we very often where no doubt is to be made.   Again; how wild and impertinent, how busy and incoherent a thing is the imagination, even in the best and wisest men; insomuch that every man may be said to be mad, but every man does not shew it. Then as to the passions; how noisy, how turbulent, and how tumultuous are they, how easy they are stirred and set a-going, how eager and hot in the pursuit, and what strange disorder and confusion do they throw a man into; so that he can neither think, nor speak, nor act as he should do, while he is under the dominion of any one of them.

Thus let every man look with a severe and impartial eye into all the distinct regions of the heart, and no doubt, several deformities and irregularities, that he never thought of, will open and disclose themselves upon so near a view; and rather make the man ashamed of himself, than proud.

Secondly: A due improvement in the knowledge of ourselves does certainly secure us from the sly and insinuating assaults of flattery. There is not in the world a baser and more hateful thing than flattery; it proceeds from so much falseness and insincerity in the man that gives it, and often discovers so much weakness and folly in the man that takes it, that it is hard to tell which of the two is most to be blamed. Every man of common sense can demonstrate in speculation, and may be fully convinced, that all the praises and commendations of the whole world can add no more to the real and intrinsic value of a man, than they can add to his stature. And yet, for all this, men of the best sense and piety, when they come down to the practice, cannot forbear thinking much better of themselves, when they have the good fortune to be spoken well of by other persons.

But the meaning of this absurd proceeding seems to be no other than this; there are few men that have so intimate an acquaintance with their own heart, as to know their own real worth, and how to set a just rate upon themselves, and therefore they do not know but that he who praises them most, may be most in the right of it. For, no doubt, if a man were ignorant of the true value of a thing he loved as well as himself, he would measure the worth of it according to the esteem of him who bids most for it, rather than of him that bids less.

Therefore, the most infallible way to disentangle a man from the snares of flattery, is, to consult and study his own heart; for whoever does that well, will hardly be so absurd, as to take another man's word, before his own sense and experience.

Thirdly: Another advantage from this kind of study, is this, that it teaches a man how to behave himself patiently, when he has the ill fortune to be censured and abused by other people. For a man who is thoroughly acquainted with his own heart, does already know more evil of himself, than anybody else can tell him; and when any one speaks ill of him, he rather thanks God that he can say no worse. For could his enemy but look into the dark and hidden recesses of the heart, he considers what a number of impure thoughts he might there see brooding and hovering, like a dark cloud, upon the face of the soul; that there he might take a prospect of the fancy, and view it acting over the several scenes of pride, of ambition, of envy, of lust, and revenge; that there he might tell how often a vicious inclination has been restrained, for no other reason but just to save the man's credit or interest in the world; and how many unbecoming ingredients have entered into the composition of his best actions. And now, what man in the whole world would be able to bear so severe a test, to have every thought and inward motion of the heart laid open and exposed to the views of his enemies? But,

Fourthly, and *Lastly:* Another advantage of this kind is, that it makes men less severe upon other people's faults, and less busy and industrious in spreading them. For a man, employed at home, inspecting into his own failings, has not leisure to take notice of every little spot and blemish that lies scattered upon others. Or if he cannot escape the sight of them, he always passes the most easy and favourable construction upon them. Thus, for instance; does the ill he knows of a man proceed from an unhappy temper and constitution of body? He then considers with himself, how hard a thing it is, not to be borne down with the current of the blood and spirits, and accordingly lays some part of the blame upon the weakness of human nature, for he has felt the force and rapidity of it within his own breast; though perhaps, in another instance, he remembers how it rages and swells by opposition; and though it may be restrained, or diverted for a while, yet it can hardly ever be totally subdued.

Or has the man sinned out of custom? He then, from his own experience, traces a habit into the very first rise and imperfect beginnings of it; and can tell by how slow and insensible advances it creeps upon the heart; how it works itself by degrees into the very frame and texture of it, and so passes into a second nature; and consequently he has a just sense of the great difficulty for him to learn to do good, who has been long accustomed to do evil.

Or, lastly, has a false opinion betrayed him into a sin? He then calls to mind what wrong apprehensions he has made of some things himself; how many opinions, that he once made no doubt of, he has, upon a stricter examination found to be doubtful and uncertain; how many more to be unreasonable and absurd. He knows further, that there are a great many more opinions that he has never yet examined into at all, and which, however, he still believes, for no other reason, but because he has believed them so long already without a reason. Thus, upon every occasion, a man intimately acquainted with himself, consults his own heart, and makes every man's case to be his own, (and so puts the most favourable interpretation upon it). Let every man therefore look into his own heart, before he beginneth to abuse the reputation of another, and then he will hardly be so absurd as to throw a dart that will so certainly rebound and wound himself. And thus, through the whole course of his conversation, let him keep an eye upon that one great comprehensive rule of Christian duty, on which hangs, not only the law and the prophets, but the very life and spirit of the Gospel too: "Whatsoever ye would that men should do unto you, do ye even so unto them." Which rule, that we may all duly observe, by throwing aside all scandal and detraction, all spite and rancour, all rudeness and contempt, all rage and violence, and whatever tends to make conversation and commerce either uneasy, or troublesome, may the God of peace grant for Jesus Christ his sake, &c.

Consider what has been said, &c.

FALSE WITNESS.

EXODUS, XX. 16.

" Thou shalt not bear false witness against thy neighbour."

I N those great changes that are made in a country by the
prevailing of one party over another, it is very convenient
that the prince, and those who are in authority under him,
should use all just and proper methods for preventing any
mischief to the public from seditious men.   And governors
do well, when they encourage any good subject to discover
(as his duty obligeth him) whatever plots or conspiracies
may be anyway dangerous to the state : Neither are they to
be blamed, even when they receive informations from bad
men, in order to find out the truth, when it concerns the
public welfare.   Every one indeed is naturally inclined to
have an ill opinion of an informer ; although it is not impossible but an honest man may be called by that name.
For whoever knoweth anything, the telling of which would
prevent some great evil to his prince, his country, or his
neighbour, is bound in conscience to reveal it.   But the
mischief is, that, when parties are violently enflamed, which
seemeth unfortunately to be our case at present, there is
never wanting a set of evil instruments, who, either out of
mad zeal, private hatred, or filthy lucre, are always ready to
offer their service to the prevailing side, and become accusers
of their brethren, without any regard to truth or charity.
Holy David numbers this among the chief of his sufferings ;
" False witnesses are risen up against me, and such as breathe
out cruelty." [1]   Our Saviour and his apostles did likewise

[1] Psalm xxvii. 12.

undergo the same distress, as we read both in the Gospels and the Acts.

Now, because the sign of false witnessing is so horrible and dangerous in itself, and so odious to God and man; and because the bitterness of too many among us is risen to such a height, that it is not easy to know where it will stop, or how far some weak and wicked minds may be carried by a mistaken zeal, a malicious temper, or hope of reward, to break this great commandment delivered in the text; therefore, in order to prevent this evil, and the consequences of it, at least among you who are my hearers, I shall,

I. *First*: Shew you several ways by which a man may be called a false witness against his neighbour.

II. *Secondly*: I shall give you some rules for your conduct and behaviour, in order to defend yourselves against the malice and cunning of false accusers.

III. And *lastly*: I shall conclude with shewing you very briefly, how far it is your duty, as good subjects and good neighbours, to bear faithful witness, when you are lawfully called to it by those in authority, or by the sincere advice of your own consciences.

I. As to the first, there are several ways by which a man may be justly called a false witness against his neighbour.

First, According to the direct meaning of the word, when a man accuseth his neighbour without the least ground of truth. So we read, that Jezebel hired two sons of Belial to accuse Naboth for blaspheming God and the King, for which, although he was entirely innocent, he was stoned to death.[1] And in our age it is not easy, to tell how many men have lost their lives, been ruined in their fortunes, and put to ignominious punishment by the downright perjury of false witnesses! The law itself in such cases being not able to protect the innocent. But this is so horrible a crime, that it doth not need to be aggravated by words.

A second way by which a man becometh a false witness is, when he mixeth falsehood and truth together, or concealeth some circumstances, which, if they were told, would

---

[1] 1 Kings, xxi. 8-13.

destroy the falsehoods he uttereth. So the two false witnesses who accused our Saviour before the chief priests, by a very little perverting his words, would have made him guilty of a capital crime: for so it was among the Jews to prophesy any evil against the Temple: " This fellow said, I am able to destroy the temple of God, and to build it in three days; " [1] whereas the words, as our Saviour spoke them, were to another end, and differently expressed : For when the Jews asked him to shew them a sign, he said, " Destroy this temple, and in three days I will raise it up." In such cases as these, an innocent man is half confounded, and looketh as if he were guilty, since he neither can deny his words, nor perhaps readily strip them from the malicious additions of a false witness.

Thirdly : A man is a false witness, when, in accusing his neighbour, he endeavoureth to aggravate by his gestures and tone of his voice, or when he chargeth a man with words which were only repeated or quoted from somebody else. As if any one should tell me that he heard another speak certain dangerous and seditious speeches, and I should immediately accuse him for speaking them himself; and so drop the only circumstance that made him innocent. This was the case of St Stephen. The false witness said, " This man ceaseth not to speak blasphemous words against this holy place and the law." [2] Whereas St Stephen said no such words; but only repeated some prophecies of Jeremiah or Malachi, which threatened Jerusalem with destruction if it did not repent. However, by the fury of the people, this innocent holy person was stoned to death for words he never spoke.

Fourthly : The blackest kind of false witnesses are those who do the office of the devil, by tempting their brethren in order to betray them. I cannot call to mind any instances of this kind mentioned in Holy Scripture. But I am afraid, this vile practice hath been too much followed in the world. When a man's temper hath been so soured by misfortunes and hard usage, that perhaps he hath reason enough to complain; then one of these seducers, under the pretence of friendship, will seem to lament his case, urge the hard-

---

[1] Mat. xxvi. 6.　　　　　[2] Acts, vi. 13.

ships he hath suffered, and endeavour to raise his passions, until he hath said something that a malicious informer can pervert or aggravate against him in a court of justice.

Fifthly: Whoever beareth witness against his neighbour, out of a principle of malice and revenge, from any old grudge, or hatred to his person; such a man is a false witness in the sight of God, although what he says be true; because the motive or cause is evil, not to serve his prince or country, but to gratify his own resentments. And therefore, although a man thus accused may be very justly punished by the law, yet this doth by no means acquit the accuser, who, instead of regarding the public service, intended only to glut his private rage and spite.

Sixthly: I number among false witnesses, all those who make a trade of being informers in hope of favour or reward; and to this end employ their time, either by listening in public places, to catch up an accidental word; or in corrupting men's servants to discover any unwary expression of their master; or thrusting themselves into company, and then using the most indecent scurrilous language; fastening a thousand falsehoods and scandals upon a whole party, on purpose to provoke such an answer as they may turn to an accusation. And truly this ungodly race is said to be grown so numerous, that men of different parties can hardly converse together with any security. Even the pulpit hath not been free from the misrepresentation of these informers; of whom the clergy have not wanted occasions to complain with holy David: "They daily mistake my words, all they imagine is to do me evil." Nor is it any wonder at all, that this trade of informing should be now in a flourishing condition, since our case is manifestly thus: We are divided into two parties, with very little charity or temper toward each other; the prevailing side may talk of past things as they please, with security; and generally do it in the most provoking words they can invent; while those who are down, are sometimes tempted to speak in favour of a lost cause, and therefore, without great caution, must needs be often caught tripping, and thereby furnish plenty of materials for witnesses and informers.

Lastly: Those may be well reckoned among false witnesses against their neighbour, who bring him into trouble

and punishment by such accusations as are of no consequence at all to the public, nor can be of any other use
but to create vexation.   Such witnesses are those who cannot hear an idle intemperate expression, but they must immediately run to the magistrate to inform ; or perhaps
wrangling in their cups over night, when they were not able
to speak or apprehend three words of common sense, will
pretend to remember everything the next morning, and
think themselves very properly qualified to be accusers of
their brethren.   God be thanked, the throne of our King [1]
is too firmly settled to be shaken by the folly and rashness
of every sottish companion.   And I do not in the least
doubt, that when those in power begin to observe the
falsehood, the prevarication, the aggravating manner, the
treachery and seducing, the malice and revenge, the love of
lucre, and lastly, the trifling accusations in too many wicked
people, they will be as ready to discourage every sort of
those whom I have numbered among false witnesses, as
they will be to countenance honest men, who, out of a true
zeal to their prince and country, do, in the innocence of their
hearts, freely discover whatever they may apprehend to be
dangerous to either.   A good Christian will think it sufficient
to reprove his brother for a rash unguarded word, where
there is neither danger nor evil example to be apprehended ;
or, if he will not amend by reproof, avoid his conversation.

II. And thus much may serve to shew the several ways
whereby a man may be said to be a false witness against his
neighbour.   I might have added one kind more, and it is of
those who inform against their neighbour out of fear of
punishment to themselves, which, although it be more excusable, and hath less of malice than any of the rest, cannot,
however, be justified.   I go on, therefore, upon the second
head, to give you some rules for your conduct and behaviour,
in order to defend yourselves against the malice and cunning
of false accusers.
   It is readily agreed, that innocence is the best protection
in the world ; yet that it is not always sufficient without
some degree of prudence, our Saviour himself intimateth to

[1] George I.

us, by instructing his disciples "to be wise as serpents, as well as innocent as doves." But if ever innocence be too weak a defence, it is chiefly so in jealous and suspicious times, when factions are arrived to an high pitch of animosity, and the minds of men, instead of being warmed by a true zeal for religion, are inflamed only by party fury. Neither is virtue itself a sufficient security in such times, because it is not allowed to be virtue, otherwise than as it hath a mixture of party.

However, although virtue and innocence are no infallible defence against perjury, malice, and subornation, yet they are great supports for enabling us to bear those evils with temper and resignation; and it is an unspeakable comfort to a good man under the malignity of evil mercenary tongues, that a few years will carry his appeal to an higher tribunal, where false witnesses, instead of daring to bring accusations before an all-seeing Judge, will call for mountains to cover them. As for earthly judges, they seldom have it in their power; and, God knows, whether they have it in their will, to mingle mercy with justice; they are so far from knowing the hearts of the accuser or the accused, that they cannot know their own; and their understanding is frequently biassed, although their intentions be just. They are often prejudiced to causes, parties, and persons, through the infirmity of human nature, without being sensible themselves that they are so: And therefore, although God may pardon their errors here, he certainly will not ratify their sentences hereafter.

However, since as we have before observed, our Saviour prescribeth to us to be not only harmless as doves, but wise as serpents; give me leave to prescribe to you some rules, which the most ignorant person may follow for the conduct of his life, with safety in perilous times, against false accusers.

1st, Let me advise you to have nothing at all to do with that which is commonly called politics, or the government of the world, in the nature of which it is certain you are utterly ignorant, and when your opinion is wrong, although it proceeds from ignorance, it shall be an accusation against you. Besides, opinions in government are right or wrong, just according to the humour and disposition of the times; and, unless you have judgment to distinguish, you may be punished at one time for what you would be rewarded in another.

2dly, Be ready at all times, in your words and actions, to shew your loyalty to the king that reigns over you. This is the plain manifest doctrine of Holy Scripture: "Submit yourselves to every ordinance of man for the Lord's sake, whether it be to the king as supreme," &c.[1] And another apostle telleth us, "The powers that be are ordained of God." Kings are the ordinances of man by the permission of God, and they are ordained of God by his instrument man. The powers that be, the present powers, which are ordained by God, and yet in some sense are the ordinances of man, are what you must obey, without presuming to examine into rights and titles; neither can it be reasonably expected, that the powers in being, or in possession, should suffer their title to be publicly disputed by subjects without severe punishment. And to say the truth, there is no duty in religion more easy to the generality of mankind, than obedience to government: I say to the generality of mankind; because while their law, and property, and religion are preserved, it is of no great consequence to them by whom they are governed, and therefore they are under no temptation to desire a change.

3dly, In order to prevent any charge from the malice of false witnesses, be sure to avoid intemperance. If it be often so hard for men to govern their tongues when they are in their right senses, how can they hope to do it when they are heated with drink? In those cases most men regard not what they say, and too many not what they swear; neither will a man's memory, disordered with drunkenness, serve to defend himself, or satisfy him whether he were guilty or no.

4thly, Avoid, as much as possible, the conversation of those people, who are given to talk of public persons and affairs, especially of those whose opinions in such matters are different from yours. I never once knew any disputes of this kind managed with tolerable temper; but on both sides they only agree as much as possible to provoke the passions of each other, indeed with this disadvantage, that

---

[1] 1 Peter, ii. 13.

he who argueth on the side of power may speak securely the utmost his malice can invent; while the other lieth every moment at the mercy of an informer; and the law, in these cases, will give no allowance at all for passion, inadvertency, or the highest provocation.

I come now in the last place to shew you how far it is your duty as good subjects and good neighbours to bear faithful witness, when you are lawfully called to it by those in authority, or by the sincere advice of your own consciences.

In what I have hitherto said, you easily find, that I do not talk of bearing witness in general, which is and may be lawful upon a thousand accounts in relation to property and other matters, and wherein there are many scandalous corruptions, almost peculiar to this country, which would require to be handled by themselves. But I have confined my discourse only to that branch of bearing false witness, whereby the public is injured in the safety or honour of the prince, or those in authority under him.

In order therefore to be a faithful witness, it is first necessary that a man doth not undertake it from the least prospect of any private advantage to himself. The smallest mixture of that leaven will sour the whole lump. Interest will infallibly bias his judgment, although he be ever so firmly resolved to say nothing but truth. He cannot serve God and Mammon; but as interest is his chief end, he will use the most effectual means to advance it. He will aggravate circumstances to make his testimony valuable; he will be sorry if the person he accuseth should be able to clear himself; in short, he is labouring a point which he thinks necessary to his own good; and it would be a disappointment to him, that his neighbour should prove innocent.

5thly, Every good subject is obliged to bear witness against his neighbour, for any action or words, the telling of which would be of advantage to the public, and the concealment dangerous, or of ill example. Of this nature are all plots and conspiracies against the peace of a nation, all disgraceful words against a prince, such as clearly discover a disloyal and rebellious heart: But where our prince and country can possibly receive no damage or disgrace; where no scandal or ill example is given; and our neighbour, it may be, provoked by us, happeneth privately to drop a rash or indiscreet word, which in strictness of law might bring him under trouble, perhaps to his utter undoing; there we are obliged, we ought, to proceed no further than warning and reproof.

In describing to you the several kinds of false witnesses, I have made it less necessary to dwell much longer upon this head; because a faithful witness like everything else is known by his contrary: Therefore it would be only a repetition of what I have already said to tell you, that the strictest truth is required in a witness; that he should be wholly free from malice against the person he accuses; that he should not aggravate the smallest circumstance against the criminal, nor conceal the smallest in his favour; and to crown all, though I have hinted it before, that the only cause or motive of his undertaking an office, so subject to censure, and so difficult to perform, should be the safety and service of his prince and country.

Under these conditions and limitations (but not otherwise,) there is no manner of doubt but a good man may lawfully and justly become a witness in behalf of the public, and may perform that office (in its own nature not very desirable) with honour and integrity. For the command in the text is positive as well as negative; that is to say, as we are directed not to bear false witness against our neighbour, so we are to bear true. Next to the word of God, and the advice of teachers, every man's conscience, strictly examined, will be his best director in this weighty point; and to that I shall leave him.

It might perhaps be thought proper to have added something by way of advice to those who are unhappily engaged in this abominable trade and sin of bearing false witness; but I am far from believing or supposing any of that destructive tribe are now my hearers. I look upon them as a sort of people that seldom frequent these holy places, where they can hardly pick up any materials to serve their turn, unless they think it worth their while to misrepresent or pervert the words of the preacher: And whoever is that way disposed, I doubt, cannot be in a very good condition to edify and reform himself by what he heareth. God in his mercy preserve us from all the guilt of this grievous sin forbidden in my text, and from the snares of those who are guilty of it !

I shall conclude with one or two precepts given by Moses, from God, to the children of Israel, in the xxiiid of Exod. 1, 2.

"Thou shalt not raise a false report : Put not thine hand with the wicked, to be an unrighteous witness.

"Thou shalt not follow a multitude to do evil, neither shalt thou speak in a cause to decline after many, to wrest judgment."

Now to God the Father, &c.

THE WISDOM OF THIS WORLD.[1]

I COR. III. 19.

" The wisdom of this world is foolishness with God."

IT is remarkable that, about the time of our Saviour's coming into the world, all kinds of learning flourished to a very great degree, insomuch that nothing is more frequent in the mouths of many men, even such who pretend to read and to know, than an extravagant praise and opinion of the wisdom and virtue of the Gentile sages of those days, and likewise of those ancient philosophers who went before them, whose doctrines are left upon record either by themselves or other writers. As far as this may be taken for granted, it may be said, that the providence of God brought this about for several very wise ends and purposes : For, it is certain that these philosophers had been a long time before searching out where to fix the true happiness of man ; and, not being able to agree upon any certainty about it, they could not possibly but conclude, if they judged impartially, that all their enquiries were, in the end, but vain and fruitless ; the consequence of which must be not only an acknowledg-ment of the weakness of all human wisdom, but likewise an open passage hereby made, for the letting in those beams of light, which the glorious sunshine of the Gospel then brought into the world, by revealing those hidden truths, which they had so long before been labouring to discover, and fixing the general happiness of mankind beyond all controversy

---

[1] The title of this sermon as given in Contents of Swift's "Works," vol. viii., pt. i. (4to, 1765) is, "A Sermon upon the Excellence of Christianity in Opposition to Heathen Philosophy." [T. S.]

and dispute. And therefore the providence of God wisely suffered men of deep genius and learning then to arise, who should search into the truth of the Gospel now made known, and canvass its doctrines with all the subtilty and knowledge they were masters of, and in the end freely acknowledge that to be the true wisdom only "which cometh from above." (James, iii. 15, 16, 17.)

However, to make a further enquiry into the truth of this observation, I doubt not but there is reason to think that a great many of those encomiums given to ancient philosophers are taken upon trust, and by a sort of men who are not very likely to be at the pains of an enquiry that would employ so much time and thinking. For the usual ends why men affect this kind of discourse, appear generally to be either out of ostentation, that they may pass upon the world for persons of great knowledge and observation; or, what is worse, there are some who highly exalt the wisdom of those Gentile sages, thereby obliquely to glance at and traduce Divine Revelation, and more especially that of the Gospel; for the consequence they would have us draw is this: That, since those ancient philosophers rose to a greater pitch of wisdom and virtue than was ever known among Christians, and all this purely upon the strength of their own reason and liberty of thinking, therefore it must follow, that either all Revelation is false, or, what is worse, that it has depraved the nature of man, and left him worse than it found him.

But this high opinion of heathen wisdom is not very ancient in the world, nor at all countenanced from primitive times: Our Saviour had but a low esteem of it, as appears by His treatment of the Pharisees and Sadducees, who followed the doctrines of Plato and Epicurus. St Paul likewise, who was well versed in all the Grecian literature, seems very much to despise their philosophy, as we find in his writings, cautioning the Colossians to "beware lest any man spoil them through philosophy and vain deceit." And, in another place, he advises Timothy to "avoid profane and vain babblings, and oppositions of science, falsely so called;" that is, not to introduce into the Christian doctrine the janglings of those vain philosophers, which they would pass upon the world for science. And the reasons he gives are, first, That those who professed them did err concerning the faith:

Secondly, Because the knowledge of them did encrease ungodliness, vain babblings being otherways expounded vanities, or empty sounds; that is, tedious disputes about words, which the philosophers were always so full of, and which were the natural product of disputes and dissensions between several sects.

Neither had the primitive fathers any great or good opinion of the heathen philosophy, as it is manifest from several passages in their writings: So that this vein of affecting to raise the reputation of those sages so high, is a mode and a vice but of yesterday, assumed chiefly, as I have said, to disparage revealed knowledge, and the consequences of it among us.

Now, because this is a prejudice which may prevail with some persons, so far as to lessen the influence of the Gospel, and whereas therefore this is an opinion which men of education are like to be encountered with, when they have produced themselves into the world; I shall endeavour to shew that their preference of heathen wisdom and virtue, before that of the Christian, is every way unjust, and grounded upon ignorance or mistake: In order to which I shall consider four things.

First, I shall produce certain points, wherein the wisdom and virtue of all unrevealed philosophy in general, fell short, and was very imperfect.

Secondly, I shall shew, in several instances, where some of the most renowned philosophers have been grossly defective in their lessons of morality.

Thirdly, I shall prove the perfection of Christian wisdom, from the proper characters and marks of it.

Lastly, I shall shew that the great examples of wisdom and virtue among the heathen wise men, were produced by personal merit, and not influenced by the doctrine of any sect; whereas, in Christianity, it is quite the contrary.

First, I shall produce certain points, wherein the wisdom and virtue of all unrevealed philosophy in general fell short, and was very imperfect.

My design is to persuade men, that Christian philosophy is in all things preferable to heathen wisdom; from which,

or its professors, I shall however have no occasion to detract.
They were as wise and as good as it was possible for them
under such disadvantages, and would have probably been
infinitely more with such aids as we enjoy: But our lessons
are certainly much better, however our practices may fall
short.

The first point I shall mention is that universal defect
which was in all their schemes, that they could not agree
about their chief good, or wherein to place the happiness of
mankind, nor had any of them a tolerable answer upon this
difficulty, to satisfy a reasonable person.   For, to say, as the
most plausible of them did, that happiness consisted in
virtue, was but vain babbling, and a mere sound of words, to
amuse others and themselves; because they were not agreed
what this virtue was, or wherein it did consist; and likewise,
because several among the best of them taught quite different
things, placing happiness in health or good fortune, in riches
or in honour, where all were agreed that virtue was not, as I
shall have occasion to shew, when I speak of their particular
tenets.

The second great defect in the Gentile philosophy was,
that it wanted some suitable reward proportioned to the
better part of man, his mind, as an encouragement for his
progress in virtue.   The difficulties they met with upon the
score of this default were great, and not to be accounted
for: Bodily goods, being only suitable to bodily wants, are
no rest at all for the mind; and, if they were, yet are they
not the proper fruits of wisdom and virtue, being equally
attainable by the ignorant and wicked. Now, human nature
is so constituted, that we can never pursue anything heartily
but upon hopes of a reward.   If we run a race, it is in expectation of a prize, and the greater the prize the faster we
run; for an incorruptible crown, if we understand it and
believe it to be such, more than a corruptible one.   But
some of the philosophers gave all this quite another turn,
and pretended to refine so far, as to call virtue its own
reward, and worthy to be followed only for itself: Whereas,
if there be anything in this more than the sound of the words,
it is at least too abstracted to become a universal influencing
principle in the world, and therefore could not be of general
use.

It was the want of assigning some happiness, proportioned
to the soul of man, that caused many of them, either, on the
one hand, to be sour and morose, supercilious and untreat-
able; or, on the other, to fall into the vulgar pursuits of
common men, to hunt after greatness and riches, to make
their court, and to serve occasions; as Plato did to the
younger Dionysius, and Aristotle to Alexander the Great.
So impossible is it for a man, who looks no further than the
present world, to fix himself long in a contemplation where
the present world has no part: He has no sure hold, no firm
footing; he can never expect to remove the earth he rests
upon, while he has no support beside for his feet, but wants,
like Archimedes, some other place whereon to stand.   To
talk of bearing pain and grief, without any sort of present or
future hope, cannot be purely greatness of spirit; there must
be a mixture in it of affectation, and an alloy of pride, or
perhaps is wholly counterfeit.

It is true there has been all along in the world a notion of
rewards and punishments in another life; but it seems to
have rather served as an entertainment to poets, or as a
terror of children, than a settled principle, by which men
pretended to govern any of their actions.   The last celebrated
words of Socrates, a little before his death, do not seem to
reckon or build much upon any such opinion; and Cæsar
made no scruple to disown it, and ridicule it in open senate.

Thirdly, The greatest and wisest of all their philosophers
were never able to give any satisfaction, to others and themselves, in their notions of a Deity.   They were often extremely gross and absurd in their conceptions; and those
who made the fairest conjectures are such as were generally
allowed by the learned to have seen the system of Moses, if
I may so call it, who was in great reputation at that time in
the heathen world, as we find by Diodorus, Justin, Longinus,
and other authors; for the rest, the wisest among them
laid aside all notions after a Deity, as a disquisition vain and
fruitless, which indeed it was, upon unrevealed principles;
and those who ventured to engage too far fell into inco-
herence and confusion.

Fourthly, Those among them who had the justest conceptions of a Divine Power, and did also admit a Providence,
had no notion at all of entirely relying and depending upon

either; they trusted in themselves for all things: But, as for a trust or dependence upon God, they would not have understood the phrase; it made no part of the profane style.

Therefore it was, that, in all issues and events, which they could not reconcile to their own sentiments of reason and justice, they were quite disconcerted: They had no retreat; but, upon every blow of adverse fortune, either affected to be indifferent, or grew sullen and severe, or else yielded and sunk like other men.

Having now produced certain points, wherein the wisdom and virtue of all unrevealed philosophy fell short, and was very imperfect; I go on, in the second place, to shew in several instances, where some of the most renowned philosophers have been grossly defective in their lessons of morality.

Thales, the founder of the Ionic sect, so celebrated for morality, being asked how a man might bear ill-fortune with greatest ease, answered, "By seeing his enemies in a worse condition." An answer truly barbarous, unworthy of human nature, and which included such consequences as must destroy all society from the world.

Solon, lamenting the death of a son, one told him, "You lament in vain:" "Therefore" (said he) "I lament, because it is in vain." This was a plain confession how imperfect all his philosophy was, and that something was still wanting. He owned that all his wisdom and morals were useless, and this upon one of the most frequent accidents in life. How much better could he have learned to support himself even from David, by his entire dependence upon God; and that before our Saviour had advanced the notions of religion to the height and perfection wherewith He hath instructed His disciples? Plato himself, with all his refinements, placed happiness in wisdom, health, good fortune, honour, and riches; and held that they who enjoyed all these were perfectly happy: Which opinion was indeed unworthy its owner, leaving the wise and the good man wholly at the mercy of uncertain chance, and to be miserable without resource.

His scholar, Aristotle, fell more grossly into the same notion; and plainly affirmed, "That virtue, without the goods of fortune, was not sufficient for happiness, but that a wise man must be miserable in poverty and sickness." Nay, Diogenes himself, from whose pride and singularity one would have looked for other notions, delivered it as his opinion, "That a poor old man was the most miserable thing in life."

Zeno also and his followers fell into many absurdities, among which nothing could be greater than that of maintaining all crimes to be equal, which, instead of making vice hateful, rendered it as a thing indifferent and familiar to all men.

Lastly: Epicurus had no notion of justice but as it was profitable ; and his placing happiness in pleasure, with all the advantages he could expound it by, was liable to very great exception : For, although he taught that pleasure did consist in virtue, yet he did not any way fix or ascertain the boundaries of virtue, as he ought to have done ; by which means he misled his followers into the greatest vices, making their names to become odious and scandalous, even in the heathen world.

I have produced these few instances from a great many others, to shew the imperfection of heathen philosophy, wherein I have confined myself wholly to their morality. And surely we may pronounce upon it in the words of St James, that "This wisdom descended not from above, but was earthly and sensual." What if I had produced their absurd notions about God and the soul ? It would then have completed the character given it by that apostle, and appeared to have been devilish too. But it is easy to observe, from the nature of these few particulars, that their defects in morals were purely the flagging and fainting of the mind, for want of a support by revelation from God.

I proceed therefore, in the third place, to shew the perfection of Christian wisdom from above, and I shall endeavour to make it appear from those proper characters and marks of it by the apostle before mentioned, in the third chapter, and 15th, 16th, and 17th verses.

The words run thus :

" This wisdom descendeth not from above, but is earthly, sensual, devilish.

"For where envying and strife is, there is confusion, and every evil work.

" But the wisdom that is from above, is first pure, then peaceable, gentle, and easy to be intreated, full of mercy and good fruits, without partiality, and without hypocrisy."

"The wisdom from above is first pure." This purity of the mind and spirit is peculiar to the Gospel. Our Saviour says, "Blessed are the pure in heart, for they shall see God." A mind free from all pollution of lusts shall have a daily vision of God, whereof unrevealed religion can form no notion. This it is which keeps us unspotted from the world ; and hereby many have been prevailed upon to live in the practice of all purity, holiness, and righteousness, far beyond the examples of the most celebrated philosophers.

It is "peaceable, gentle, and easy to be intreated." The Christian doctrine teacheth us all those dispositions that make us affable and courteous, gentle and kind, without any morose leaven of pride or vanity, which entered into the composition of most heathen schemes : So we are taught to be meek and lowly. Our Saviour's last legacy was peace ; and He commands us to forgive our offending brother unto seventy times seven. Christian wisdom is full of mercy and good works, teaching the height of all moral virtues, of which the heathens fall infinitely short. Plato indeed (and it is worth observing) has somewhere a dialogue, or part of one, about forgiving our enemies, which was perhaps the highest strain ever reached by man, without divine assistance ; yet how little is that to what our Saviour commands us ? " To love them that hate us ; to bless them that curse us ; and do good to them that despitefully use us."

Christian wisdom is " without partiality ;" it is not calculated for this or that nation of people, but the whole race of mankind : Not so the philosophical schemes, which were narrow and confined, adapted to their peculiar towns, governments, or sects ; but, " in every nation, he that feareth God and worketh righteousness, is accepted with Him."

Lastly : It is " without hypocrisy : " It appears to be what it really is ; it is all of a piece. By the doctrines of the Gospel we are so far from being allowed to publish to the world those virtues we have not, that we are commanded to hide, even from ourselves, those we really have, and not to let our right hand know what our left hand does ; unlike several branches of the heathen wisdom, which pretended to teach insensibility and indifference, magnanimity and contempt of life, while, at the same time, in other parts it belied its own doctrines.

I come now, in the last place, to shew that the great examples of wisdom and virtue, among the Grecian sages, were produced by personal merit, and not influenced by the doctrine of any particular sect; whereas, in Christianity, it is quite the contrary.

The two virtues most celebrated by ancient moralists were Fortitude and Temperance, as relating to the government of man in his private capacity, to which their schemes were generally addressed and confined; and the two instances, wherein those virtues arrived at the greatest height, were Socrates and Cato.   But neither those, nor any other virtues possessed by these two, were at all owing to any lessons or doctrines of a sect.   For Socrates himself was of none at all ; and although Cato was called a Stoic, it was more from a resemblance of manners in his worst qualities, than that he avowed himself one of their disciples.   The same may be affirmed of many other great men of antiquity.   From whence I infer, that those who were renowned for virtue among them, were more obliged to the good natural dispositions of their own minds, than to the doctrines of any sect they pretended to follow.

On the other side, As the examples of fortitude and patience, among the primitive Christians, have been infinitely greater and more numerous, so they were altogether the product of their principles and doctrine; and were such as the same persons, without those aids, would never have arrived to.   Of this truth most of the apostles, with many thousand martyrs, are a cloud of witnesses beyond exception. Having therefore spoken so largely upon the former heads, I shall dwell no longer upon this.

And, if it should here be objected, Why does not Christianity still produce the same effects ? it is easy to answer, First, That although the number of pretended Christians be great, yet that of true believers, in proportion to the other, was never so small ; and it is a true lively faith alone, that by the assistance of God's grace, can influence our practice.

Secondly, we may answer, That Christianity itself has very much suffered by being blended up with Gentile philosophy. The Platonic system, first taken into religion, was thought to have given matter for some early heresies in the Church. When disputes began to arise, the Peripatetic forms were introduced by Scotus, as best fitted for controversy. And, however this may now have become necessary, it was surely the author of a litigious vein, which has since occasioned very pernicious consequences, stopped the progress of Christianity, and been a great promoter of vice, verifying that sentence given by St James, and mentioned before, "Where envying and strife is, there is confusion, and every evil work." This was the fatal stop to the Grecians, in their progress both of arts and arms: Their wise men were divided under several sects, and their governments under several commonwealths, all in opposition to each other; which engaged them in eternal quarrels among themselves, while they should have been armed against the common enemy. And I wish we had no other examples from the like causes, less foreign or ancient than that. Diogenes said Socrates was a madman; the disciples of Zeno and Epicurus, nay of Plato and Aristotle, were engaged in fierce disputes about the most insignificant trifles. And, if this be the present language and practice among us Christians, no wonder that Christianity does not still produce the same effects which it did at first, when it was received and embraced in its utmost purity and perfection. For such a wisdom as this cannot "descend from above," but must be "earthly, sensual, devilish; full of confusion and every evil work": Whereas "the wisdom from above, is first pure, then peaceable, gentle, and easy to be intreated, full of mercy and good fruits, without partiality, and without hypocrisy." This is the true heavenly wisdom, which Christianity only can boast of, and which the greatest of the heathen wise men could never arrive at.

Now to God the Father, &c. &c.

DOING GOOD:

A SERMON, ON THE OCCASION OF WOOD'S PROJECT.[1]

WRITTEN IN THE YEAR MDCCXXIV.

GALATIANS, VI. 10.

"As we have therefore opportunity, let us do good unto all men."

NATURE directs every one of us, and God permits us, to consult our own private good before the private good of any other person whatsoever. We are, indeed, commanded to love our neighbour as ourselves, but not as well as ourselves. The love we have for ourselves is to be the pattern of that love we ought to have towards our neighbour: But, as the copy doth not equal the original, so my

---

[1] "I did very lately, as I thought it my duty, preach to the people under my inspection, upon the subject of Mr. Wood's coin; and although I never heard that my sermon gave the least offence, as I am sure none was intended; yet, if it were now printed and published, I cannot say, I would insure it from the hands of the common hangman; or my own person from those of a messenger." See "The Drapier's Letters," No. VI.

" 'I never' (said the Dean in a jocular conversation), 'preached but twice in my life; and then they were not sermons, but pamphlets.' Being asked on what subject, he replied, 'They were against Wood's halfpence.' "—Pilkington's *Memoirs*, vol. i. p. 56.

"The pieces relating to Ireland are those of a public nature; in which the Dean appears, as usual, in the best light, because they do honour to his heart as well as to his head; furnishing some additional proofs, that, though he was very free in his abuse of the inhabitants of that country, as well natives as foreigners, he had their interest sincerely at heart, and perfectly understood it. His sermon upon Doing Good, though peculiarly adapted to Ireland and Wood's designs upon it, contains perhaps the best motives to patriotism that were ever delivered within so small a compass."—BURKE.

neighbour cannot think it hard, if I prefer myself, who am
the original, before him, who is only the copy.   Thus, if
any matter equally concern the life, the reputation, the
profit of my neighbour, and my own ; the law of nature,
which is the law of God, obligeth me to take care of myself
first, and afterwards of him.   And this I need not be at
much pains in persuading you to ; for the want of self-love,
with regard to things of this world, is not among the faults
of mankind.   But then, on the other side, if, by a small
hurt and loss to myself, I can procure a great good to my
neighbour, in that case his interest is to be preferred.   For
example, if I can be sure of saving his life, without great
danger to my own ; if I can preserve him from being undone, without ruining myself, or recover his reputation
without blasting mine ; all this I am obliged to do : and, if
I sincerely perform it, I do then obey the command of God,
in loving my neighbour as myself.

But, beside this love we owe to every man in his particular capacity under the title of our neighbour, there is yet
a duty of a more large extensive nature incumbent on us ;
which is, our love to our neighbour in his public capacity,
as he is a member of that great body the commonwealth,
under the same government with ourselves ; and this is
usually called love of the public, and is a duty to which we
are more strictly obliged than even that of loving ourselves ;
because therein ourselves are also contained, as well as all
our neighbours, in one great body.   This love of the public,
or of the commonwealth, or love of our country, was in
ancient times properly known by the name of virtue, because
it was the greatest of all virtues, and was supposed to con-
tain all virtues in it : And many great examples of this
virtue are left us on record, scarcely to be believed, or even
conceived, in such a base, corrupted, wicked age as this we
live in.   In those times it was common for men to sacrifice
their lives for the good of their country, although they had
neither hope or belief of future rewards ; whereas, in our
days, very few make the least scruple of sacrificing a whole
nation, as well as their own souls, for a little present gain ;
which often hath been known to end in their own ruin in
this world, as it certainly must in that to come.

Have we not seen men, for the sake of some petty employment, give up the very natural rights and liberties of their country, and of mankind, in the ruin of which themselves must at last be involved? Are not these corruptions gotten among the meanest of our people, who, for a piece of money, will give their votes at a venture, for the disposal of their own lives and fortunes, without considering whether it be to those who are most likely to betray or defend them? But, if I were to produce only one instance of a hundred wherein we fail in this duty of loving our country, it would be an endless labour; and therefore I shall not attempt it.

But here I would not be misunderstood: By the love of our country I do not mean loyalty to our king, for that is a duty of another nature; and a man may be very loyal, in the common sense of the word, without one grain of public good at his heart. Witness this very kingdom we live in. I verily believe, that, since the beginning of the world, no nation upon earth ever shewed (all circumstances considered) such high constant marks of loyalty in all their actions and behaviour, as we have done: And, at the same time, no people ever appeared more utterly void of what is called a public spirit. When I say the people, I mean the bulk or mass of the people, for I have nothing to do with those in power.

Therefore I shall think my time not ill spent, if I can persuade most or all of you who hear me, to shew the love you have for your country, by endeavouring, in your several stations, to do all the public good you are able. For I am certainly persuaded, that all our misfortunes arise from no other original cause than that general disregard among us to the public welfare.

I therefore undertake to shew you three things.

First: That there are few people so weak or mean, who have it not sometimes in their power to be useful to the public.
Secondly: That it is often in the power of the meanest among mankind to do mischief to the public.
And, *Lastly:* That all wilful injuries done to the public are very great and aggravated sins in the sight of God.

First: There are few people so weak or mean, who have it not sometimes in their power to be useful to the public.

Solomon tells us of a poor wise man who saved a city by his counsel. It hath often happened that a private soldier, by some unexpected brave attempt, hath been instrumental in obtaining a great victory. How many obscure men have been authors of very useful inventions, whereof the world now reaps the benefit? The very example of honesty and industry in a poor tradesman will sometimes spread through a neighbourhood, when others see how successful he is ; and thus so many useful members are gained, for which the whole body of the public is the better. Whoever is blessed with a true public spirit, God will certainly put it into his way to make use of that blessing, for the ends it was given him, by some means or other : And therefore it hath been observed in most ages, that the greatest actions, for the benefit of the commonwealth, have been performed by the wisdom or courage, the contrivance or industry, of particular men, and not of numbers ; and that the safety of a kingdom hath often been owing to those hands from whence it was least expected.

But, *Secondly :* It is often in the power of the meanest among mankind to do mischief to the public : And hence arise most of those miseries with which the states and kingdoms of the earth are infested. How many great princes have been murdered by the meanest ruffians ? The weakest hand can open a flood-gate to drown a country, which a thousand of the strongest cannot stop. Those who have thrown off all regard for public good, will often have it in their way to do public evil, and will not fail to exercise that power whenever they can. The greatest blow given of late to this kingdom, was by the dishonesty of a few manufacturers ; who, by imposing bad ware at foreign markets, in almost the only traffic permitted to us, did half ruin that trade ; by which this poor unhappy kingdom now suffers in the midst of sufferings. I speak not here of persons in high stations, who ought to be free from all reflection, and are supposed always to intend the welfare of the community : But we now find by experience, that the meanest instrument may, by the concurrence of accidents, have it in his power to bring a whole kingdom to the very brink of destruction, and is, at this present, endeavouring to finish his work ; and hath agents among ourselves, who are contented to see their own country undone, to be small sharers in that iniquitous gain, which at last must end in their own ruin as well as ours. I confess, it was chiefly the consideration of that great danger we are in, which engaged me to discourse to you on this subject; to exhort you to a love of your country, and a public spirit, when all you have is at stake; to prefer the interest of your prince and your fellow-subjects before that of one destructive impostor, and a few of his adherents.

Perhaps it may be thought by some, that this way of discoursing is not so proper from the pulpit. But surely, when an open attempt is made, and far carried on, to make a great kingdom one large poorhouse, to deprive us of all means to exercise hospitality or charity, to turn our cities and churches into ruins, to make the country a desert for wild beasts and robbers, to destroy all arts and sciences, all trades and manufactures, and the very tillage of the ground, only to enrich one obscure ill-designing projector, and his followers; it is time for the pastor to cry out that the wolf is getting into his flock, to warn them to stand together, and all to consult the common safety. And God be praised for His infinite goodness in raising such a spirit of union among us, at least in this point, in the midst of all our former divisions; which union, if it continue, will, in all probability, defeat the pernicious design of this pestilent enemy to the nation.

But, from hence, it clearly follows how necessary the love of our country, or a public spirit, is in every particular man, since the wicked have so many opportunities of doing public mischief. Every man is upon his guard for his private advantage; but, where the public is concerned, he is apt to be negligent, considering himself only as one among two or three millions, among whom the loss is equally shared, and thus, he thinks, he can be no great sufferer. Meanwhile the trader, the farmer, and the shopkeeper, complain of the hardness and deadness of the times, and wonder whence it comes; while it is, in a great measure, owing to their own folly, for want of that love of their country, and public spirit and firm union among themselves, which are so necessary to the prosperity of every nation.

Another method by which the meanest wicked man, may

have it in his power to injure the public, is false accusation, whereof this kingdom hath afforded too many examples: Neither is it long since no man, whose opinions were thought to differ from those in fashion, could safely converse beyond his nearest friends, for fear of being sworn against, as a traitor, by those who made a traffic of perjury and subornation; by which the very peace of the nation was disturbed, and men fled from each other as they would from a lion or a bear got loose. And, it is very remarkable, that the pernicious project now in hand to reduce us to beggary, was forwarded by one of these false accusers, who had been convicted of endeavouring, by perjury and subornation, to take away the lives of several innocent persons here among us; and, indeed, there could not be a more proper instrument for such a work.

Another method by which the meanest people may do injury to the public, is the spreading of lies and false rumours, thus raising a distrust among the people of a nation, causing them to mistake their true interest, and their enemies for their friends: And this hath been likewise too successful a practice among us, where we have known the whole kingdom misled by the grossest lies, raised upon occasion to serve some particular turn. As it hath also happened in the case I lately mentioned, where one obscure man, by representing our wants where they were least, and concealing them where they were greatest, had almost succeeded in a project of utterly ruining this whole kingdom; and may still succeed, if God doth not continue that public spirit, which He hath almost miraculously kindled in us upon this occasion.

Thus we see the public is many times, as it were, at the mercy of the meanest instrument, who can be wicked enough to watch opportunities of doing it mischief, upon the principles of avarice or malice; which, I am afraid, are deeply rooted in too many breasts, and against which there can be no defence, but a firm resolution in all honest men, to be closely united and active in shewing their love to their country, by preferring the public interest to their present private advantage. If a passenger, in a great storm at sea, should hide his goods that they might not be thrown overboard to lighten the ship, what would be the consequence? The ship is cast away, and he loses his life and goods together.

We have heard of men, who, through greediness of gain, have brought infected goods into a nation, which bred a plague, whereof the owners and their families perished first. Let those among us consider this and tremble, whose houses are privately stored with those materials of beggary and desolation, lately brought over to be scattered like a pestilence among their countrymen, which may probably first seize upon themselves and their families, until their houses shall be made a dunghill.

I shall mention one practice more, by which the meanest instruments often succeed in doing public mischief; and this is by deceiving us with plausible arguments, to make us believe that the most ruinous project they can offer is intended for our good, as it happened in the case so often mentioned. For the poor ignorant people, allured by the appearing convenience in their small dealings, did not discover the serpent in the brass,[1] but were ready, like the Israelites, to offer incense to it; neither could the wisdom of the nation convince them, until some, of good intentions, made the cheat so plain to their sight, that those who run may read. And thus the design was to treat us, in every point, as the Philistines treated Samson, (I mean when he was betrayed by Delilah) first to put out our eyes, and then bind us with fetters of brass.

I proceed to the last thing I proposed, which was to shew you that all wilful injuries done to the public, are very great and aggravated sins in the sight of God.

First : It is apparent from Scripture, and most agreeable to reason, that the safety and welfare of nations are under the most peculiar care of God's providence. Thus He promised Abraham to save Sodom, if only ten righteous men could be found in it. Thus the reason which God gave to Jonas for not destroying Nineveh was, because there were six score thousand men in that city.

All government is from God, Who is the God of order, and therefore whoever attempts to breed confusion or disturbance among a people, doth his utmost to take the

---

[1] " Brass " may be read " Wood's halfpence." [T. S.]

government of the world out of God's hands, and to put it into the hands of the Devil, who is the author of confusion. By which it is plain, that no crime, how heinous soever, committed against particular persons, can equal the guilt of him who does injury to the public.

Secondly : All offenders against their country lie under this grievous difficulty, that it is next to impossible to obtain a pardon, or make restitution. The bulk of mankind are very quick at resenting injuries, and very slow in forgiving them : And how shall one man be able to obtain the pardon of millions, or repair the injuries he hath done to millions? How shall those, who, by a most destructive fraud, got the whole wealth of our neighbouring kingdom into their hands, be ever able to make a recompence? How will the authors and promoters of that villainous project, for the ruin of this poor country, be able to account with us for the injuries they have already done, although they should no farther succeed? The deplorable case of such wretches, must entirely be left to the unfathomable mercies of God : For those who know the least in religion are not ignorant that, without our utmost endeavours to make restitution to the person injured, and to obtain his pardon, added to a sincere repentance, there is no hope of salvation given in the Gospel.

Lastly : All offences against our own country have this aggravation, that they are ungrateful and unnatural. It is to our country we owe those laws which protect us in our lives, our liberties, our properties, and our religion. Our country produced us into the world, and continues to nourish us so, that it is usually called our mother ; and there have been examples of great magistrates, who have put their own children to death for endeavouring to betray their country, as if they had attempted the life of their natural parent.

Thus I have briefly shewn you how terrible a sin it is to be an enemy to our country, in order to incite you to the contrary virtue, which at this juncture is so highly necessary, when every man's endeavour will be of use. We have hitherto been just able to support ourselves under many hardships ; but now the axe is laid to the root of the tree, and nothing but a firm union among us can prevent our utter undoing. This we are obliged to, in duty to our gracious King, as well as to ourselves. Let us therefore preserve that public spirit, which God hath raised in us for our own temporal interest. For, if this wicked project should succeed, which it cannot do but by our own folly; if we sell ourselves for nought; the merchant, the shopkeeper, the artificer, must fly to the desert with their miserable families, there to starve or live upon rapine, or at least exchange their country for one more hospitable than that where they were born.

Thus much I thought it my duty to say to you, who are under my care, to warn you against those temporal evils, which may draw the worst of spiritual evils after them; such as heart-burnings, murmurings, discontents, and all manner of wickedness which a desperate condition of life may tempt men to.

I am sensible that what I have now said will not go very far, being confined to this assembly; but I hope it may stir up others of my brethren to exhort their several congregations, after a more effectual manner, to shew their love for their country on this important occasion. And this, I am sure, cannot be called meddling in affairs of state.

I pray God protect his Most Gracious Majesty, and this kingdom, long under his government, and defend us from all ruinous projectors, deceivers, suborners, perjurers, false accusers, and oppressors; from the virulence of party and faction; and unite us in loyalty to our King, love to our country, and charity to each other.

And this we beg for Jesus Christ His sake : To Whom, &c.

THE MARTYRDOM OF KING CHARLES I.

PREACHED AT ST PATRICK'S, DUBLIN, JAN. 30, 1725-26,
BEING SUNDAY.

GENESIS, XLIX. 5, 6, 7.

" Simeon and Levi are brethren; instruments of cruelty are in their habitations.

"O my soul, come not thou into their secret; unto their assembly, mine honour, be not thou united: for in their anger they slew a man, and in their self-will they digged down a wall.

"Cursed be their anger, for it was fierce; and their wrath, for it was cruel. I will divide them in Jacob, and scatter them in Israel."

I KNOW very well, that the Church hath been often censured for keeping holy this day of humiliation, in memory of that excellent king and blessed martyr, Charles I., who rather chose to die on a scaffold, than betray the religion and liberties of his people, wherewith God and the laws had entrusted him. But, at the same time, it is manifest that those who make such censures are either people without any religion at all, or who derive their principles, and perhaps their birth, from the abettors of those who contrived the murder of that prince, and have not yet shewn the world that their opinions are changed. It is alleged, that the observation of this day hath served to continue and increase the animosity and enmity among our countrymen, and to disunite Protestants; that a law was made, upon the restoration of the Martyr's son, for a general pardon and oblivion, forbidding all reproaches upon that occasion; and, since none are now alive who were actors or instruments in that tragedy, it is thought hard and uncharitable to keep up the memory of it for all generations.

Now, because I conceive most of you to be ignorant in many particulars concerning that horrid murder, and the rebellion which preceded it ; I will,

First, relate to you so much of the story as may be sufficient for your information :

Secondly, I will tell you the consequences which this bloody deed had upon these kingdoms :

And, *Lastly*, I will shew you to what good uses this solemn day of humiliation may be applied.

As to the first : In the reign of this prince, Charles the Martyr, the power and prerogative of the king were much greater than they are in our times, and so had been for at least seven hundred years before ; And the best princes we ever had, carried their power much farther than the blessed Martyr offered to do in the most blameable part of his reign.   But, the lands of the Crown having been prodigally bestowed to favourites, in the preceding reigns, the succeeding kings could not support themselves without taxes raised by Parliament ; which put them under a necessity of frequently calling those assemblies : And, the crown lands being gotten into the hands of the nobility and gentry, beside the possessions of which the Church had been robbed by King Henry the Eighth, power, which always follows property, grew to lean to the side of the people, by whom even the just rights of the Crown were often disputed.

But further : Upon the cruel persecution raised against the Protestants, under Queen Mary, among great numbers who fled the kingdom to seek for shelter, several went and resided at Geneva, which is a commonwealth, governed without a king, and where the religion, contrived by Calvin, is without the order of bishops.   When the Protestant faith was restored by Queen Elizabeth, those who fled to Geneva returned among the rest home to England, and were grown so fond of the government and religion of the place they had left, that they used all possible endeavours to introduce both into their own country ; at the same time continually preaching and railing against ceremonies and distinct habits of the clergy, taxing whatever they disliked, as a remnant of Popery, and continued extremely troublesome to the Church and state, under that great Queen, as well as her successor King James I. These people called themselves Puritans, as pretending to a purer faith than those of the Church established. And these were the founders of our Dissenters. They did not think it sufficient to leave all the errors of Popery, but threw off many laudable and edifying institutions of the primitive Church, and, at last, even the government of bishops; which, having been ordained by the apostles themselves, had continued without interruption, in all Christian churches, for above fifteen hundred years. And all this they did, not because those things were evil, but because they were kept by the Papists. From thence they proceeded, by degrees, to quarrel with the kingly government; because, as I have already said, the city of Geneva, to which their fathers had flown for refuge, was a commonwealth, or government of the people.

These Puritans, about the middle of the Martyr's reign, were grown to a considerable faction in the kingdom, and in the Lower House of Parliament. They filled the public with the most false and bitter libels against the bishops and the clergy, accusing chiefly the very best among them of Popery; and, at the same time, the House of Commons grew so insolent and uneasy to the King, that they refused to furnish him with necessary supplies for the support of his family, unless upon such conditions as he could not submit to without forfeiting his conscience and honour, and even his coronation oath. And, in such an extremity, he was forced upon a practice, no way justifiable, of raising money; for which, however, he had the opinion of the judges on his side; for, wicked judges there were in those times as well as in ours. There were likewise many complaints, and sometimes justly, made against the proceedings of a certain court, called the Star-chamber, a judicature of great antiquity, but had suffered some corruptions, for which, however, the King was nowise answerable. I cannot recollect any more subjects of complaint with the least ground of reason, nor is it needful to recollect them, because this gracious King did, upon the first application, redress all grievances by an act of Parliament, and put it out of his power to do any hardships for the future. But that wicked faction in the House of Commons, not content with all those marks of his justice and condescension, urged still for more; and joining with a factious party from Scotland, who had the same fancies in religion, forced him to pass an act for cutting off the head of his best and chief minister; and, at the same time, compelled him, by tumults and threatenings of a packed rabble, poisoned with the same doctrines, to pass another law, by which it should not be in his power to dissolve that Parliament without their own consent. Thus, by the greatest weakness and infatuation that ever possessed any man's spirit, this Prince did in effect sign his own destruction. For the House of Commons, having the reins in their own hands, drove on furiously; sent him every day some unreasonable demand, and when he refused to grant it, made use of their own power, and declared that an ordinance of both Houses, without the King's consent, should be obeyed as a law, contrary to all reason and equity, as well as to the fundamental constitution of the kingdom.

About this time the rebellion in Ireland broke out, wherein his Parliament refused to assist him; nor would accept his offer to come hither in person to subdue those rebels. These, and a thousand other barbarities, forced the King to summon his loyal subjects to his standard in his own defence. Meanwhile the English Parliament, instead of helping the poor Protestants here, seized on the very army that his Majesty was sending over for our relief, and turned them against their own Sovereign. The rebellion in England continued for four or five years: At last the King was forced to fly in disguise to the Scots, who sold him to the rebels. And these Puritans had the impudent cruelty to try his sacred person in a mock court of justice, and cut off his head; which he might have saved, if he would have yielded to betray the constitution in Church and state.

In this whole proceeding, Simeon and Levi were brethren; the wicked insinuations of those fanatical preachers stirring up the cruelty of the soldiers, who, by force of arms, excluded from the house every member of Parliament, whom they apprehended to bear the least inclination towards an agreement with the King, suffering only those to enter who thirsted chiefly for his blood; and this is the very account given by their own writers : From whence it is clear that this Prince was, in all respects, a real martyr for the true religion and the liberty of the people.   That odious Parliament had first turned the bishops out of the House of Lords; in a few years after, they murdered their King; then immediately abolished the whole House of Lords; and so, at last, obtained their wishes, of having a government of the people, and a new religion, both after the manner of Geneva, without a king, a bishop, or a nobleman; and this they blasphemously called "The kingdom of Christ and his saints."

This is enough for your information on the first head : I shall therefore proceed to the second, wherein I will shew you the miserable consequences which that abominable rebellion and murder produced in these nations.

First: The Irish rebellion was wholly owing to that wicked English Parliament. For the leaders in the Irish Popish massacre would never have dared to stir a finger, if they had not been encouraged by that rebellious spirit in the English House of Commons, which they very well knew must disable the King from sending any supplies to his Protestant subjects here; and, therefore, we may truly say that the English Parliament held the King's hands, while the Irish Papists here were cutting our grandfathers' throats.

Secondly: That murderous Puritan Parliament, when they had all in their own power, could not agree upon any one method of settling a form either of religion or civil government; but changed every day from schism to schism, from heresy to heresy, and from one faction to another: From whence arose that wild confusion, still continuing in our several ways of serving God, and those absurd notions of civil power, which have so often torn us with factions more than any other nation in Europe.

Thirdly: To this rebellion and murder have been owing the rise and progress of atheism among us. For, men observing what numberless villainies of all kinds were committed during twenty years, under pretence of zeal and the reformation of God's Church, were easily tempted to doubt that all religion was a mere imposture : And the same spirit of infidelity, so far spread among us at this present, is nothing but the fruit of the seeds sown by those rebellious hypocritical saints.

Fourthly : The old virtue and loyalty, and generous spirit of the English nation, were wholly corrupted by the power, the doctrine, and the example of those wicked people. Many of the ancient nobility were killed, and their families extinct, in defence of their Prince and country, or murdered by the merciless courts of justice. Some of the worst among them favoured, or complied with the reigning iniquities, and not a few of the new set created, when the Martyr's son was restored, were such who had drunk too deep of the bad principles then prevailing.

Fifthly : The children of the murdered Prince were forced to fly, for the safety of their lives, to foreign countries ; where one of them at least, I mean King James II., was seduced to Popery ; which ended in the loss of his kingdoms, the misery and desolation of this country, and a long and expensive war abroad. Our deliverance was owing to the valour and conduct of the late King ; and, therefore, we ought to remember him with gratitude, but not mingled with blasphemy or idolatry. It was happy that his interests and ours were the same : And God gave him greater success than our sins deserved. But, as a house thrown down by a storm, is seldom rebuilt without some change in the foundation ; so it hath happened, that, since the late Revolution, men have sat much looser in the true fundamentals both of religion and government, and factions have been more violent, treacherous, and malicious than ever, men running naturally from one extreme into another ; and, for private ends, taking up those very opinions professed by the leaders in that rebellion, which carried the blessed Martyr to the scaffold.

Sixthly : Another consequence of this horrid rebellion and murder was the destroying or defacing of such vast number of God's houses. " In their self-will they digged down a wall." If a stranger should now travel in England, and observe the churches in his way, he could not otherwise conclude, than that some vast army of Turks or heathens had been sent on purpose to ruin and blot out all marks of

Christianity. They spared neither the statues of saints, nor ancient prelates, nor kings, nor benefactors ; broke down the tombs and monuments of men famous in their generations, seized the vessels of silver set apart for the holiest use, tore down the most innocent ornaments both within and without, made the houses of prayer dens of thieves, or stables for cattle. These were the mildest effects of Puritan zeal, and devotion for Christ ; and this was what themselves affected to call a thorough reformation. In this kingdom those ravages were not so easily seen ; for the people here being too poor to raise such noble temples, the mean ones we had were not defaced, but totally destroyed.

Upon the whole, it is certain, that although God might have found out many other ways to have punished a sinful people, without permitting this rebellion and murder, yet as the course of the world hath run ever since, we need seek for no other causes, of all the public evils we have hitherto suffered, or may suffer for the future, by the misconduct of princes, or wickedness of the people.

I go on now upon the third head, to shew you to what good uses this solemn day of humiliation may be applied.

First : It may be an instruction to princes themselves, to be careful in the choice of those who are their advisers in matters of law. All the judges of England, except one or two, advised the King, that he might legally raise money upon the subjects for building of ships without consent of Parliament ; which, as it was the greatest oversight of his reign, so it proved the principal foundation of all his misfortunes. Princes may likewise learn from hence, not to sacrifice a faithful servant to the rage of a faction, nor to trust any body of men with a greater share of power than the laws of the land have appointed them, much less to deposit it in their hands until they shall please to restore it.

Secondly : By bringing to mind the tragedy of this day, and the consequences that have arisen from it, we shall be convinced how necessary it is for those in power to curb, in season, all such unruly spirits as desire to introduce new doctrines and discipline in the Church, or new forms of government in the state. Those wicked Puritans began, in Queen Elizabeth's time, to quarrel only with surplices and other habits, with the ring in matrimony, the cross in baptism, and the like; thence they went on to further matters of higher importance, and, at last, they must needs have the whole government of the Church dissolved. This great work they compassed, first, by depriving the bishops of their seats in Parliament, then they abolished the whole order; and, at last, which was their original design, they seized on all the Church-lands, and divided the spoil among themselves; and, like Jeroboam, made priests of the very dregs of the people. This was their way of reforming the Church. As to the civil government, you have already heard how they modelled it upon the murder of their King, and discarding the nobility. Yet, clearly to shew what a Babel they had built, after twelve years' trial and twenty several sorts of government; the nation grown weary of their tyranny, was forced to call in the son of him whom those reformers had sacrificed. And thus were Simeon and Levi divided in Jacob and scattered in Israel.

Thirdly: Although the successors of these Puritans, I mean our present Dissenters, do not think fit to observe this day of humiliation; yet, since it would be very proper in them, upon some occasions, to renounce in a public manner those principles upon which their predecessors acted; and it will be more prudent in them to do so, because those very Puritans, of whom ours are followers, found by experience, that after they had overturned the Church and state, murdered their King, and were projecting what they called a kingdom of the saints, they were cheated of the power and possessions they only panted after, by an upstart sect of religion that grew out of their own bowels, who subjected them to one tyrant, while they were endeavouring to set up a thousand.

Fourthly: Those who profess to be followers of our Church established, and yet presume in discourse to justify or excuse that rebellion, and murder of the King, ought to consider, how utterly contrary all such opinions are to the doctrine of Christ and his apostles, as well as to the articles of our Church, and to the preaching and practice of its true professors for above a hundred years. Of late times, indeed, and I speak it with grief of heart, we have heard even sermons of a strange nature; although reason would make one think it a very unaccountable way of procuring favour under a monarchy, by palliating and lessening the guilt of those who murdered the best of kings in cold blood, and, for a time, destroyed the very monarchy itself. Pray God, we may never more hear such doctrine from the pulpit, nor have it scattered about in print, to poison the people!

Fifthly : Some general knowledge of this horrid rebellion and murder, with the consequences they had upon these nations, may be a warning to our people not to believe a lie, and to mistrust those deluding spirits, who, under pretence of a purer and more reformed religion, would lead them from their duty to God and the laws. Politicians may say what they please, but it is no hard thing at all for the meanest person, who hath common understanding, to know whether he be well or ill governed. If he be freely allowed to follow his trade and calling ; if he be secure in his property, and hath the benefit of the law to defend himself against injustice and oppression ; if his religion be different from that of his country, and the government think fit to tolerate it, (which he may be very secure of, let it be what it will ;) he ought to be fully satisfied, and give no offence, by writing or discourse, to the worship established, as the dissenting preachers are too apt to do. But, if he hath any new visions of his own, it is his duty to be quiet, and possess them in silence, without disturbing the community by a furious zeal for making proselytes. This was the folly and madness of those ancient puritan fanatics: They must needs overturn heaven and earth, violate all the laws of God and man, make their country a field of blood, to propagate whatever wild or wicked opinions came into their heads, declaring all their absurdities and blasphemies to proceed from the Holy Ghost.

To conclude this head. In answer to that objection of keeping up animosity and hatred between Protestants, by the observation of this day ; if there be any sect or sort of people among us, who profess the same principles in religion and government which those puritan rebels put in practice, I think it is the interest of all those who love the Church and King, to keep up as strong a party against them as possible, until they shall, in a body, renounce all those wicked opinions upon which their predecessors acted, to the disgrace of Christianity, and the perpetual infamy of the English nation.

When we accuse the Papists of the horrid doctrine, "that

no faith ought to be kept with heretics," they deny it to a man ; and yet we justly think it dangerous to trust them, because we know their actions have been sometimes suitable to that opinion. But the followers of those who beheaded the Martyr have not yet renounced their principles; and, till they do, they may be justly suspected. Neither will the bare name of Protestants set them right. For surely Christ requires more from us than a profession of hating Popery, which a Turk or an atheist may do as well as a Protestant.

If an enslaved people should recover their liberty from a tyrannical power of any sort, who could blame them for commemorating their deliverance by a day of joy and thanksgiving? And doth not the destruction of a Church, a King, and three kingdoms, by the artifices, hypocrisy, and cruelty of a wicked race of soldiers and preachers, and other sons of Belial, equally require a solemn time of humiliation? Especially since the consequences of that bloody scene still continue, as I have already shewn, in their effects upon us.

Thus I have done with the three heads I proposed to discourse on. But before I conclude, I must give a caution to those who hear me, that they may not think I am pleading for absolute unlimited power in any one man. It is true, all power is from God, and, as the apostle says, "the powers that be are ordained of God ; " but this is in the same sense that all we have is from God, our food and raiment, and whatever possessions we hold by lawful means. Nothing can be meant in those, or any other words of Scripture, to justify tyrannical power, or the savage cruelties of those heathen emperors who lived in the time of the apostles. And so St Paul concludes, "The powers that be are ordained of God:" For what? Why, "for the punishment of evil doers, and the praise, the reward, of them that do well." There is no more inward value in the greatest emperor, than in the meanest of his subjects: His body is composed of the same substance, the same parts, and with the same or greater, infirmities: His education is generally worse, by flattery, and idleness, and luxury, and those evil dispositions that early power is apt to give. It is therefore against common sense, that his private personal interest, or pleasure, should be put in the balance with the safety of millions, every one of which is his equal by nature, equal in the sight of God, equally capable of salvation; and it is for their sakes, not his own, that he is entrusted with the government over them. He hath as high trust as can safely be reposed in one man, and, if he discharge it as he ought, he deserves all the honour and duty that a mortal may be allowed to receive. His personal failings we have nothing to do with, and errors in government are to be imputed to his ministers in the state. To what height those errors may be suffered to proceed, is not the business of this day, or this place, or of my function, to determine. When oppressions grow too great and universal to be borne, nature or necessity may find a remedy. But, if a private person reasonably expects pardon, upon his amendment, for all faults that are not capital, it would be a hard condition indeed, not to give the same allowance to a prince, who must see with other men's eyes, and hear with other men's ears, which are often wilfully blind and deaf. Such was the condition of the Martyr, and is so, in some degree, of all other princes. Yet this we may justly say in defence of the common people, in all civilized nations, that it must be a very bad government indeed, where the body of the subjects will not rather choose to live in peace and obedience, than take up arms on pretence of faults in the administration, unless where the vulgar are deluded by false preachers to grow fond of new visions and fancies in religion; which, managed by dexterous men, for sinister ends of malice, envy, or ambition, have often made whole nations run mad. This was exactly the case in the whole progress of that great rebellion, and the murder of King Charles I. But the late Revolution under the Prince of Orange was occasioned by a proceeding directly contrary, the oppression and injustice there beginning from the throne: For that unhappy prince, King James II., did not only invade our laws and liberties, but would have forced a false religion upon his subjects, for which he was deservedly rejected, since there could be no other remedy found, or at least agreed on. But, under the blessed Martyr, the deluded people would have forced many false religions, not only on their fellow-subjects, but even upon their sovereign himself, and at the same time invaded all his undoubted rights; and, because he would not comply, raised a horrid rebellion, wherein, by the permission of God, they prevailed, and put their sovereign to death, like a common criminal, in the face of the world.

Therefore, those who seem to think they cannot otherwise justify the late Revolution, and the change of the succession, than by lessening the guilt of the Puritans, do certainly put the greatest affront imaginable upon the present powers, by supposing any relation, or resemblance, between that rebellion and the late Revolution; and, consequently, that the present establishment is to be defended by the same arguments which those usurpers made use of, who, to obtain their tyranny, trampled under foot all the laws of both God and man.

One great design of my discourse was to give you warning against running into either extreme of two bad opinions, with relation to obedience. As kings are called gods upon earth, so some would allow them an equal power with God, over all laws and ordinances; and that the liberty, and property, and life, and religion of the subject, depended wholly upon the breath of the prince; which, however, I hope was never meant by those who pleaded for passive obedience. And this opinion hath not been confined to that party which was first charged with it, but hath sometimes gone over to the other, to serve many an evil turn of interest or ambition, who have been as ready to enlarge prerogative, where they could find their own account, as the highest maintainers of it.

On the other side, some look upon kings as answerable for every mistake or omission in government, and bound to comply with the most unreasonable demands of an unquiet faction; which was the case of those who persecuted the blessed Martyr of this day from his throne to the scaffold.

Between these two extremes, it is easy, from what hath been said, to choose a middle; to be good and loyal subjects, yet, according to your power, faithful assertors of your religion and liberties; to avoid all broachers and preachers of new-fangled doctrines in the Church; to be strict observers of the laws, which cannot be justly taken from you without your own consent: In short, "to obey God and the King, and meddle not with those who are given to change."

Which that you may all do, &c.

THE POOR MAN'S CONTENTMENT.

PHILIPPIANS, CHAP. IV. PART OF THE 11TH VERSE.

"I have learned, in whatsoever state I am, therewith to be content."

THE holy Scripture is full of expressions to set forth the miserable·condition of man during the whole progress of his life; his weakness, pride, and vanity; his unmeasurable desires, and perpetual disappointments; the prevalency of his passions, and the corruptions of his reason; his deluding hopes, and his real, as well as imaginary, fears; his natural and artificial wants; his cares and anxieties; the diseases of his body, and the diseases of his mind; the shortness of his life; his dread of a future state, with his carelessness to prepare for it : And the wise men of all ages have made the same reflections.

But all these are general calamities, from which none are excepted; and being without remedy, it is vain to bewail them. The great question, long debated in the world, is, whether the rich or the poor are the least miserable of the two? It is certain, that no rich man ever desired to be poor, and that most, if not all, poor men, desire to be rich; whence it may be argued, that, in all appearance, the advantage lieth on the side of wealth, because both parties agree in preferring it before poverty. But this reasoning will be found to be false: For, I lay it down as a certain truth, that God Almighty hath placed all men upon an equal foot, with respect to their happiness in this world, and the capacity of attaining their salvation in the next; or, at least, if there be any difference, it is not to the advantage of the rich and the mighty. Now, since a great part of those who usually make up our congregations, are not of considerable station, and many among them of the lower sort, and since the meaner people are generally and justly charged with the sin of repining and murmuring at their own condition, to which, however, their betters are sufficiently subject (although, perhaps, for shame, not always so loud in their complaints) I thought it might be useful to reason upon this point in as plain a manner as I can. I shall therefore shew, first, that the poor enjoy many temporal blessings, which are not common to the rich and the great: And, likewise, that the rich and the great are subject to many temporal evils, which are not common to the poor.

But here I would not be misunderstood; perhaps there is not a word more abused than that of the poor, or wherein the world is more generally mistaken. Among the number of those who beg in our streets, or are half-starved at home, or languish in prison for debt, there is hardly one in a hundred who doth not owe his misfortunes to his own laziness, or drunkenness, or worse vices.

To these he owes those very diseases which often disable him from getting his bread. Such wretches are deservedly unhappy: They can only blame themselves; and when we are commanded to have pity on the poor, these are not understood to be of the number.

It is true, indeed, that sometimes honest, endeavouring men are reduced to extreme want, even to the begging of alms, by losses, by accidents, by diseases, and old age, without any fault of their own: But these are very few in comparison of the other; nor would their support be any sensible burthen to the public, if the charity of well-disposed persons were not intercepted by those common strollers, who are most importunate, and who least deserve it. These, indeed, are properly and justly called the poor, whom it should be our study to find out and distinguish, by making them partake of our superfluity and abundance.

But neither have these anything to do with my present subject; For, by the poor, I only intend the honest, industrious artificer, the meaner sort of tradesmen, and the labouring man, who getteth his bread by the sweat of his brows, in town or country, and who make the bulk of mankind among us.

First: I shall therefore shew, first, that the poor (in the sense
I understand the word) do enjoy many temporal blessings,
which are not common to the rich and great; and likewise, that the rich and great are subject to many temporal
evils, which are not common to the poor.

Secondly: From the arguments offered to prove the foregoing
head, I shall draw some observations that may be useful
for your practice.

I. As to the first: Health, we know, is generally allowed
to be the best of all earthly possessions, because it is that,
without which we can have no satisfaction in any of the rest.
For riches are of no use, if sickness taketh from us the ability
of enjoying them, and power and greatness are then only a
burthen. Now, if we would look for health, it must be in
the humble habitation of the labouring man, or industrious
artificer, who earn their bread by the sweat of their brows,
and usually live to a good old age, with a great degree of
strength and vigour.

The refreshment of the body by sleep is another great
happiness of the meaner sort. Their rest is not disturbed
by the fear of thieves and robbers, nor is it interrupted by
surfeits of intemperance. Labour and plain food supply the
want of quieting draughts; and the wise man telleth us, that
the sleep of the labouring man is sweet. As to children,
which are certainly accounted of as a blessing, even to the
poor, where industry is not wanting; they are an assistance
to honest parents, instead of being a burthen; they are
healthy and strong, and fit for labour; neither is the father
in fear, lest his heir should be ruined by an unequal match:
Nor is he solicitous about his rising in the world, farther than
to be able to get his bread.

The poorer sort are not the objects of general hatred or
envy; they have no twinges of ambition, nor trouble themselves with party quarrels, or state divisions. The idle rabble,
who follow their ambitious leaders in such cases, do not fall
within my description of the poorer sort; for, it is plain, I
mean only the the honest industrious poor in town or country,
who are safest in times of public disturbance, in perilous
seasons, and public revolutions, if they will be quiet, and do
their business; for artificers and husbandmen are necessary

in all governments: But in such seasons, the rich are the public mark, because they are oftentimes of no use, but to be plundered; like some sort of birds, who are good for nothing, but their feathers; and so fall a prey to the strongest side.

Let us proceed, on the other side to examine the disadvantages which the rich and the great lie under, with respect to the happiness of the present life.

First, then; While health, as we have said, is the general portion of the lower sort, the gout, the dropsy, the stone, the cholic, and all other diseases, are continually haunting the palaces of the rich and the great, as the natural attendants upon laziness and luxury. Neither does the rich man eat his sumptuous fare with half the appetite and relish, that even the beggars do the crumbs which fall from his table: But, on the contrary, he is full of loathing and disgust, or at best of indifference, in the midst of plenty. Thus their intemperance shortens their lives, without pleasing their appetites.

Business, fear, guilt, design, anguish, and vexation are continually buzzing about the curtains of the rich and the powerful, and will hardly suffer them to close their eyes, unless when they are dosed with the fumes of strong liquors.

It is a great mistake to imagine that the rich want but few things; their wants are more numerous, more craving, and urgent, than those of poorer men : For these endeavour only at the necessaries of life, which make them happy, and they think no farther: But the desire of power and wealth is endless, and therefore impossible to be satisfied with any acquisitions.

If riches were so great a blessing as they are commonly thought, they would at least have this advantage, to give their owners cheerful hearts and countenances; they would often stir them up to express their thankfulness to God, and discover their satisfaction to the world. But, in fact, the contrary to all this is true. For where are there more cloudy brows, more melancholy hearts, or more ingratitude to their great Benefactor, than among those who abound in wealth? And, indeed, it is natural that it should be so, because those men, who covet things that are hard to be got, must be hard to please; whereas a small thing maketh a poor man happy, and great losses cannot befall him.

It is likewise worth considering, how few among the rich have procured their wealth by just measures; how many owe their fortunes to the sins of their parents, how many more to their own? If men's titles were to be tried before a true court of conscience, where false swearing, and a thousand vile artifices, (that are well known, and can hardly be avoided in human courts of justice) would avail nothing; how many would be ejected with infamy and disgrace? How many grow considerable by breach of trust, by bribery and corruption? How many have sold their religion, with the rights and liberties of themselves and others, for power and employments?

And, it is a mistake to think, that the most hardened sinner, who oweth his possessions or titles to any such wicked arts of thieving, can have true peace of mind, under the reproaches of a guilty conscience, and amid the cries of ruined widows and orphans.

I know not one real advantage that the rich have over the poor, except the power of doing good to others. But this is an advantage which God hath not given wicked men the grace to make use of. The wealth acquired by evil means was never employed to good ends; for that would be to divide the kingdom of Satan against itself. Whatever hath been gained by fraud, avarice, oppression, and the like, must be preserved and increased by the same methods.

I shall add but one thing more upon this head, which I hope will convince you, that God (whose thoughts are not as our thoughts) never intended riches or power to be necessary for the happiness of mankind in this life; because it is certain, that there is not one single good quality of the mind absolutely necessary to obtain them, where men are resolved to be rich at any rate; neither honour, justice, temperance, wisdom, religion, truth, or learning; for a slight acquaintance of the world will inform us, that there have been many instances of men, in all ages, who have arrived at great possessions and great dignities, by cunning, fraud, or flattery, without any of these, or any other virtues that can be named. Now, if riches and greatness were such blessings, that good men without them could not have their share of happiness in this life; how cometh it to pass, that God should suffer them to be often dealt to the worst, and most profligate of mankind; that they should be generally procured by the most abominable means, and applied to the basest and most wicked uses? This ought not to be conceived of a just, a merciful, a wise, and Almighty Being. We must therefore conclude, that wealth and power are in their own nature, at best, but things indifferent, and that a good man may be equally happy without them, provided that he hath a sufficiency of the common blessings of human life to answer all the reasonable and virtuous demands of nature, which his industry will provide, and sobriety will prevent his wanting. Agur's prayer, with the reasons of his wish, are full to this purpose: "Give me neither poverty nor riches. Feed me with food convenient for me; lest I be full and deny thee, and say, 'Who is the Lord?' Or, lest I be poor, and steal, and take the name of my God in vain."

From what hath been said, I shall, in the second place, offer some considerations, that may be useful for your practice.

And here I shall apply myself chiefly to those of the lower sort, for whose comfort and satisfaction this discourse is principally intended. For, having observed the great sin of those, who do not abound in wealth, to be that of murmuring and repining, that God hath dealt his blessings unequally to the sons of men, I thought it would be of great use to remove out of your minds so false and wicked an opinion, by shewing that your condition is really happier than most of you imagine.

First: Therefore, it hath been always agreed in the world, that the present happiness of mankind consisted in the ease of our body and the quiet of our mind; but, from what has been already said, it plainly appears, that neither wealth nor power do in any sort contribute to either of these two blessings. If, on the contrary, by multiplying our desires, they increase our discontents; if they destroy our health, gall us with painful diseases, and shorten our life; if they expose us to hatred, to envy, to censure, to a thousand temptations, it is not easy to see why a wise man should make them his choice, for their own sake, although it were in his power. Would any of you, who are in health and strength of body, with moderate food and raiment earned by your own labour,

rather choose to be in the rich man's bed, under the torture
of the gout, unable to take your natural rest, or natural
nourishment, with the additional load of a guilty conscience,
reproaching you for injustice, oppressions, covetousness, and
fraud? No; but you would take the riches and power, and
leave behind the inconveniences that attend them; and so
would every man living. But that is more than our share,
and God never intended this world for such a place of rest
as we would make it; for the Scripture assureth us that it
was only designed as a place of trial. Nothing is more
frequent, than a man to wish himself in another's condition;
yet he seldom doth it without some reserve: He would not
be so old; he would not be so sickly; he would not be so
cruel; he would not be so insolent; he would not be so
vicious; he would not be so oppressive, so griping, and so
on. From whence it is plain, that, in their own judgment,
men are not so unequally dealt with, as they would at first
sight imagine: For, if I would not change my condition
with another man, without any exception or reservation at
all, I am, in reality, more happy than he.

Secondly: You of the meaner sort are subject to fewer
temptations than the rich; and therefore your vices are
more unpardonable. Labour subdueth your appetites to be
satisfied with common things; the business of your several
callings filleth up your whole time; so that idleness, which
is the bane and destruction of virtue, doth not lead you into
the neighbourhood of sin: Your passions are cooler, by not
being inflamed with excess, and therefore the gate and the
way that lead to life are not so straight and so narrow to
you, as to those who live among all the allurements to
wickedness. To serve God with the best of your care and
understanding, and to be just and true in your dealings, is
the short sum of your duty, and will be the more strictly
required of you, because nothing lieth in the way to divert
you from it.

Thirdly: It is plain from what I have said, that you of the
lower rank have no just reason to complain of your condition: Because, as you plainly see, it affordeth you so many
advantages, and freeth you from so many vexations, so
many distempers both of body and mind, which pursue and
torment the rich and powerful.

Fourthly: You are to remember and apply, that the poorest person is not excused from doing good to others, and even relieving the wants of his distressed neighbour, according to his abilities; and if you perform your duty in this point, you far outdo the greatest liberalities of the rich, and will accordingly be accepted of by God, and get your reward: For it is our Saviour's own doctrine, when the widow gave her two mites. The rich give out of their abundance; that is to say, what they give, they do not feel it in their way of living: But the poor man, who giveth out of his little stock, must spare it from the necessary food and raiment of himself and his family. And, therefore, our Saviour adds, " That the widow gave more than all who went before her; for she gave all she had, even all her living;" and so went home utterly unprovided to supply her necessities.

Lastly: As it appeareth from what hath been said, that you in the lower rank have, in reality, a greater share of happiness, your work of salvation is easier, by your being liable to fewer temptations; and as your reward in Heaven is much more certain than it is to the rich, if you seriously perform your duty, for yours is the Kingdom of Heaven; so your neglect of it will be less excusable, will meet with fewer allowances from God, and will be punished with double stripes: For the most unknowing among you cannot plead ignorance of what you have been so early taught, I hope, so often instructed in, and which is so easy to be understood, I mean the art of leading a life agreeable to the plain and positive laws of God. Perhaps you may think you lie under one disadvantage, which the great and rich have not; that idleness will certainly reduce you to beggary; whereas those who abound in wealth lie under no necessity either of labour or temperance to keep enough to live on. But this is indeed one part of your happiness, that the lowness of your condition, in a manner, forceth you to what is pleasing to God, and necessary for your daily support. Thus your duty and interest are always the same.

To conclude: Since our blessed Lord, instead of a rich and honourable station in this world, was pleased to choose his lot among men of the lower condition; let not those, on whom the bounty of Providence hath bestowed wealth and honours, despise the men who are placed in a humble and

IV.   P

inferior station; but rather, with their utmost power, by their countenance, by their protection, by just payment of their honest labour, encourage their daily endeavours for the support of themselves and their families.   On the other hand, let the poor labour to provide things honest in the sight of all men; and so, with diligence in their several employments, live soberly, righteously, and godlily in this present world, that they may obtain that glorious reward promised in the Gospel to the poor, I mean the kingdom of Heaven.

Now, to God the Father, &c.

WRETCHED CONDITION OF IRELAND.[1]

PSALM CXLIV. PART OF THE 14TH AND 15TH VERSES.

" That there be no complaining in our streets. Happy is the people
that is in such a case."

IT is a very melancholy reflection, that such a country as
ours, which is capable of producing all things necessary,
and most things convenient for life, sufficient for the support
of four times the number of its inhabitants, should yet lie
under the heaviest load of misery and want, our streets
crowded with beggars, so many of our lower sort of tradesmen, labourers, and artificers, not able to find clothes and
food for their families.

I think it may therefore be of some use to lay before you
the chief causes of this wretched condition we are in, and
then it will be easier to assign what remedies are in our
power toward removing, at least, some part of these evils.

For it is ever to be lamented, that we lie under many disadvantages, not by our own faults, which are peculiar to
ourselves, and which no other nation under heaven hath any
reason to complain of.

I shall, therefore, first mention some causes of our miseries,

---

[1] This is not very properly styled a sermon; but, considered as a
political dissertation, it has great merit, and it is highly worthy of the
subject, and the author. Most of the circumstances here founded upon,
as the causes of national distress, are the subject of separate disquisi-
tions in those political writings connected with Ireland. But they are
here summed up, and brought into one view; and the opinions expressed form a sort of index to the Dean's tenets upon the state of that
country. [S.]

which I doubt are not to be remedied, until God shall put it in the hearts of those who are stronger to allow us the common rights and privileges of brethren, fellow-subjects, and even of mankind.

The first cause of our misery is the intolerable hardships we lie under in every branch of our trade, by which we are become as hewers of wood, and drawers of water, to our rigorous neighbours.

The second cause of our miserable state is the folly, the vanity, and ingratitude of those vast numbers, who think themselves too good to live in the country which gave them birth, and still gives them bread; and rather choose to pass their days, and consume their wealth, and draw out the very vitals of their mother kingdom, among those who heartily despise them.

These I have but lightly touched on, because I fear they are not to be redressed, and, besides, I am very sensible how ready some people are to take offence at the honest truth; and, for that reason, I shall omit several other grievances, under which we are long likely to groan.

I shall therefore go on to relate some other causes of this nation's poverty, by which, if they continue much longer, it must infallibly sink to utter ruin.

The first is, that monstrous pride and vanity in both sexes, especially the weaker sex, who, in the midst of poverty, are suffered to run into all kind of expense and extravagance in dress, and particularly priding themselves to wear nothing but what cometh from abroad, disdaining the growth or manufacture of their own country, in those articles where they can be better served at home with half the expense; and this is grown to such a height, that they will carry the whole yearly rent of a good estate at once on their body. And, as there is in that sex a spirit of envy, by which they cannot endure to see others in a better habit than themselves, so those, whose fortunes can hardly support their families in the necessaries of life, will needs vie with the richest and greatest amongst us, to the ruin of themselves and their posterity.

Neither are the men less guilty of this pernicious folly, who, in imitation of a gaudiness and foppery of dress, introduced of late years into our neighbouring kingdom, (as fools are apt to imitate only the defects of their betters,) cannot find materials in their own country worthy to adorn their bodies of clay, while their minds are naked of every valuable quality.

Thus our tradesmen and shopkeepers, who deal in home goods, are left in a starving condition, and only those encouraged who ruin the kingdom by importing among us foreign vanities.

Another cause of our low condition is our great luxury, the chief support of which is the materials of it brought to the nation in exchange for the few valuable things left us, whereby so many thousand families want the very necessaries of life.

Thirdly, In most parts of this kingdom the natives are from their infancy so given up to idleness and sloth, that they often choose to beg or steal, rather than support themselves with their own labour ; they marry without the least view or thought of being able to make any provision for their families ; and whereas, in all industrious nations, children are looked on as a help to their parents ; with us, for want of being early trained to work, they are an intolerable burthen at home, and a grievous charge upon the public, as appeareth from the vast number of ragged and naked children in town and country, led about by strolling women, trained up in ignorance and all manner of vice.

Lastly, A great cause of this nation's misery, is that Egyptian bondage of cruel, oppressing, covetous landlords, expecting that all who live under them should make bricks without straw, who grieve and envy when they see a tenant of their own in a whole coat, or able to afford one comfortable meal in a month, by which the spirits of the people are broken, and made for slavery; the farmers and cottagers, almost through the whole kingdom, being to all intents and purposes as real beggars as any of those to whom we give our charity in the streets.   And these cruel landlords are every day unpeopling their kingdom, by forbidding their miserable tenants to till the earth, against common reason and justice, and contrary to the practice and prudence of all other nations, by which numberless families have been forced either to leave the kingdom, or stroll about, and increase the number of our thieves and beggars.

Such, and much worse, is our condition at present, if I had leisure or liberty to lay it before you; and, therefore, the next thing which might be considered is, whether there may be any probable remedy found, at the least against some part of these evils; for most of them are wholly desperate.

But this being too large a subject to be now handled, and the intent of my discourse confining me to give some directions concerning the poor of this city, I shall keep myself within those limits. It is indeed in the power of the law-givers to found a school in every parish of the kingdom, for teaching the meaner and poorer sort of children to speak and read the English tongue, and to provide a reasonable maintenance for the teachers. This would, in time, abolish that part of barbarity and ignorance, for which our natives are so despised by all foreigners: this would bring them to think and act according to the rules of reason, by which a spirit of industry, and thrift, and honesty would be introduced among them. And, indeed, considering how small a tax would suffice for such a work, it is a public scandal that such a thing should never have been endeavoured, or, perhaps, so much as thought on.

To supply the want of such a law, several pious persons, in many parts of this kingdom, have been prevailed on, by the great endeavours and good example set them by the clergy, to erect charity-schools in several parishes, to which very often the richest parishioners contribute the least. In those schools, children are, or ought to be, trained up to read and write, and cast accounts; and these children should, if possible, be of honest parents, gone to decay through age, sickness, or other unavoidable calamity, by the hand of God; not the brood of wicked strollers; for it is by no means reasonable, that the charity of well-inclined people should be applied to encourage the lewdness of those profligate, abandoned women, who crowd our streets with their borrowed or spurious issue.

In those hospitals which have good foundations and rents to support them, whereof, to the scandal of Christianity, there are very few in this kingdom; I say, in such hospitals, the children maintained ought to be only of decayed citizens, and freemen, and be bred up to good trades. But in these small parish charity-schools which have no support, but the casual goodwill of charitable people, I do altogether disapprove the custom of putting the children 'prentice, except to the very meanest trades; otherwise the poor honest citizen, who is just able to bring up his child, and pay a small sum of money with him to a good master, is wholly defeated, and the bastard issue, perhaps, of some beggar preferred before him.   And hence we come to be so overstocked with 'prentices and journeymen, more than our discouraged country can employ; and, I fear, the greatest part of our thieves, pickpockets, and other vagabonds are of this number.

Therefore, in order to make these parish charity-schools of great and universal use, I agree with the opinion of many wise persons, that a new turn should be given to this whole matter.

I think there is no complaint more just than what we find in almost every family, of the folly and ignorance, the fraud and knavery, the idleness and viciousness, the wasteful squandering temper of servants, who are, indeed, become one of the many public grievances of the kingdom; whereof, I believe, there are few masters that now hear me who are not convinced by their own experience.   And I am not very confident, that more families, of all degrees, have been ruined by the corruptions of servants, than by all other causes put together.   Neither is this to be wondered at, when we consider from what nurseries so many of them are received into our houses.   The first is the tribe of wicked boys, wherewith most corners of this town are pestered, who haunt public doors.   These, having been born of beggars, and bred to pilfer as soon as they can go or speak, as years come on, are employed in the lowest offices to get themselves bread, are practised in all manner of villainy, and when they are grown up, if they are not entertained in a gang of thieves, are forced to seek for a service.   The other nursery is the barbarous and desert part of the country, from whence such lads come up hither to seek their fortunes, who are bred up from the dunghill in idleness, ignorance, lying, and thieving. From these two nurseries, I say, a great number of our servants come to us, sufficient to corrupt all the rest.   Thus, the whole race of servants in this kingdom have gotten so ill a reputation, that some persons from England, come over hither into great stations, are said to have absolutely refused admitting any servant born among us into their families. Neither can they be justly blamed; for although it is not impossible to find an honest native fit for a good service, yet the inquiry is too troublesome, and the hazard too great for a stranger to attempt.

If we consider the many misfortunes that befall private families, it will be found that servants are the causes and instruments of them all: Are our goods embezzled, wasted and destroyed? Is our house burnt down to the ground? It is by the sloth, the drunkenness or the villainy of servants. Are we robbed and murdered in our beds? It is by confederacy with our servants. Are we engaged in quarrels and misunderstandings with our neighbours? These were all begun and inflamed by the false, malicious tongues of our servants. Are the secrets of our families betrayed, and evil repute spread of us? Our servants were the authors. Do false accusers rise up against us (an evil too frequent in this country)? They have been tampering with our servants. Do our children discover folly, malice, pride, cruelty, revenge, undutifulness in their words and actions? Are they seduced to lewdness or scandalous marriages? It is all by our servants. Nay, the very mistakes, follies, blunders, and absurdities of those in our service, are able to ruffle and discompose the mildest nature, and are often of such consequence, as to put whole families into confusion.

Since therefore not only our domestic peace and quiet, and the welfare of our children, but even the very safety of our lives, reputations, and fortunes have so great a dependence upon the choice of our servants, I think it would well become the wisdom of the nation to make some provision in so important an affair. But in the meantime, and, perhaps, to better purpose, it were to be wished, that the children of both sexes, entertained in the parish charity-schools, were bred up in such a manner as would give them a teachable disposition, and qualify them to learn whatever is required in any sort of service. For instance, they should be taught to read and write, to know somewhat in casting accounts, to understand the principles of religion, to practise cleanliness, to get a spirit of honesty, industry, and thrift, and be severely punished for every neglect in any of these particulars. For, it is the misfortune of mankind, that if they are not used to be taught in their early childhood, whereby to acquire what I call a teachable disposition, they cannot, without great difficulty, learn the easiest thing in the course of their lives, but are always awkward and unhandy; their minds, as well as bodies, for want of early practice, growing stiff and unmanageable, as we observe in the sort of gentlemen, who, kept from school by the indulgence of their parents but a few years, are never able to recover the time they have lost, and grow up in ignorance and all manner of vice, whereof we have too many examples all over the nation. But to return to what I was saying: If these charity children were trained up in the manner I mentioned, and then bound apprentices in the families of gentlemen and citizens, (for which a late law giveth great encouragement) being accustomed from their first entrance to be always learning some useful thing, [they] would learn, in a month, more than another, without those advantages, can do in a year; and, in the meantime, be very useful in a family, as far as their age and strength would allow. And when such children come to years of discretion, they will probably be a useful example to their fellow-servants, at least they will prove a strong check upon the rest; for, I suppose, everybody will allow, that one good, honest, diligent servant in a house may prevent abundance of mischief in the family.

These are the reasons for which I urge this matter so strongly, and I hope those who listen to me will consider them.

I shall now say something about that great number of poor, who, under the name of common beggars, infest our streets, and fill our ears with their continual cries, and craving importunity. This I shall venture to call an unnecessary evil, brought upon us for the gross neglect, and want of proper management, in those whose duty it is to prevent it. But before I proceed farther, let me humbly presume to vindicate the justice and mercy of God and His dealings with mankind. Upon this particular He hath not dealt so hardly with His creatures as some would imagine, when they see so many miserable objects ready to perish for want: For it would infallibly be found, upon strict enquiry, that there is hardly one in twenty of those miserable objects who do not owe their present poverty to their own faults, to their present sloth and negligence, to their indiscreet marriage without the least prospect of supporting a family, to their foolish expensiveness, to their drunkenness, and other vices, by which they have squandered their gettings, and contracted diseases in their old age. And, to speak freely, is it any way reasonable or just, that those who have denied themselves many lawful satisfactions and conveniences of life, from a principle of conscience, as well as prudence, that they might not be a burthen to the public, should be charged with supporting others, who have brought themselves to less than a morsel of bread by their idleness, extravagance, and vice? Yet such, and no other, are far the greatest number not only in those who beg in our streets, but even of what we call poor decayed housekeepers, whom we are apt to pity as real objects of charity, and distinguish them from common beggars, although, in truth, they both owe their undoing to the same causes; only the former is either too nicely bred to endure walking half naked in the streets, or too proud to own their wants. For the artificer or other tradesman, who pleadeth he is grown too old to work or look after business, and therefore expecteth assistance as a decayed housekeeper; may we not ask him, why he did not take care, in his youth and strength of days, to make some provision against old age, when he saw so many examples before him of people undone by their idleness and vicious extravagance? And to go a little higher; whence cometh it that so many citizens and shopkeepers, of the most creditable trade, who once made a good figure, go to decay by their expensive pride and vanity, affecting to educate and dress their children above their abilities, or the state of life they ought to expect?

However, since the best of us have too many infirmities to answer for, we ought not to be severe upon those of others; and therefore if our brother, through grief, or sickness, or other incapacity, is not in a condition to preserve his being, we ought to support him to the best of our power, without reflecting over seriously on the causes that brought him to his misery. But in order to this, and to turn our charity into its proper channel, we ought to consider who and where those objects are, whom it is chiefly incumbent upon us to support.

By the ancient law of this realm, still in force, every parish is obliged to maintain its own poor, which although some may think to be not very equal, because many parishes are very rich, and have few poor among them, and others the contrary; yet, I think, may be justly defended: For as to remote country parishes in the desert part of the kingdom, the necessaries of life are there so cheap, that the infirm poor may be provided for with little burden to the inhabitants. But in what I am going to say, I shall confine myself only to this city, where we are overrun not only with our own poor, but with a far greater number from every part of the nation. Now, I say, this evil of being encumbered with so many foreign beggars, who have not the least title to our charity, and whom it is impossible for us to support, may be easily remedied, if the government of this city, in conjunction with the clergy and parish officers, would think it worth their care; and I am sure few things deserve it better. For, if every parish would take a list of those begging poor which properly belong to it, and compel each of them to wear a badge, marked and numbered, so as to be seen and known by all they meet, and confine them to beg within the limits of their own parish, severely punishing them when they offend, and driving out all interlopers from other parishes, we could then make a computation of their numbers; and the strollers from the country being driven away, the remainder would not be too many for the charity of those who pass by to maintain; neither would any beggar, although confined to his own parish, be hindered from receiving the charity of the whole town; because, in this case, those well-disposed persons who walk the streets will give their charity to such whom they think proper objects, wherever they meet them, provided they are found in their own parishes, and wearing their badges of distinction. And, as to those parishes which bordered upon the skirts and suburbs of the town, where country strollers are used to harbour themselves, they must be forced to go back to their homes, when they find nobody to relieve them, because they want that mark which only gives them licence to beg. Upon this point, it were to be wished, that inferior parish officers had better encouragement given them to perform their duty in driving away all beggars who do not belong to the parish, instead of conniving at them, as it is said they do for some small contribution: For the whole city would save much more by ridding themselves of many hundred beggars, than they would lose by giving parish officers a reasonable support.

It should seem a strange, unaccountable thing, that those who have probably been reduced to want by riot, lewdness, and idleness, although they have assurance enough to beg alms publicly from all they meet, should yet be too proud to wear the parish badge, which would turn so much to their own advantage, by ridding them of such great numbers, who now intercept the greatest part of what belongeth to them : Yet it is certain, that there are very many who publicly declare they will never wear those badges, and many others who either hide or throw them away: But the remedy for this is very short, easy, and just, by trying them like vagabonds and sturdy beggars, and forcibly driving them out of the town.

Therefore, as soon as this expedient of wearing badges shall be put in practice, I do earnestly exhort all those who hear me, never to give their alms to any public beggar who doth not fully comply with this order, by which our number of poor will be so reduced, that it will be much easier to provide for the rest. Our shop-doors will be no longer crowded with so many thieves and pickpockets, in beggars' habits, nor our streets so dangerous to those who are forced to walk in the night.

Thus I have, with great freedom, delivered my thoughts upon this subject, which so nearly concerneth us. It is certainly a bad scheme, to any Christian country, which God hath blessed with fruitfulness, and where the people enjoy the just rights and privileges of mankind, that there should be any beggars at all. But, alas! among us, where the whole nation itself is almost reduced to beggary by the disadvantages we lie under, and the hardships we are forced to bear ; the laziness, ignorance, thoughtlessness, squandering temper, slavish nature, and uncleanly manner of living in the poor Popish natives, together with the cruel oppressions of their landlords, who delight to see their vassals in the dust ; I say, that, in such a nation, how can we otherwise

expect than to be over-run with objects of misery and want?
Therefore, there can be no other method to free this city
from so intolerable a grievance, than by endeavouring, as
far as in us lies, that the burthen may be more equally
divided, by contributing to maintain our own poor, and
forcing the strollers and vagabonds to return to their several
homes in the country, there to smite the conscience of those
oppressors, who first stripped them of all their substance.

I might here, if the time would permit, offer many arguments to persuade to works of charity; but you hear them
so often from the pulpit, that I am willing to hope you may
not now want them.   Besides, my present design was only
to shew where your alms would be best bestowed, to the
honour of God, your own ease and advantage, the service of
your country, and the benefit of the poor.   I desire you will
all weigh and consider what I have spoken, and, according
to your several stations and abilities, endeavour to put it in
practice; and God give you good success.   To Whom, with
the Son and Holy Ghost, be all honour, &c.

The grace of our Lord Jesus Christ, &c.

SLEEPING IN CHURCH.

ACTS, CHAP. XX. VER. 9.

"And there sat in a window a certain young man, named *Eutychus*, being fallen into a deep sleep; and as *Paul* was long preaching, he sunk down with sleep, and fell down from the third loft, and was taken up dead."

I HAVE chosen these words with design, if possible, to disturb some part in this audience of half an hour's sleep, for the convenience and exercise whereof this place, at this season of the day, is very much celebrated.

There is indeed one mortal disadvantage to which all preaching is subject; that those who, by the wickedness of their lives, stand in greatest need, have usually the smallest share; for either they are absent upon the account of idleness, or spleen, or hatred to religion, or in order to doze away the intemperance of the week; or, if they do come, they are sure to employ their minds rather any other way, than regarding or attending to the business of the place.

The accident which happened to this young man in the text, hath not been sufficient to discourage his successors: But because the preachers now in the world, however they may exceed St Paul in the art of setting men to sleep, do extremely fall short of him in the working of miracles; therefore men are become so cautious as to choose more safe and convenient stations and postures for taking their repose, without hazard of their persons; and, upon the whole matter, choose rather to trust their destruction to a miracle, than their safety. However, this being not the only way by which the lukewarm Christians and scorners of the age discover their neglect and contempt of preaching, I shall enter expressly into consideration of this matter, and order my discourse in the following method :

First : I shall produce several instances to shew the great neglect of preaching now amongst us.

Secondly : I shall reckon up some of the usual quarrels men have against preaching.

Thirdly : I shall set forth the great evil of this neglect and contempt of preaching, and discover the real causes from whence it proceedeth.

Lastly : I shall offer some remedies against this great and spreading evil.

First : I shall produce certain instances to shew the great neglect of preaching now among us.

These may be reduced under two heads.   First, men's absence from the service of the Church ; and secondly, their misbehaviour when they are here.

The first instance of men's neglect, is in their frequent absence from the church.

There is no excuse so trivial, that will not pass upon some men's consciences to excuse their attendance at the public worship of God.   Some are so unfortunate as to be always indisposed on the Lord's day, and think nothing so unwholesome as the air of a church.   Others have their affairs so oddly contrived, as to be always unluckily prevented by business.   With some it is a great mark of wit, and deep understanding, to stay at home on Sundays. Others again discover strange fits of laziness, that seize them, particularly on that day, and confine them to their beds.   Others are absent out of mere contempt of religion. And, lastly, there are not a few who look upon it as a day of rest, and therefore claim the privilege of their cattle, to keep the Sabbath by eating, drinking, and sleeping, after the toil and labour of the week.   Now in all this the worst circumstance is, that these persons are such whose companies are most required, and who stand most in need of a physician.

Secondly : Men's great neglect and contempt of preaching, appear by their misbehaviour when at church.

If the audience were to be ranked under several heads, according to their behaviour, when the word of God is delivered, how small a number would appear of those who receive it as they ought? How much of the seed then sown would be found to fall by the way-side, upon stony ground or among thorns? And how little good ground would there be to take it? A preacher cannot look round from the pulpit, without observing, that some are in a perpetual whisper, and, by their air and gesture, give occasion to suspect, that they are in those very minutes defaming their neighbour. Others have their eyes and imagination constantly engaged in such a circle of objects, perhaps to gratify the most unwarrantable desires, that they never once attend to the business of the place; the sound of the preacher's words doth not so much as once interrupt them. Some have their minds wandering among idle, worldly, or vicious thoughts. Some lie at catch to ridicule whatever they hear, and with much wit and humour provide a stock of laughter, by furnishing themselves from the pulpit. But, of all misbehaviour, none is comparable to that of those who come here to sleep; opium is not so stupefying to many persons as an afternoon sermon. Perpetual custom hath so brought it about, that the words, of whatever preacher, become only a sort of uniform sound at a distance, than which nothing is more effectual to lull the senses. For, that it is the very sound of the sermon which bindeth up their faculties, is manifest from hence, because they all awake so very regularly as soon as it ceaseth, and with much devotion receive the blessing, dozed and besotted with indecencies I am ashamed to repeat.

I proceed, *Secondly*, to reckon up some of the usual quarrels men have against preaching, and to shew the unreasonableness of them.

Such unwarrantable demeanour as I have described, among Christians, in the house of God, in a solemn assembly, while their faith and duty are explained and delivered, have put those who are guilty upon inventing some excuses to extenuate their fault: This they do by turning the blame either upon the particular preacher, or upon preaching in general. First, they object against the par-

ticular preacher; his manner, his delivery, his voice are disagreeable, his style and expression are flat and low; sometimes improper and absurd; the matter is heavy, trivial and
insipid; sometimes despicable, and perfectly ridiculous; or
else, on the other side, he runs up into unintelligible speculation, empty notions, and abstracted flights, all clad in words
above usual understandings.

Secondly, They object against preaching in general; it is
a perfect road of talk; they know already whatever can be
said; they have heard the same an hundred times over.
They quarrel that preachers do not relieve an old beaten
subject with wit and invention; and that now the art is lost
of moving men's passions, so common among the ancient
orators of Greece and Rome. These, and the like objections, are frequently in the mouths of men who despise
the "foolishness of preaching." But let us examine the
reasonableness of them.

The doctrine delivered by all preachers is the same: "So
we preach, and so ye believe:" But the manner of deliver
ing is suited to the skill and abilities of each, which differ
in preachers just as in the rest of mankind. However, in
personal dislikes of a particular preacher, are these men
sure they are always in the right? Do they consider how
mixed a thing is every audience, whose taste and judgment
differ, perhaps, every day, not only from each other, but
themselves? And how to calculate a discourse, that shall
exactly suit them all, is beyond the force and reach of
human reason, knowledge, or invention. Wit and eloquence
are shining qualities, that God hath imparted, in great
degrees, to very few, nor any more to be expected, in the
generality of any rank among men, than riches and honour.
But further: If preaching in general be all old and beaten,
and that they are already so well acquainted with it, more
shame and guilt to them who so little edify by it. But
these men, whose ears are so delicate as not to endure a
plain discourse of religion, who expect a constant supply of
wit and eloquence on a subject handled so many thousand
times; what will they say when we turn the objection upon
themselves, who, with all the rude and profane liberty of
discourse they take, upon so many thousand subjects, are so
dull as to furnish nothing but tedious repetitions, and little

paltry, nauseous common-places, so vulgar, so worn, or so obvious, as, upon any other occasion, but that of advancing vice, would be hooted off the stage ? Nor, lastly, are preachers justly blamed for neglecting human oratory to move the passions, which is not the business of a Christian orator, whose office it is only to work upon faith and reason. All other eloquence hath been a perfect cheat, to stir up men's passions against truth and justice, for the service of a faction, to put false colours upon things, and by an amusement of agreeable words, make the worse reason appear to be the better. This is certainly not to be allowed in Christian eloquence, and, therefore, St Paul took quite the other course; he "came not with excellency of words, or enticing speech of men's wisdom, but in plain evidence of the Spirit and power." And perhaps it was for that reason the young man Eutychus, used to the Grecian eloquence, grew tired and fell so fast asleep.

I go on, *Thirdly*, to set forth the great evil of this neglect and scorn of preaching, and to discover the real causes from whence it proceedeth.

I think it is obvious,[1] that this neglect of preaching hath very much occasioned the great decay of religion among us. To this may be imputed no small part of that contempt some men bestow on the clergy; for, whoever talketh without being regarded, is sure to be despised. To this we owe, in a great measure, the spreading of atheism and infidelity among us; for religion, like all other things, is soonest put out of countenance by being ridiculed. The scorn of preaching might perhaps have been at first introduced by men of nice ears and refined taste; but it is now become a spreading evil, through all degrees, and both sexes; for, since sleeping, talking, and laughing are qualities sufficient to furnish out a critic, the meanest and most ignorant have set up a title, and succeeded in it as well as their betters. Thus are the last efforts of reforming mankind rendered wholly useless: "How shall they hear," saith the apostle, "without a preacher?" But, if they have a preacher, and make it a point of wit or breeding not to hear him, what remedy is

---

[1] Hawkesworth (Swift's "Works," vol. xiii., 1762) inserts here "to believe." [T. S.]

left? To this neglect of preaching, we may also entirely impute that gross ignorance among us in the very principles of religion, which it is amazing to find in persons who very much value their own knowledge and understanding in other things; yet, it is a visible, inexcusable ignorance, even in the meanest among us, considering the many advantages they have of learning their duty. And it hath been the great encouragement to all manner of vice: For, in vain we preach down sin to a people, "whose hearts are waxed gross, whose ears are dull of hearing, and whose eyes are closed." Therefore Christ Himself, in His discourses, frequently rouseth up the attention of the multitude, and of His disciples themselves, with this expression, "He that hath ears to hear, let him hear." But, among all neglects of preaching, none is so fatal as that of sleeping in the house of God; a scorner may listen to truth and reason, and in time grow serious; an unbeliever may feel the pangs of a guilty conscience; one whose thoughts or eyes wander among other objects, may, by a lucky word, be called back to attention: But the sleeper shuts up all avenues to his soul: He is "like the deaf adder, that hearkeneth not to the voice of the charmer, charm he never so wisely." And, we may preach with as good success to the grave that is under his feet.

But the great evil of this neglect will further yet appear, from considering the real causes whence it proceedeth; whereof the first, I take to be, an evil conscience. Many men come to church to save or gain a reputation; or because they will not be singular, but comply with an established custom; yet, all the while, they are loaded with the guilt of old rooted sins. These men can expect to hear of nothing but terrors and threatenings, their sins laid open in true colours, and eternal misery the reward of them; therefore, no wonder they stop their ears, and divert their thoughts, and seek any amusement rather than stir the hell within them.

Another cause of this neglect is, a heart set upon worldly things. Men whose minds are much enslaved to earthly affairs all the week, cannot disengage or break the chain of their thoughts so suddenly, as to apply to a discourse that is wholly foreign to what they have most at heart. Tell a usurer of charity, and mercy, and restitution, you talk to the deaf; his heart and soul, with all his senses, are got among his bags, or he is gravely asleep, and dreaming of a mortgage. Tell a man of business, that the cares of the world choke the good seed; that we must not encumber ourselves with much serving; that the salvation of his soul is the one thing necessary: You see, indeed, the shape of a man before you, but his faculties are all gone off among clients and papers, thinking how to defend a bad cause, or find flaws in a good one; or, he weareth out the time in drowsy nods.

A third cause of the great neglect and scorn of preaching, ariseth from the practice of men who set up to decry and disparage religion; these, being zealous to promote infidelity and vice, learn a rote of buffoonery that serveth all occasions, and refutes the strongest arguments for piety and good manners. These have a set of ridicule calculated for all sermons, and all preachers, and can be extreme witty as often as they please upon the same fund.

Let me now, in the last place, offer some remedies against this great evil.

It will be one remedy against the contempt of preaching, rightly to consider the end for which it was designed. There are many who place abundance of merit in going to church, although it be with no other prospect but that of being well entertained, wherein if they happen to fail, they return wholly disappointed. Hence it is become an impertinent vein among people of all sorts to hunt after what they call a good sermon, as if it were a matter of pastime and diversion. Our business, alas! is quite another thing, either to learn, or, at least, be reminded of our duty, to apply the doctrines delivered, compare the rules we hear with our lives and actions, and find wherein we have transgressed. These are the dispositions men should bring into the house of God, and then they will be little concerned about the preacher's wit or eloquence, nor be curious to enquire out his faults and infirmities, but consider how to correct their own.

Another remedy against the contempt of preaching, is, that men would consider, whether it be not reasonable to give more allowances for the different abilities of preachers than they usually do; refinements of style, and flights of wit, as they are not properly the business of any preacher, so they cannot possibly be the talents of all. In most other discourses, men are satisfied with sober sense and plain reason; and, as understandings usually go, even that is not over frequent. Then why they should be so over nice in expectation of eloquence,[1] where it is neither necessary nor convenient, is hard to imagine.

Lastly : The scorners of preaching would do well to consider, that this talent of ridicule, they value so much, is a perfection very easily acquired, and applied to all things whatsoever; neither is anything at all the worse, because it is capable of being perverted to burlesque : Perhaps it may be the more perfect upon that score ; since we know, the most celebrated pieces have been thus treated with greatest success. It is in any man's power to suppose a fool's cap on the wisest head, and then laugh at his own supposition. I think there are not many things cheaper than supposing and laughing ; and if the uniting these two talents can bring a thing into contempt, it is hard to know where it may end.

To conclude: These considerations may, perhaps, have some effect while men are awake ; but what arguments shall we use to the sleeper ? What methods shall we take to hold open his eyes ? Will he be moved by considerations of common civility ? We know it is reckoned a point of very bad manners to sleep in private company, when, perhaps, the tedious impertinence of many talkers would render it at least as excusable as at the dullest sermon. Do they think it a small thing to watch four hours at a play, where all virtue and religion are openly reviled ; and can they not watch one half hour to hear them defended ? Is this to deal like a judge, (I mean like a good judge) to listen on one side of the cause, and sleep on the other ? I shall add but one word more : That this indecent sloth is very much owing to that luxury and excess men usually practise upon this day, by which half the service thereof is turned to sin ; men dividing the time between God and their bellies, when after a gluttonous meal, their senses dozed and stupefied,

---

[1] Hawkesworth (1762 edit.) has " over nice and expecting for sense " ; but both the 4to and the 8vo of 1764 agree with Scott as above. [T. S.]

they retire to God's house to sleep out the afternoon.   Surely, brethren, these things ought not so to be.

"He that hath ears to hear, let him hear."   And God give us all grace to hear and receive His holy word to the salvation of our own souls.

APPENDIX I.

SWIFT'S REMARKS ON DR GIBBS'S PARAPHRASE OF THE PSALMS.

NOTE.

" THE following manuscript was literally copied from the printed
original found in the library of Dr. J. Swift, Dean of St Patrick's,
Dublin, in the year 1745. The marginal notes and parodies were
written by the Dean's own hand, except such as are distinguished with
this mark (φ) with which I am only chargeable. Witness my hand,
this 25th day of February, 1745.   WILLIAM DUNKIN.
" N.B.—The original was by me presented to his excellency Philip
Dormer Stanhope, Earl of Chesterfield, lord lieutenant general and
general governor of Ireland.   W. D."
The manuscript to which Dr. Dunkin refers is in the library of
Trinity College, Dublin. The present text is taken from a transcript
which is at the South Kensington Museum, and which appears to be the
identical transcript used by Nichols for his reprint in the quarto edition,
vol. xiv. At the end of this MS. is the following note :

" The above was written from the manuscript mentioned in the first
page, now in the hands of Nicholas Coyne, Esq., being the only copy
in the kingdom of Ireland ; he having purchased the original, and afterwards generously given it to his friend Dr. Dunkin, finding the doctor
extremely uneasy at the disappointment the Earl of Chesterfield was
like to meet with, as he had promised the earl to attend the auction,
and procure it for him at any price ; and is now transcribed by Neale
Molloy, of Dublin, Esqr, by the favour of the said Nicholas Coyne,
his brother-in-law; and sent by him to his kinsman, and dear friend,
Charles Molloy, of London, Esqre.

" *Dublin, 26th of May,* 1748."   .

The " Epistle Dedicatory " to Princess Anne, in Dr. Gibbs's volume,
has also been annotated, chiefly by Dr. Dunkin; but as these are mostly
too filthy to be published, I have omitted the few notes by Swift, which
consist merely of marginalia corrections of words and a few satirical in-
terpolations of no great consequence. I have corrected Dr. Gibbs's text
by the original edition of his " Paraphrase " (1701). The corrections
were necessary, since the transcript could not be absolutely relied on.
                                                           [T. S.]

APPENDIX I.

DR SWIFT'S REMARKS

ON "The first Fifteen Psalms of David, translated into Lyric Verse: Proposed as an Essay, supplying the Perspicuity and Coherence according to the Modern Art of Poetry; not known to have been attempted before in any Language. With a Preface containing some Observations of the great and general Defectiveness of former Versions in Greek, Latin, and English. By Dr. [James] Gibbs. London: printed by J. Mathews, for John Hartley, over-against Gray's-Inn, in Holborn. MDCCI."

THE FIRST FIFTEEN PSALMS, TRANSLATED INTO ENGLISH VERSE.

DR GIBBS.

DR SWIFT.

I. PSALM OF DAVID. (1)

Comparing the different state of the righteous and the wicked, both in this and the next world.

1 THRICE happy he! that does refuse
    With *impious* (2) *sinners* to combine;
Who ne'er their wicked way pursues,
    And does the scorner's *seat* (3) *decline:*

2 But still to learn, and to obey
    The Law of God is his delight;
In that employs himself all day,
    And reads and thinks thereon at (4) night. (5)

(1) I warn the reader that this is a lie, both here and all over the book; for these are not Psalms of David, but of Dr. Gibbs.

(2) But I suppose with *pious* sinners a man may combine safely enough.
(3) What part of speech is it?

(4) All.
(5) A man must have some time to sleep; so that I will change the verse thus:
"And thinks and dreams thereon all night."

DR GIBBS.	DR SWIFT.

3 For as a tree, whose spreading root
   By some prolific stream is fed,
   Produces (6) fair and timely fruit,
   And numerous boughs adorn its head :
	(6) Look ye ; you must thin the boughs at the top, or your fruit will be neither fair or timely.

Whose (7) very leaves, tho' storms descend,
   In lively verdure still appear ;
Such blessings always shall attend
   The man that does the Lord revere.
	(7) Why, what other part of a tree appears in lively verdure, beside the leaves?
	These very leaves on which you penn'd
	Your woful stuff, may serve for squibs :
	Such blessings always shall attend
	The madrigals of Dr. Gibbs.

. . . . . . 4 Like chaff with every wind disperst : (1) [rhyming with " curst "]	(1) " Dispurst," Pronounce this like a blockhead.
. . . . . . 6 And these to punishment may go. (2)	(2) If they please.

["The above may serve for a tolerable specimen of Swift's remarks. The whole should be given, if it were possible to make them intelligible, without copying the version which is ridiculed ; a labour for which our readers would scarcely thank us. A few detached stanzas, however, with the Dean's notes on them, shall be transcribed."] Thus writes Scott ; but I have added a great many more, which deserve reprinting, if only for their humour. [T. S.]

DR GIBBS.	DR SWIFT.
II. PSALM OF DAVID.	

1 Why do the heathen nations rise,
   And in mad tumults join !
2 Confederate kings vain plots (1) devise
   Against the Almighty's reign :
	(1) I do not believe that ever kings entered into plots and confederacies against the reign of God Almighty.

His Royal Title they deny,
   Whom God appointed Christ ;
3 Let us reject their (2) laws, they cry,
   Their binding force resist.
	(2) What word does that plural number belong to ?

. . . . . . 7 And thus to Him was pleased to say, As I His words declare ; (3)	(3) An excellent druggerman.

DR GIBBS.	DR SWIFT.

9 But those, that do thy laws refuse,
   In pieces thou shalt break ;
And with an iron sceptre bruise (4)
   Their disobedient (5) *neck*.

(4) After a man is broken in pieces, 'tis no great matter to have his neck bruised.
(5) Neak.

10 Ye earthly kings, the caution *hear ;*
   Ye rulers, *learn* the same ; (6)
11 Serve God with reverence, and with
      fear (7)
   His joyful praise proclaim ;

(6) Rulers must *learn* it, but kings may only *hear* it.
(7) Very proper to make a joyful proclamation with fear.

12 Confess the Son, and own His (8) reign,
   Ere He to wrath inclines ;
And, so resenting your disdain,
   Confound your vain designs : (9)

(8) Of Blackmore's reign.

(9) You with his lines.

For should the madness of His foes (1)
   Th' avenging God incense,
Happy are they that can repose
   In Him their confidence. (2)

(1) For should the foes of David's ape Provoke his grey goose quills, Happy are they that can escape The vengeance of his pills.
(2) Admirably reasoned and connected !

III. PSALM OF DAVID.

When he fled from his son Absalom.

To Dr. Gibbs, *ex aquâ in igneni.*

.   .   .   .   .   .

4 When to the Lord for help I cry,
   He hears me from the Throne on high ;
5 And thus I sleep and wake secure, (3)
   Guarded by His almighty Power. (4)

(3) Sec*o*ure.
(4) By this I think it is clear that he cries in his sleep.

6 No fears shall then my soul depress,*
   Though thus my enemies increase ;
7 And (5) therefore, now arise, O Lord,*
   And graciously thy help afford :

* Depre*a*se, L*o*ard, Scoticé.
(5) He desires God's help, because he is not afraid of his enemies ; others, I think, usually desire it when they *are* afraid.

.   .   .   .   .   .

8 And *thus* (6) to grant a sure defence,

(6) The doctor hath a mighty affection for the particle *thus :* he uses it

DR GIBBS.

DR SWIFT.

four times in this Psalm, and 100 times in other places, and always wrong.

Belongs to God's (7) omnipotence ;

(7) That is as much as to say, he that can do all things can defend a man ; which I take to be an undoubted truth.

IV. Psalm of David.

Reproving and admonishing his enemies.

Not to burlesque his Psalms.

1 As Thou hast always taken care
  My sufferings to remove.

A pretty phrase !

2 But you, my frail (1) malicious foes,
  Who do my power despise ;
  Vainly how long will ye oppose,
  And (2) falsely calumnize !

(1) Are they malicious out of frailty, or frail out of malice ?

(2) That is, they say *false* things *falsely.*

I will discover the doctor's secret of making the coherence and connection in the Psalms that he brags of in his title and preface: he lays violent hands on certain particles, (such as *and, when, since, for, but, thus, so,* &c.) and presses them to his service on all occasions sore against their wills, and without any regard whether the sense will admit them or no.

3 Since those alone the Lord has blest,
  That do from sin refrain ;
  He therefore grants what I request, (3)
  And hears when I (4) complain :

(3) 'Tis plain the doctor never requested to be a poet.

(4) If your requests be granted, why do you complain ?

But of Thy face to us do Thou
The favour still dispense ;

What is it, to dispense the favour of his face ?

DR GIBBS.	DR SWIFT.
7 Then shall my soul with more divine And solid joys abound, Than they with stores of corn and wine, Those earthly riches, crown'd : (5)	(5) I have heard of a crown or garland of corn, but a crown of wine is new, and can hardly be explained, unless we suppose the wine to be in icicles.
8 And thus confiding, Lord, in thee I take my calm repose ; (6) For thou each night protectest me From all my (7) treacherous foes.	(6) And yet, to shew I tell no fibs, Thou hast left me in thrall To Hopkins, eke, and Doctor Gibbs, The vilest rogue of all. (7) Aye, and *open* foes too ; or his repose would not be very calm.

V. PSALM OF DAVID :

Trusting in God, he implores protection from his enemies.

	Especially Doctor Gibbs.
1 O Lord, receive my fervent prayer, Relieve my soul opprest with care, And hear my loud (1) complaint ; 2 On Thee alone I can rely, Do Thou, my God, to whom I fly, My sad (2) petition grant :	(1) I suppose he thought it would be heard the better for being loud. Οἶον ἦν τὸ μέγα κεκραγέναι καὶ ὀχληρὸν ἔιναι.— Luc. Tim., *Misanth.* (2) My poor petition. Ay, a sad one indeed.

. . . . . .

| 5 They on thy favour can't rely,
That practice such iniquity, (3)
For Thou wilt punish those
6 That do malicious lies (4) invent,
And would to death the innocent
By treacherous means (5) expose. | (3) Such vile poetry. What is the meaning of that word, *such*, in this place ?
(4) Malicious lines.
(5) By doggrel rhimes. |

. . . . . .

| 8 Lord, in Thy Laws (6) direct my ways,
Since those my watchful foe surveys,
And make me persevere : | (6) He perseveres—not that he values the Laws, but because his foes watch him. A good principle ! |

. . . . . .

| 9   They flatter to destroy :
10 But let, O Lord, the vengeance due
Those in their horrid crimes (7) pursue,
Who do Thy power defy : (8) | (7) Horrid rhimes.
(8) De*foy*. |

. . . . . .

DR GIBBS.	DR SWIFT.

VI. Psalm of David:

Penitently complaining of his sufferings.   By this translator.

1   Thy heavy hand restrain,
   (9) With mercy, Lord, correct;
Do not, (1) as if in high disdain,
   My helpless soul reject:

(9) Thy heavy hand re-
     strain;
Have mercy, Dr Gibbs:
Do not, I pray thee, paper
    stain
With rhymes retail'd in
    dribbs.
(1) That bit is a most
glorious botch.

2   For how shall I sustain
   (2) Those ills, which now I bear!
My vitals are consumed with pain,
   (3) My soul oppress'd with care:

   (2) The squeaking of a
     hogrel.
   (3) To listen to thy
     doggrel.

. . . . . .

5 For in the silent grave,
   When there I lie obscure,
No gracious favours I can have,
   Nor magnify Thy power:

} Very true all that.

6   Lord, I have pray'd in (1) vain
So long, so much opprest;
My very (2) cries increase my pain,
And tears prevent my rest;

(1) The doctor must
mean himself, for I hope
David never thought so.
(2) Then he's a dunce
for crying.
(3) That is, he is afraid
of becoming a prey to his
enemies while his eyes
are sore.

7   These do my sight impair,
My flowing eyes decay,
While to my enemies I fear
Thus (3) to become a prey.

8 But, ye vain forces! fly, (4)
   For God, Whom I adore,
9 My impious foes does still destroy,
   When I His aid implore.

(4) Fly.
   Why then does he
tell us just before that
he has prayed in vain,
and is afraid of be-
coming a prey to his
enemies?

. . . . . .

10 O Lord, by Thy fierce hand repell'd,
   With sudden shame retire. (5)

(5) A very proper word
for a man that is repell'd
by a fierce hand.

VII. Psalm of David:

When unjustly persecuted, (6) *and accused of*
treachery against King Saul.

(6) By Doctor Gibbs.

1 O Lord my God, since I repose
   My trust in Thee alone, (7)

(7) By chance.

DR GIBBS.

Save and defend me from my foes,
  That furiously come on : (8)

2 Lest, like a ravenous lion, they
  My captive soul devour,

　　.　　.　　.　　.　　.　　.

4 If I've not spared him though he's
    grown (9)
  My causeless (1) enemy,
5 Then let my life, and future (2) crown
  Become to him a prey :

6 But, Lord, thy kind assistance (1) lend,
  Arise in my defence;
  According to Thy laws, (2) contend
  For injured innocence :

7 That all the nations, that oppose, (3)
    May then confess Thy power :
  Therefore assert my righteous cause,
    That they may Thee adore : (4)

8 For equal judgment, Lord, to Thee
    The nations (5) all submit;
  Be therefore (6) merciful to me,
    And my just soul acquit : (7)

9 Destroy the wicked in their plots :
    The just with blessings crown :
  For all the ways and secret thoughts (8)
    Of both to Thee are known.

DR SWIFT.

(8) Advance.

What sort of lions are
they that devour souls ?

(9) Grow*n*.
(1) If he be grown his
causeless enemy I presume
he is no longer *guiltless*.
(2) He gives a thing
before he has it, and gives
it to him that has it
already; for Saul is the
person meant.
(1) But why *lend?*
Does he design to return
it back when he has done
with it ?
(2) Profane rascal ! he
makes it a struggle and
contention between God
and the wicked.

(3) Opp*a*use.
(4) Ado*u*re.

(5) Yet in the very
verse before he tells of
nations that *oppose.*
(6) Because all nations
submit to God, therefore
God must be merciful to
Dr. Gibbs.
(7) Of what ?

Poor David never could
    acquit
  A criminal like thee,
Against his Psalms who
    couldst commit
  Such wicked poetry.

(8) Thots.

DR GIBBS.

10 Thus by God's gracious providence (9)
   I'm still preserved secure, (1)
   Who all the good and just defends
   With a resistless (2) power.

11 All men He does with justice view,
   And their iniquity
   With direful vengeance can pursue,
   Or patiently (1) pass by:

13 For He the artillery directs,
   The sudden charge ordains,
   .   .   .   .   .   .

15 Lo! now th'inflictions (2) they design'd
   By others to be borne,
   Even all the mischiefs (3) in their mind
   Do on themselves return: (4)

16 By their own treachery betray'd
   To the same ills, (5) that they
   Invented, and with those essay'd
   To make the poor (6) their prey:

17 O Lord, how glorious are the ways
   Of Thy good Providence!
   Thou, Lord, Whose blessed Name I
        praise,
   True justice dost dispense.

DR SWIFT.

(9) Observe the con-
nection.
(1) Sec*oure*.
(2) That's right, doc-
tor; but then there will
be no *contending*, as you
desired a while ago.

'Tis wonderful that Provi-
        dence
   Should save thee from
        the halter,
Who hast in numbers
        without sense
   Burlesqued the holy
        Psalter.
(1) That's no great
mark of viewing them
with justice. God has
wiser ends for passing by
His vengeance on the
wicked, you profane
dunce!
   What's that charge? it
must allude to a charge
of gunpowder, or it is
nonsense.

(2) Ay, but what sort
of things are these in-
flictions?
(3) If the mischiefs be
in their mind, what need
they return on themselves?
are they not there already?
(4) Ret*orn*.

(5) Pills.
(6) Rich.
Does this verse end
according to the more
modern art of poetry, as
the author speaks in his
preface?

Do not these verses end
very sublimely?

DR GIBBS.

VIII. Psalm of David:

. . . . .

1 The mighty powers, that celebrate
Thy endless praises, can't relate
The glory they in Heaven survey:
2 *Young* helpless *infants* at the breast
Their great Creator have confest,
And in their weakness spoke Thy
pow'r,

. . . . .

4 Lord, what is wretched (7) man, I cry,
Or all his sinful progeny,
That thou to them dost prove so kind !
5 To honour Thou dost them prefer,
To angels scarce inferior,
6   They over all Thy works command :
7 The flocks and herds o'er every field
To their just lords obedience yield,
And all (1) in full subjection stand :

8 O'er all the birds, that mount the air,
And fish, that in the floods appear, (2)
Man bears an arbitrary sway :

. . . . .

IX. Psalm of David :

3 Confounded at the sight of Thee
My foes are put to flight ; (3)
4 Thus thou, great God of equity,
Dost still assert my right. (4)

. . . . .

6 Insulting foes, how long can ye
Of ruin'd cities boast ! (5)
Your plunderings now as well as they
Are in oblivion lost :

7 But God eternally remains
(6) Fixt in His throne on high,
8 And to the world from thence ordains
(7) Impartial equity :

. . . . .

9 And for their injured souls extend
A refuge most secure.

. . . . . .

DR SWIFT.

That's a lie; for if they
can survey it they can
easily relate it.
Young younglings.
[The italics are Swift's.]
This stanza is just upon
the purlieus between sense
and nonsense.

(7) A very proper epi-
thet for those who are
scarce inferior to angels.

A fine cadence that.

(1) That's a lie, for
sometimes they trespass
on other men's grounds.

(2) App*ai*r.
Those, I think, are
not very many: they are
good fish when they are
caught, but till then we
have no great sway over
them.

(3) The doctor's mis-
taken; for, when people
are confounded, they can-
not fly.
(4) Against Sternhold
and Hopkins.

(5) b*o*st.
Blunderings, *Sic corrige
meo periculo*. That's a
lie, for Gibbs remembers
them.

(6) That's false and
profane; God is not fixed
anywhere.
(7) Did anybody ever
hear of *partial* equity ?

That extending a re-
fuge, is pretty.

DR GIBBS.	DR SWIFT.
12 He hears the injured poor, and then 　　Does all their cries resent.	*i.e.* is angry at their cries.

13 And thus consider still, O Lord, 　　The justice of my cause; Who often hast my life (8) restor'd From death's devouring jaws : 　.　　.　　.　　.　　.　　.	(8) Nothing is restored but what has been taken away; so that he has been often raised from the dead, if this be true.
15 The heathen nations are dismay'd (9) 　　They're all to ruin brought, For in the treacherous nets, they laid, Ev'n they themselves are caught : 16 Lo, thus the Lord to execute 　　True judgment still inclines ; 　.　　.　　.　　.　　.　　.	(9) We heard a while ago their very names were dead,[1] now (it seems) they're only dismay'd. 　This is profane, as if it were only an inclination in God to be just.

X. PSALM OF DAVID :

1 Lord, why in times of deep distress 　　Dost Thou from us retire, When dismal woes our souls oppress, 　　And Thy kind aid require !	If the woes require aid it is to increase them, they cannot require it against themselves.
2 The wicked do with lawless pride (1) 　　The helpless persecute; But let them be themselves destroy'd, 　　And fall in their pursuit :	(1) Proide. Pronounce it like the Scotch. 　Ay, let them !
3 For still they triumph, when success 　　Does their designs attend, And then their ways, who thus oppress, 　　Profanely they commend : 　.　　.　　.　　.　　.　　.	I cannot crock this stave.
5 And from the barbarous (2) paths they 　　　　tread, 　　No acts of Providence Can e'er oblige them to recede,	(2) The author should first have premised what sort of paths were properly barbarous. I suppose they must be very deep and dirty, or very rugged and stony; both which I myself have heard travellers call barbarous roads.

---

[1] Ver. 5. "They and their very names are dead."

DR GIBBS.

Or stop (3) their bold offence;

.   .   .   .   .

And for the poor in secret they
Do treacherously lay wait:

As hungry lions do their prey
  Observe with watchful eyes,
So heedless innocents would they
  With sudden force surprise;

And then, like lions merciless,
  Their trembling souls devour;
And thus the helpless do oppress (4)
  When captives to their power;

.   .   .   .   .

no more
[rhyming with pow'r.]

.   .   .   .   .

deserts
[rhyming with hearts.]

.   .   .   .   .

XI. PSALM OF DAVID:

come on,
[rhyming with shun.]

.   .   .   .   .

For if the Power, in which they trust,
  Should fail, how helpless are the just!

.   .   .   .   .

And on their impious heads will pour
  Of snares (1) and flames a dismal
    shower;
And this their bitter cup must be
  (2) To drink to all eternity:

.   .   .   .   .

XII. PSALM OF DAVID:

O Lord, some help for me provide,
For in but few I can confide,
  All men are so perfidious grown;

DR SWIFT.

(3) Which is the way to
stop an offence? Would
you have it stopped like a
bottle, or a thief?
  For what end? is it to
catch a louse, better lay
wait for the rich by half.
  As a lion observes with
watchful eyes, just so a
wicked man surprises
with sudden force—a very
just simile.
  They surprise them like
lions, but then they devour
them [like] lions.
  (4) This line is dry
nonsense or false gram-
mar, and will bear no jest.

No mour. Pronounce
this like my lady's woman.

Desarts. Pronounce
this like my lady's house-
maid.

Come un. Pronounce
this like a chambermaid.
  The force of his argu-
ment lies here: he does
not fear his enemies, be-
cause if God's power
should fail he has no
help.
  (1) A shower of snares
on a man's head would
do wonderful execution.
However, I grant it is a
scurvy thing enough to
swallow them.
  (2) To taste the doc-
tor's poetry.

He can confide in but
few because all are per-
fidious. Smoke that!

DR GIBBS.	DR SWIFT.
2 True mutual kindness they pretend, ...	Did ever any man pretend mutual kindness to another?
3 But God those flatterers will confound, That with abusive lies abound, And proudly boast their vicious ways,	Qu : whether flatterers usually abound with abusive lies ?
4 That say, with our deceitful tongues	If they say thus they are silly flatterers.
6 And since He thus was pleased to say, Like gold refined from base alloy, His promise never can deceive ; (3)	That comparison is well applied. (3) Deceeve. Pronounce this like a beau.
7 And therefore will their cause assert, Who thus are pure and true of heart, And save them from the enemy ;	Examine well the grammar and sense and the elegance of this stanza.
8 For, when th' ungodly meet success, The wicked more and more increase, (1) And proudly all their foes defy.	Here the author separates the wicked from the ungodly. (1) Incress.

XIII. PSALM OF DAVID :

1 How long wilt Thou neglect, O Lord, to hear me pray !	A civil question that !
3 Attend, and hear my cries, Some comfort now disclose, E'er grief has shut my weeping eyes In death's obscure repose :	Mind me, Sir ! Which would be nonsense, put in prose.
4 Lest my proud enemy, If now my trust should fail, And those that persecute me cry ; See, thus we still prevail :	A pretty speech, that !

XIV. PSALM OF DAVID :

1 Hence virtue in the world declines, And all men vicious grow.	Without question virtue declines with a vengeance when all men grow vicious.
2 And see who would His being own, And Him, as God, adore :	What other way is there of adoring ?
3 (2) But they were all perverted grown, Polluted all with blood,	(2) But they were all perverted grown,

DR GIBBS.

And other impious crimes; not one
  Was either just (3) or good.

4 Are they so stupid (4) then, said (5) God,
  Who thus My (6) saints devour !
  These (7) crimes have they not under-
      stood,
  Nor thought upon My power !

. . . . . .

7 (1) O, that His aid we now might have
  From Sion's holy hill,
  That God the captive just would save,
  And glad all Israel.

DR SWIFT.

In spite of Dr. Gibbs
      his blood :
Of all his impious rhimes
      not one
  Was either just or good.

(3) For a man (it seems)
may be good and not just.
(4) The fault was not
that they devoured saints,
but that they were stupid.
Qu : Whether stupidity
makes men devour saints,
or devouring saints makes
a man stupid ? I believe
the latter, because they
may be apt to lie heavy
in one's stomach.
  (5) Clod.
  (6) Strains.
  (7) Rhimes.

(1) And O that every
      parish clerk,
  Who hums what Brady
      cribs
  From Hopkins, would
      read this work,
  And glad the heart with
      Gibbs.

XV. Psalm of David :

Representing the character of a good man.

. . . . . .

2 Sincere, and just, who never lie ;

3 And so their neighbour ne'er deceive,

. . . . . .

5 All those that lead a life like this
  Shall reign in everlasting bliss. (2)

And a bad poet.

How *so ?*

(2) And so the doctor
now may kiss —— !

FINIS.

F iddling I mpudent N auseous I lliterate S coundrel Scot.
  oolish   dle   onsensical gnorant   ot.

APPENDIX II.

A

PROPOSAL

HUMBLY OFFERED TO THE

P   T

FOR THE MORE EFFECTUAL PREVENTING THE FURTHER GROWTH OF POPERY.

WITH THE

DESCRIPTION AND USE OF THE ECCLESIASTICAL THERMO-METER, VERY PROPER FOR ALL FAMILIES.

" Insani sanus nomen ferat, æquus iniqui,
Ultra quàm satis est, virtutem si petat ipsam."
HOR. Epist. I. vi. 16.

THIS "Proposal," which has not been included in the editions of Swift's Works issued by Scott, Faulkner, or Hawkesworth, appeared originally, but in a shorter form, in the "Tatler" (No. 220, September 4th, 1710). In this form the whole of the first portion, from the beginning to the paragraph commencing "The Church thermometer," is omitted, as are also the last paragraphs of the essay, including the "Advertisement." The text of the present reprint I have taken from the "Miscellanies," vol. viii., 1745 (pp. 217-229). In all modern editions of the "Tatler" this paper is ascribed to Addison; but the style and the subject are so characteristic of Swift that, although I am not in a position to say definitely that it is by him, I think it deserves a place in the form of an Appendix. The date of its appearance in the "Tatler" is somewhat against Swift having written it, since he was at that time on his way to London; and of the few contributions he sent to the "Tatler" it is agreed by all editors that the first is the paper on the same subject as the letter to the Lord High Treasurer, which appeared in No. 230 (September 28th, 1710).

[T. S.]

APPENDIX II.

PROPOSAL FOR PREVENTING THE FURTHER GROWTH OF POPERY.

HAVING, with great sorrow of heart, observed the increase of Popery among us of late years, and how ineffectual the penal laws and statutes of this realm have been, for near forty years last past, towards reclaiming that blind and deluded people from their errors, notwithstanding the good intentions of the legislators, and the pious and unwearied labours of the many learned divines of the Established Church, who have preached to them without ceasing, although hitherto without success:

Having also remarked, in his Grace's speech to both Houses of Parliament, most kind offers of his Grace's good offices towards obtaining such further laws as shall be thought necessary towards bringing home the said wandering sheep into the fold of the Church, as also a good disposition in the parliament to join in the laudable work, towards which every good Protestant ought to contribute at least his advice: I think it a proper time to lay before the public a scheme which was writ some years since, and laid by to be ready on a fit occasion.

That, whereas the several penal laws and statutes now in being against Papists, have been found ineffectual, and rather tend to confirm, than reclaim men from their errors, as calling a man coward, is a ready way to make him fight; It is humbly proposed,

I. That the said penal laws and statutes against Papists, except the law of Gavelkind, and that which disqualifies them for places, be repealed, abrogated, annulled, destroyed, and obliterated, to all intents and purposes.

II. That, in the room of the said penal laws and statutes, all ecclesiastical jurisdiction be taken from out of the hands of the clergy of the established Church, and the same be vested in the several popish archbishops, bishops, deans and arch-deacons; nevertheless so as such jurisdiction be exercised over persons of the Popish religion only.

III. That a Popish priest shall be settled by law in each and every parish in Ireland.

IV. That the said Popish priest shall, on taking the oath of allegiance to his majesty, be entitled to a tenth part or tithe of all things tithable in Ireland, belonging to the papists, within their respective parishes, yet so as such grant of tithes to such Popish priests, shall not be construed, in law or equity, to hinder the Protestant clergyman of such parish from receiving and collecting his tithes in like manner as he does at present.

V. That, in case of detention or subtraction of tithes by any Papist, the parish priest do have his remedy at law in any of his majesty's courts, in the same manner as now practised by the clergy of the Established Church; together with all other ecclesiastical dues. And, for their further discovery to vex their people at law, it might not be amiss to oblige the solicitor-general, or some other able king's counsel, to give his advice, or assistance to such priests gratis, for which he might receive a salary out of the Barrack Fund, Military Contingencies, or Concordatum; having observed the exceedings there better paid than of the army, or any other branch of the establishment; and I would have no delay in payment in a matter of this importance.

VI. That the archbishops and bishops have power to visit the inferior clergy, and to extort proxies, exhibits, and all other perquisites usual in Popish and Protestant countries.

VII. That the convocation having been found, by long experience, to be hurtful to true religion, be for ever hereafter abolished among Protestants.

VIII. That, in the room thereof, the Popish archbishops, bishops, priests, deans, arch-deacons, and proctors, have liberty to assemble themselves in convocation, and be im-

powered to make such canons as they shall think proper for
the government of the Papists in Ireland:

IX. And that, the secular arm being necessary to enforce
obedience to ecclesiastical censure, the sheriffs, constables,
and other officers, be commanded to execute the decrees
and sentences of the said popish convocation, with secrecy
and dispatch, or, in lieu thereof, they may·be at liberty to
erect an inquisition, with proper officers of their own.

X. That, as Papists declare themselves converts to the
Established Church, all spiritual power over them shall
cease.

XI. That as soon as any whole parish shall renounce the
Popish religion, the priest of such parish shall, for his good
services, have a pension of £200 per ann. settled on him
for life, and that he be from such time exempt from preaching and praying, and other duties of his function, in like
manner as protestant divines, with equal incomes, are at
present.

XII. That each bishop, so soon as his diocese shall become protestants, be called, My Lord, and have a pension
of two thousand pounds per annum during life.

XIII. That when a whole province shall be reclaimed,
the archbishop shall be called His Grace, and have a
pension of three thousand pounds per ann. during life, and
be admitted a member of his majesty's most honourable
privy council.

The good consequences of this scheme, (which will execute
itself without murmurings against the government) are very
visible: I shall mention a few of the most obvious.

I. The giving the priest a right to the tithe would produce
law-suits and wrangles; his reverence, being entituled to a
certain income at all events, would consider himself as a
legal incumbent, and behave accordingly, and apply himself
more to fleecing than feeding his flock; his necessary
attendance on the courts of justice would leave his people
without a spiritual guide; by which means protestant curates,
who have no suits about tithes, would be furnished with
proper opportunities for making converts, which is very much
wanted.

II. The erecting a spiritual jurisdiction amongst them
would, in all probability, drive as many out of that commu-

nion, as a due execution of such jurisdiction hath hitherto drove from amongst ourselves.

III. An inquisition would still be a further improvement, and most certainly would expedite the conversion of Papists.

I know it may be objected to this scheme, and with some shew of reason, that, should the Popish princes abroad pursue the same methods, with regard to their protestant subjects, the Protestant interest in Europe would thereby be considerably weakened: but as we have no reason to suspect Popish counsels will ever produce so much moderation, I think the objection ought to have but little weight.

A due execution of this scheme will soon produce many converts from Popery; nevertheless, to the end may it be known, when they shall be of the true Church, I have ordered a large parcel of ecclesiastical or Church thermometers to be made, one of which is to be hung up in each parish church, the description and use of which take as follows, in the words of the ingenious Isaac Bickerstaff, Esq.

The [1] Church thermometer, which I am now to treat of, is supposed have been invented in the reign of Henry the Eighth, about the time when that religious prince put some to death for owning the Pope's supremacy, and others for denying transubstantiation. I do not find, however, any great use made of this instrument till it fell into the hand of a learned and vigilant priest or minister, (for he frequently wrote himself both the one and the other) who was some time Vicar of Bray. This gentleman lived in his vicarage to a good old age; and after having seen several successions of his neighbouring clergy either burnt or banished, departed this life with the satisfaction of having never deserted his flock,

---

[1] In the "Tatler" this paragraph is preceded by the following:

"*From my own apartment, Sept.* 4.—Having received many letters filled with compliments and acknowledgments for my late useful discovery of the political barometer, I shall here communicate to the public an account of my ecclesiastical thermometer, the latter giving as manifest prognostications of the changes and revolutions in Church, as the former does of those in State, and both of them being absolutely necessary for every prudent subject who is resolved to keep what he has, and get what he can." [T. S.]

and died Vicar of Bray. As this glass was first designed to calculate the different degrees of heat in religion, as it raged in Popery, or as it cooled, and grew temperate in the Reformation, it was marked at several distances, after the manner our ordinary thermometer is to this day, viz. extreme hot sultry hot, very hot, hot, warm, temperate, cold, just freezing, frost, hard frost, great frost, extreme cold.

It is well known, that Torricellius,[1] the inventor of the common weather-glass, made the experiment of a long tube which held thirty-two foot of water ; and that a more modern virtuoso finding such a machine altogether unwieldly and useless, and considering that thirty-two inches of quicksilver weighed as much as so many foot of water in a tube of the same circumference, invented that sizeable instrument which is now in use. After this manner, that I might adapt the thermometer I am now speaking of to the present constitution of our Church, as divided into High and Low, I have made some necessary variations both in the tube and the fluid it contains. In the first place I ordered a tube to be cast in a planetary hour, and took care to seal it hermetically, when the sun was in conjunction with Saturn. I then took the proper precautions about the fluid, which is a compound of two different liquors ; one of them a spirit drawn out of a strong heady wine ; the other a particular sort of rock-water, colder than ice, and clearer than crystal. The spirit is of a red, fiery colour, and so very apt to ferment, that, unless it be mingled with a proportion of the water, or pent up very close, it will burst the vessel that holds it, and fly up in a fume and smoke. The water, on the contrary, is of such a subtile, piercing cold, that, unless it be mingled with a proportion of the spirits, it will sink almost through every thing it is put into, and seems to be of the same nature as the water mentioned by Quintus Curtius, which says the historian, could be contained in nothing but in the hoof, or (as the Oxford Manuscript has it) the skull of an ass. The thermometer is marked according to the following figure, which I set down at length, not only to give my reader a clear idea of it, but also to fill up my paper.

---

[1] Evangelista Torricelli (1608-1647) was assistant to Galileo, and is famous as the discoverer of the phenomena on which he made the barometer. In 1644 he published "Opera Geometrica." [T. S.]

> Ignorance.
> Persecution.
> Wrath.
> Zeal.
> CHURCH.
> Moderation.
> Lukewarmness.
> Infidelity.
> Ignorance.

The reader will observe, that the Church is placed in the middle point of the glass between Zeal and Moderation, the situation in which she always flourishes, and in which every good Englishman wishes her, who is a friend to the constitution of his country.   However, when it mounts to Zeal, it is not amiss; and, when it sinks to Moderation, it is still in admirable temper.   The worst of it is, that when once it begins to rise, it has still an inclination to ascend, insomuch that it is apt to climb from Zeal to Wrath, and from Wrath to Persecution, which often ends in Ignorance, and very often proceeds from it.   In the same manner it frequently takes its progress through the lower half of the glass; and, when it has a tendency to fall, will gradually descend from Moderation to Lukewarmness, and from Lukewarmness to Infidelity, which very often terminates in Ignorance, and always proceeds from it.

It is a common observation, that the ordinary thermometer will be affected by the breathing of people who are in the room where it stands, and indeed it is almost incredible to conceive how the glass I am now describing, will fall by the breath of the multitude crying Popery; or, on the contrary, how it will rise when the same multitude (as it sometimes happens) cry out in the same breath, *The Church is in Danger*.

As soon as I have finished this my glass, and adjusted it to the above-mentioned scale of religion, that I might make proper experiments with it, I carried it under my cloak to several coffee-houses, and other places of resort, about this great city.   At Saint James's Coffee-house the liquor stood at Moderation; but at Will's, to my extreme surprise, it subsided to the very lowest mark of the glass.   At the

Grecian it mounted but just one point higher; at the Rainbow it still ascended two degrees; Child's fetched it up to Zeal, and other adjacent coffee-houses to Wrath.

It fell in the lower half of the glass as I went further into the City, till at length it settled at Moderation, where it continued all the time I stayed about the Change, as also whilst I passed by the Bank. And here I cannot but take notice, that, through the whole course of my remarks, I never observed my glass to rise at the same time that the stocks did.

To complete the experiment, I prevailed upon a friend of mine, who works under me in the occult sciences, to make a progress with my glass through the whole Island of Great Britain; and, after his return, to present me with a register of his observations. I guessed beforehand at the temper of several places he passed through, by the characters they have had time out of mind. Thus that facetious divine, Dr. Fuller,[1] speaking of the town of Banbury near a hundred years ago, tells us, it was a place famous for cakes and zeal, which I find by my glass is true to this day, as to the latter part of his description; though I must confess, it is not in the same reputation for cakes that it was in the time of that learned author; and thus of other places. In short, I have now by me, digested in an alphabetical order, all the counties, corporations, and boroughs in Great Britain, with their respective tempers, as they stand related to my thermometer. But this I shall keep to myself, because I would by no means do any thing that may seem to influence any ensuing election.

The point of doctrine which I would propagate by this my invention, is the same which was long ago advanced by that able teacher Horace, out of whom I have taken my text for this discourse: We should be careful not to over-shoot ourselves in the pursuits even of virtue. Whether zeal or moderation be the point we aim at, let us keep fire out of the one, and frost out of the other. But, alas! the world is too wise to want such a precaution. The terms High-Church and Low-Church, as commonly used, do not so much denote

---

[1] Thomas Fuller, D.D. (1608-1661) was the author of "History of the Worthies of England," "History of the Holy War," and many other works distinguished for their humour and style. [T. S.]

a principle, as they distinguish a party.   They are like words
of battle, they have nothing to do with their original signifi-,
cation, but are only given out to keep a body of men together,
and to let them know friends from enemies.

I must confess I have considered, with some attention,
the influence which the opinions of these great national sects
have upon their practice ; and do look upon it as one of
the unaccountable things of our times, that multitudes of
honest gentlemen, who entirely agree in their lives, should
take it in their heads to differ in their religion.[1]

I shall conclude this paper with an account of a confer-
ence which happened between a very excellent divine (whose
doctrine was easy, and formerly much respected) and a lawyer.

And behold a certain lawyer stood up, and tempted him,
saying, Master, what shall I do to inherit eternal life ?

He said unto him, What is written in the law?   How
readest thou ?

And he answering said, Thou shalt love the Lord thy
God with all thy heart, and with all thy soul, and with
all thy strength, and with all thy mind ; and thy neighbour
as thyself.

And he said unto him, Thou hast answered right; this do,
and thou shalt live.

But he, willing to justify himself, said unto Jesus, And
who is my neighbour ?

And Jesus answering, said ; A certain man went down
from Jerusalem to Jericho, and fell among thieves, which
stripped him of his raiment, and wounded him, and departed,
leaving him half dead.

And by chance there came down a certain priest that
way ; and, when he saw him, he passed by on the other side.

And likewise a Levite, when he was at the place, came and
looked on him, and passed by on the other side.

But a certain Samaritan, as he journeyed, came where he
was ; and, when he saw him, he had compassion on him.

And went to him, and bound up his wounds, pouring in
oil and wine ; and set him on his own beast, and brought
him to an inn, and took care of him.

[1] Here the " Tatler " paper ends.   [T. S.]

And on the morrow, when he departed, he took out two pence, and gave them to the host, and said unto him, Take care of him, and whatsoever thou spendest more, when I come again, I will repay thee.

Which now of these three, thinkest thou, was neighbour unto him that fell among the thieves?

And he said, He that shewed mercy on him. Then said Jesus unto him, Go, and do thou likewise. Luke x. 25 to 38.

Advertisement.

There is now in the press a proposal for raising a fund towards paying the National Debt by the following means: The author would have commissioners appointed to search all the public and private libraries, booksellers shops and warehouses, in this kingdom, for such books as are of no use to the owner, or to the public, viz. all comments on the Holy Scriptures, whether called sermons, creeds, bodies of divinity, tomes of casuistry, vindications, confutations, essays, answers, replies, rejoinders, or sur-rejoinders, together with all other learned treatises and books of divinity, of what denomination or class soever; as also all comments on the laws of the land, such as reports, law-cases, decrees, guides for attorneys and young clerks, and, in fine, all the books now in being in this kingdom (whether of divinity, law, physic, metaphysics, logics or politics) except the pure text of the Holy Scriptures, the naked text of the laws, a few books of morality, poetry, music, architecture, agriculture, mathematics, merchandise and history; the author would have the aforesaid useless books carried to the several paper-mills, there to be wrought into white paper, which, to prevent damage or complaints, he would have performed by the commentators, critics, popular preachers, apothecaries, learned lawyers, attorneys, solicitors, logicians, physicians, almanac-makers, and others of the like wrong turn of mind; the said paper to be sold, and the produce applied to discharge the National Debt; what should remain of the said debt unsatisfied, might be paid by a tax on the salaries or estates of bankers, common cheats, usurers, treasurers, embezzelers of public money, general officers, sharpers, pensioners, pick-pockets, &c.

IV. S

APPENDIX III.

SWIFT AND SERJEANT BETTESWORTH.

APPENDIX III.

SWIFT AND SERJEANT BETTESWORTH.

THE *rencontre* with Serjeant Bettesworth, to which reference has already been made in the note prefixed to "The Presbyterians' Plea of Merit," is further illustrated by the Resolution which the inhabitants of the Liberty of St. Patrick's passed, and which they presented to the Dean. Bettesworth, as a note in the thirteenth volume of Swift's works (1762) states, "engaged his footman and two ruffians to attend him, in order to secure the dean wherever they met him, until he had gratified his resentment either by maiming or stabbing him." Accordingly, he went directly to the deanery, and hearing the Dean was at a friend's house (Rev. Mr. John Worrall's in Big Ship Street), followed him thither, charged him with writing the said verses, but had not courage enough to put his bloody design in execution. However, as he had the assurance to relate this affair to several noblemen and gentlemen, the inhabitants of the Liberty of St. Patrick's waited upon the Dean, and presented the following paper, signed by above thirty of them, in the name of themselves, and the rest of their neighbourhood:

"We the inhabitants of the Liberty of the Dean and Chapter of St Patrick's Dublin, and the neighbourhood of the same, having been informed, by universal report, that a certain man of this city hath openly threatened, and sworn before many hundred people, as well persons of quality as others, that he resolves upon the first opportunity, by the help of several ruffians, to murder or maim the Reverend the Dean of St. Patrick, our neighbour, benefactor, and the head of the Liberty of St Patrick, upon a frivolous unproved suspicion of the said Dean's having written some lines in verse reflecting on the said man.

"Therefore, we, the said inhabitants of the said Liberty, and in the neighbourhood thereof, from our great love and respect to the said Dean, to whom the whole kingdom hath so many obligations, as well as we of the Liberty, do unanimously declare, that we will endeavour to defend the life and limbs of the said Dean against the said man, and all his ruffians and murderers, as far as the law will allow, if he or any of them presume to come into the said Liberty with any wicked malicious intent against the house, or family, or person, or goods of the said Dean.   To which we have cheerfully, sincerely, and heartily set our hands."

Swift, at the time of receiving this Resolution lay very ill in bed, and was unable to receive the deputation in person. He, however, dictated the following reply :

"GENTLEMEN,
        "I receive, with great thankfulness, these many kind expressions of your concern for my safety, as well as your declared resolution to defend me (as far as the laws of God and man will allow) against all murderers and ruffians, who shall attempt to enter into the liberty with any bloody or wicked designs upon my life, my limbs, my house, or my goods.   Gentlemen, my life is in the hand of God, and whether it may be cut off by treachery or open violence, or by the common way of other men ; as long as it continueth, I shall ever bear a grateful memory for this favour you have shewn, beyond my expectation, and almost exceeding my wishes.

"The inhabitants of the liberty, as well as those of the neighbourhood, have lived with me in great amity for near twenty years; which I am confident will never diminish during my life.   I am chiefly sorry, that by two cruel disorders of deafness and giddiness, which have pursued me for four months, I am not in condition either to hear, or to receive you, much less to return my most sincere acknowledgements, which in justice and gratitude I ought to do. May God bless you and your families in this world, and make you for ever happy in the next."

The poem itself to which Bettesworth took exception is herewith reprinted, as well as three others occasioned by the Bettesworth action.

ON THE WORDS

BROTHER PROTESTANTS AND FELLOW CHRISTIANS,

SO FAMILIARLY USED BY THE ADVOCATES FOR THE REPEAL

OF THE TEST-ACT IN IRELAND.   1733.

" AN inundation, says the fable,
Overflow'd a farmer's barn and stable ;
Whole ricks of hay and sacks of corn
Were down the sudden current borne ;
While things of heterogeneous kind
Together float with tide and wind.
The generous wheat forgot its pride,
And sail'd with litter side by side ;
Uniting all, to shew their amity,
As in a general calamity.
A ball of new-dropp'd horse's dung,
Mingling with apples in the throng,
Said to the pippin plump and prim,
' See, brother, how we apples swim.'
    Thus Lamb, renown'd for cutting corns,
An offer'd fee from Radcliff scorns,
' Not for the world—we doctors, brother,
Must take no fees of one another.'
Thus to a dean some curate sloven
Subscribes, ' Dear sir, your brother loving.'
Thus all the footmen, shoeboys, porters,
About St James's cry, ' We courtiers.'
Thus Horace in the house will prate,
' Sir, we, the ministers of state.'
Thus at the bar the booby Bettesworth,
Though half a crown o'erpays his sweat's worth ;
Who knows in law nor text nor margent,

Calls Singleton [1] his brother sergeant.[2]
And thus fanatic saints, though neither in
Doctrine nor discipline our brethren,
Are brother Protestants and Christians,
As much as Hebrews and Philistines:
But in no other sense, than nature
Has made a rat our fellow-creature.
Lice from your body suck their food;
But is a louse your flesh and blood?
Though born of human filth and sweat, it
As well may say man did beget it.
And maggots in your nose and chin
As well may claim you for their kin.
   Yet critics may object, why not?
Since lice are brethren to a Scot:
Which made our swarm of sects determine
Employments for their brother vermin.
But be they English, Irish, Scottish,
What Protestant can be so sottish,
While o'er the church these clouds are gathering,
To call a swarm of lice his brethren?
   " As Moses, by divine advice,
In Egypt turn'd the dust to lice;
And as our sects, by all descriptions,
Have hearts more harden'd than Egyptians;
As from the trodden dust they spring,
And, turn'd to lice, infest the king:
For pity's sake, it would be just,
A rod should turn them back to dust.
   Let folks in high or holy stations
Be proud of owning such relations;
Let courtiers hug them in their bosom,
As if they were afraid to lose 'em:
While I, with humble Job, had rather
Say to corruption—'Thou 'rt my father.'
For he that has so little wit
To nourish vermin, may be bit."

---

[1] Henry Singleton, Esq., then prime sergeant, afterwards lord-chief-justice of the common pleas, which he resigned, and was some time after made master of the rolls. [F.]
  [2] These lines occasioned the personal attack upon the Dean. [T. S.]

AN EPIGRAM.[1]

INSCRIBED TO THE HONOURABLE SERGEANT KITE.

" In your indignation what mercy appears,
While Jonathan's threaten'd with loss of his ears ;
For who would not think it a much better choice,
By your knife to be mangled than rack'd with your voice.
If truly you [would] be revenged on the parson,
Command his attendance while you act your farce on ;
Instead of your maiming, your shooting, or banging,
Bid *Povey*[2] secure him while you are haranguing.
Had this been your method to torture him, long since,
He had cut his own ears to be deaf to your nonsense."

"THE YAHOO'S OVERTHROW ; OR, THE KEVAN BAYL'S NEW BALLAD.[3]

UPON SERGEANT KITE'S INSULTING THE DEAN.

To the Tune of " Derry Down."

" Jolly boys of St Kevan's,[4] St Patrick's, Donore,
And Smithfield, I'll tell you, if not told before,
How Bettesworth, that booby, and scoundrel in grain,
Has insulted us all by insulting the Dean.
     Knock him down, down, down, knock him down.

[1] Now first published from a copy in the Dean's handwriting, in possession of J. Connill, Esq. [S.]
[2] Povey was sergeant-at-arms to the House of Commons.
[3] " Grub Street Journal," No. 189, August 9th, 1734. — " In December last, Mr Bettesworth of the city of Dublin, serjeant-at-law, and member of parliament, openly swore, before many hundreds of people, that, upon the first opportunity, by the help of ruffians, he would murder or maim the Dean of St. Patrick's, (Dr Swift).   Upon which thirty-one of the principal inhabitants of that liberty signed a paper to this effect : ' That, out of their great love and respect to the Dean, to whom the

[4] Kevan Bayl was a cant expression for the mob of this district of Dublin.

" The Dean and his merits we every one know,
But this skip of a lawyer, where the de'il did he grow?
How greater his merit at Four Courts or House,
Than the barking of Towzer, or leap of a louse !
                              Knock him down, &c.

" That he came from the Temple, his morals do show ;
But where his deep law is, few mortals yet know :
His rhetoric, bombast, silly jests, are by far
More like to lampooning, than pleading at bar.
                              Knock him down, &c.

" This pedlar, at speaking and making of laws,
Has met with returns of all sorts but applause ;
Has, with noise and odd gestures, been prating some years,
What honester folk never durst for their ears.
                              Knock him down, &c.

" Of all sizes and sorts, the fanatical crew
Are his brother Protestants, good men and true ;
Red hat, and blue bonnet, and turban's the same,
What the de'il is't to him whence the devil they came.
                              Knock him down, &c.

" Hobbes, Tindal, and Woolston, and Collins, and Nayler,
And Muggleton, Toland, and Bradley the tailor,
Are Christians alike ; and it may be averr'd,
He's a Christian as good as the rest of the herd.
                              Knock him down, &c.

" He only the rights of the clergy debates ;
Their rights ! their importance !   We'll set on new rates
On their tithes at half-nothing, their priesthood at less ; .
What's next to be voted with ease you may guess.
                              Knock him down, &c.

whole kingdom hath so many obligations, they would endeavour to
defend the life and limbs of the said Dean against a certain man and all
his ruffians and murderers.' With which paper they, in the name of
themselves and all the inhabitants of the city, attended the Dean on
January 8, who being extremely ill in bed of a giddiness and deafness,
and not able to receive them, immediately dictated a very grateful
answer. The occasion of a certain man's declaration of his villainous
design against the Dean, was a frivolous unproved suspicion that he
had written some lines in verse reflecting upon him."

" At length his old master, (I need not him name,)
To this damnable speaker had long owed a shame ;
When his speech came abroad, he paid him off clean,
By leaving him under the pen of the Dean.
Knock him down, &c.

" He kindled, as if the whole satire had been
The oppression of virtue, not wages of sin :
He began, as he bragg'd, with a rant and a roar ;
He bragg'd how he bounced, and he swore how he swore.[1]
Knock him down, &c.

" Though he cringed to his deanship in very low strains,
To others he boasted of knocking out brains,
And slitting of noses, and cropping of ears,
While his own ass's zags were more fit for the shears.
Knock him down, &c.

" On this worrier of deans whene'er we can hit,
We'll shew him the way how to crop and to slit ;
We'll teach him some better address to afford
To the dean of all deans, though he wears not a sword.
Knock him down, &c.

" We'll colt him through Kevan, St Patrick's, Donore,
And Smithfield, as rap was ne'er colted before ;
We'll oil him with kennel, and powder him with grains,
A modus right fit for insulters of deans.
Knock him down, &c.

" And, when this is over, we'll make him amends,
To the Dean he shall go ; they shall kiss and be friends :
But how ?   Why, the Dean shall to him disclose
A face for to kiss, without eyes, ears, or nose.
Knock him down, &c.

" If you say this is hard on a man that is reckon'd
That sergeant-at-law whom we call Kite the Second,

---

[1] See the Dean's letter to the Duke of Dorset, in which he gives an account of his interview with Bettesworth, about which he alleges the serjeant had spread abroad five hundred falsehoods.   [S.]

You mistake ; for a slave, who will coax his superiors,
May be proud to be licking a great man's posteriors.
                         Knock him down, &c.

"What care we how high runs his passion or pride?
Though his soul he despises, he values his hide ;
Then fear not his tongue, or his sword, or his knife ;
He'll take his revenge on his innocent wife.
         Knock him down, down, down, keep him down."

"ON THE ARCHBISHOP OF CASHEL,[1] AND BETTESWORTH.

"DEAR DICK, pr'ythee tell by what passion you move?
The world is in doubt whether hatred or love ;
And, while at good Cashel you rail with such spite,
They shrewdly suspect it is all but a bite.
You certainly know, though so loudly you vapour,
His spite cannot wound who attempted the Drapier.
Then, pr'ythee, reflect, take a word of advice ;
And, as your old wont is, change sides in a trice :
On his virtues hold forth ; 'tis the very best way ;
And say of the man what all honest men say.
But if, still obdurate, your anger remains,
If still your foul bosom more rancour contains,
Say then more than they, nay, lavishly flatter ;
'Tis your gross panegyrics alone can bespatter ;
For thine, my dear Dick, give me leave to speak plain,
Like very foul mops, dirty more than they clean."

             [1] Dr. Theophilus Bolton. [T. S.]

The letter to the Earl of Dorset, containing Swift's version of the story is as follows :

"January, 1734.

"MY LORD,

"It has been my great misfortune that since your grace's return to this kingdom I have not been able to attend you, as my duty and gratitude for your favours as well as the honour of having been so many years known to you obliged me to do. I have been pursued by two old disorders, a giddiness and deafness, which used to leave me in three or four weeks, but now have continued four months. Thus I am put under a necessity to write what I would rather have chosen to say in your grace's presence.

"On Monday last week towards evening there came to the deanery one Mr. Bettesworth; who, being told by the servants that I was gone to a friend's house,¹ went thither to inquire for me, and was admitted into the street parlour. I left my company in the back room and went to him. He began with asking me 'whether I were the author of certain verses wherein he was reflected on.' The singularity of the man, in his countenance, manner, action, style, and tone of voice, made me call to mind that I had once seen him about two or three years ago at Mr. Ludlow's country-house. But I could not recollect his name; and of what calling he might be I had never heard. I therefore desired to know who and what he was; said 'I had heard of some such verses, but knew no more.' He then signified to me 'that he was a serjeant-at-law and a member of parliament.' After which he repeated the lines that concerned him with great emphasis; said 'I was mistaken in one thing, for he assured me he was no booby, but owned himself to be a coxcomb.' However, that being a point of controversy wherein I had no concern, I let it drop. As to the verses, he insisted, 'that by his taste and skill in poetry he was as sure I wrote them as if he had seen them fall from my pen.' But I found the chief weight of his argument lay upon two words that rhymed to his name, which he knew could come from none but me. He then told me 'that, since I would not own the verses, and

¹ The Rev. Mr. Worrall's. [T. S.]

that since he could not get satisfaction by any course of law, he would get it by his pen, and show the world what a man I was.' When he began to grow over-warm and eloquent I called in the gentleman of the house from the room adjoining; and the serjeant, going on with less turbulence, went away.   He had a footman in the hall during all his talk, who was to have opened the door for one or more fellows, as he has since reported; and likewise that he had a sharp knife in his pocket, ready to stab or maim me.   But the master and mistress of the house, who knew his character and could hear every word from the room they were in, had prepared a sufficient defence in such a case, as they afterward told me.   He has since related to five hundred persons of all ranks about five hundred falsehoods of this conversation, of my fears and his own brutalities, against all probability as well as fact; and some of them, as I have been assured, even in the presence of your grace.   His meanings and his movements were indeed peevish enough, but his words were not.   He threatened me with nothing but his pen, yet owned he had no pretence to wit.   And indeed I am heartily glad for his own sake that he proceeded no farther, for the least uproar would have called his nearest neighbours first to my assistance, and next to the manifest danger of his life; and I would not willingly have even a dog killed upon my account.   Ever since he has amused himself with declaring in all companies, especially before bishops and lords and members of parliament, his resolutions for vengeance and the several manners by which he will put it in execution.

"It is only to the advice of some judicious friends that your grace owes the trouble of this letter; for though I may be dispirited enough by sickness and years, yet I have little reason to apprehend any danger from that man; and those who seem to have most regard for my safety are no more apprehensive than myself, especially such as best know his character; for his very enemies and even his ridiculers, who are of the two by far the greater number, allow him to be a peaceable man in all things except his words, his rhetorical actions, his looks, and his hatred to the clergy; which however are all known by abundance of experience to be perfectly harmless, and particularly as to the clergy.   I do not doubt but, if he will be so good to continue steadfast in his principles and practices, he may at proper junctures contribute very much to the honour and interests of that reverend body, as well as employ and improve the wit of many young gentlemen in the city, the university, and the rest of the kingdom.

"What I have said to your grace is only meant as a poor endeavour to preserve myself in your good opinion and in the continuance of your favour. I am, with the highest respect, etc.

"JONATHAN SWIFT."

APPENDIX IV.

A TRUE AND FAITHFUL NARRATIVE OF WHAT PASSED IN LONDON, DURING THE GENERAL CONSTERNATION OF ALL RANKS AND DEGREES OF MANKIND;

ON TUESDAY, WEDNESDAY, THURSDAY, AND FRIDAY LAST.

NOTE.

WILLIAM WHISTON (1667-1752), born at Norton, Leicestershire, was educated at Tamworth School and Clare College, Cambridge. He resigned the living at Lowestoft, presented to him by his patron and friend, Bishop Moore, of Norwich, on accepting the Professorship of Mathematics, vacated by Sir Isaac Newton. He was a profound scholar and mathematician, but obtained a somewhat harassing fame by his propagation of Arianism. Indeed, his public lectures and sermons, as well as his publications vindicating his attitude, forced the authorities to deprive him of his lectureship, and expel him from the university.

In 1717 Whiston founded a Society for Promoting Primitive Christianity, and its meetings were held at his house in Cross Street, Hatton Garden. But the society lived only for two years. In that curious medley, "Memoirs of the Life of Mr. William Whiston, by himself," we are told that he had a model made of the original Tabernacle of Moses from his own plans, and toured the country giving lectures on the coming of the Messiah, the restoration of the Jews to their own country, and the rebuilding of the Temple according to the model. The Millennium he foretold would commence in 1766.

He wrote a prodigious number of tracts, pamphlets, commentaries, and biblical expositions in support of his particular view of Christianity; but the works for which he is now remembered are his astronomical and mechanical papers and his well-known translation of Josephus's "History of the Jews."

The pamphlet which follows is written in ridicule of Whiston's prophetic pronouncements. Scott ascribes its authorship to Swift; but the "Miscellanies" of 1747 and Hawkesworth in the edition of 1766 of Swift's Works place it in the list of "Contents," with other pieces, under the heading, "By Mr. Pope and Mr. Gay."

The present text is practically that given by Scott, which is based on that in the third edition of the "Miscellanies" of 1732.

[T. S.]

APPENDIX IV.

A TRUE AND FAITHFUL

NARRATIVE

OF

What passed in London, *during the General Con-sternation of all Ranks and Degrees of Mankind;*

ON TUESDAY, WEDNESDAY, THURSDAY, *and*
FRIDAY *last.*

ON Tuesday the 13th of October, Mr Whiston held his lecture, near the Royal Exchange, to an audience of fourteen worthy citizens, his subscribers and constant hearers. Besides these, there were five chance auditors for that night only, who had paid their shillings a-piece. I think myself obliged to be very particular in this relation, lest my veracity should be suspected; which makes me appeal to the men who were present; of which number I myself was one. Their names are,

> Henry Watson, *Haberdasher.*
> George Hancock, *Druggist.*
> John Lewis, *Dry-Salter.*
> William Jones, *Corn-Chandler.*
> Henry Theobald, *Watchmaker.*
> James Peters, *Draper.*
> Thomas Floyer, *Silver-Smith.*
> John Wells, *Brewer.*
> Samuel Greg, *Soap-Boiler.*

William Cooley, *Fish-monger*.
James Harper, *Hosier*.
Robert Tucker, *Stationer*.
George Ford, *Iron-monger*.
Daniel Lynch, *Apothecary*.

William Bennet,
David Somers,
Charles Lock,   } *Apprentices.*
Leonard Daval,
Henry Croft,

Mr Whiston began by acquainting us, that (contrary to his advertisement) he thought himself in duty and conscience obliged to change the subject matter of his intended discourse. Here he paused, and seemed, for a short space, as it were, lost in devotion and mental prayer; after which, with great earnestness and vehemence, he spake as follows:

"Friends and fellow-citizens, all speculative science is at an end: the period of all things is at hand; on Friday next this world shall be no more. Put not your confidence in me, brethren; for to-morrow morning, five minutes after five, the truth will be evident; in that instant the comet shall appear, of which I have heretofore warned you. As ye have heard, believe. Go hence, and prepare your wives, your families, and friends, for the universal change."

At this solemn and dreadful prediction, the whole society appeared in the utmost astonishment: but it would be unjust not to remember, that Mr Whiston himself was in so calm a temper, as to return a shilling a-piece to the youths, who had been disappointed of their lecture, which I thought, from a man of his integrity, a convincing proof of his own faith in the prediction.

As we thought it a duty in charity to warn all men, in two or three hours the news had spread through the city. At first, indeed, our report met with but little credit; it being, by our greatest dealers in stocks, thought only a court artifice to sink them, that some choice favourites might purchase at a lower rate; for the South Sea, that very evening, fell five *per cent.*, the India, eleven, and all the other funds in proportion. But, at the Court end of the town, our attestations were entirely disbelieved, or turned into ridicule; yet nevertheless the news spread everywhere, and was the subject matter of all conversation.

That very night, (as I was credibly informed) Mr Whiston was sent for to a great lady, who is very curious in the learned sciences, and addicted to all the speculative doubts of the most able philosophers; but he was not now to be found; and since, at other times, he has been known not to decline that honour, I make no doubt he concealed himself to attend the great business of his soul: but whether it was the lady's faith, or inquisitiveness, that occasioned her to send, is a point I shall not presume to determine. As for his being sent for to the secretary's office by a messenger, it is now known to be a matter notoriously false, and indeed at first it had little credit with me, that so zealous and honest a man should be ordered into custody, as a seditious preacher, who is known to be so well-affected to the present happy establishment.

'Twas now I reflected, with exceeding trouble and sorrow, that I had disused family prayers for above five years, and (though it has been a custom of late entirely neglected by men of any business or station) I determined within myself no longer to omit so reasonable and religious a duty. I acquainted my wife with my intentions: But two or three neighbours having been engaged to sup with us that night, and many hours being unwarily spent at cards, I was prevailed upon by her to put it off till the next day; she reasoning, that it would be time enough to take off the servants from their business (which this practice must infallibly occasion for an hour or two every day) after the comet had made its appearance.

Zachery Bowen, a Quaker, and my next neighbour, had no sooner heard of the prophecy, but he made me a visit. I informed him of everything I had heard, but found him quite obstinate in his unbelief; for, said he, be comforted, friend, thy tidings are impossibilities; for, were these things to happen, they must have been foreseen by some of our brethren. This indeed (as in all other spiritual cases with this set of people) was his only reason against believing me; and, as he was fully persuaded that the prediction was erroneous, he in a very neighbourly manner admonished me against selling my stock at the present low price, which, he said, beyond dispute, must have a rise before Monday, when this unreasonable consternation should be over.

But on Wednesday morning (I believe to the exact calculation of Mr Whiston) the comet appeared; for, at three minutes after five by my own watch, I saw it. He indeed foretold, that it would be seen at five minutes after five; but, as the best watches may be a minute or two too slow, I am apt to think his calculation just to a minute.

In less than a quarter of an hour, all Cheapside was crowded with a vast concourse of people, and notwithstanding it was so early, it is thought that, through all that part of the town, there was not man, woman, or child, except the sick or infirm, left in their beds. From my own balcony, I am confident, I saw several thousands in the street, and counted at least seventeen, who were upon their knees, and seemed in actual devotion. Eleven of them, indeed, appeared to be old women of about fourscore; the six others were men in advanced life, but (as I could guess) two of them might be under seventy.

It is highly probable, that an event of this nature may be passed over by the greater historians of our times, as conducing very little or nothing to the unravelling and laying open the deep schemes of politicians, and mysteries of state; for which reason, I thought it might not be unacceptable to record the facts, which, in the space of three days, came to my knowledge, either as an eye-witness, or from unquestionable authorities; nor can I think this narrative will be entirely without its use, as it may enable us to form a more just idea of our countrymen in general, particularly in regard to their faith, religion, morals, and politics.

Before Wednesday noon, the belief was universal, that the day of judgment was at hand, insomuch, that a waterman of my acquaintance told me, he counted no less than one hundred and twenty-three clergymen, who had been ferried over to Lambeth before twelve o'clock: these, it is said, went thither to petition, that a short prayer might be penned, and ordered, there being none in the service upon that occasion. But, as in things of this nature, it is necessary that the council be consulted, their request was not immediately complied with; and this I affirm to be the true and only reason, that the churches were not that morning so well attended, and is in noways to be imputed to the fears and consternation of the clergy, with which the freethinkers have since very unjustly reproached them.

My wife and I went to church, (where we had not been for many years on a week-day,) and, with a very large congregation, were disappointed of the service. But (what will be scarce credible) by the carelessness of a 'prentice, in our absence, we had a piece of fine cambric carried off by a shop-lifter : so little impression was yet made on the minds of those wicked women !

I cannot omit the care of a particular director of the Bank ; I hope the worthy and wealthy knight will forgive me, that I endeavour to do him justice ; for it was unquestionably owing to Sir Gilbert Heathcote's [1] sagacity, that all the fire-offices were required to have a particular eye upon the Bank of England. Let it be recorded to his praise, that in the general hurry, this struck him as his nearest and tenderest concern ; but the next day in the evening, after having taken due care of all his books, bills, and bonds, I was informed, his mind was wholly turned upon spiritual matters ; yet, ever and anon, he could not help expressing his resentment against the Tories and Jacobites, to whom he imputed that sudden run upon the Bank, which happened on this occasion.

A great man (whom at this time it may not be prudent to name) employed all the Wednesday morning to make up such an account, as might appear fair, in case he should be called upon to produce it on the Friday ; but was forced to desist, after having for several hours together attempted it, not being able to bring himself to a resolution to trust the many hundred articles of his secret transactions upon paper.

Another seemed to be very melancholy, which his flatterers imputed to his dread of losing his power in a day or two ; but I rather take it, that his chief concern was the terror of being tried in a court, that could not be influenced, and where a majority of voices could avail him nothing. It was observed, too, that he had but few visitors that day.

[1] Sir Gilbert Heathcote had before signalized his care for the Bank when in equal danger, by petitioning against the Lord-Treasurer Godolphin's being removed, as a measure that would destroy the public credit. [H.]

This added so much to his mortification, that he read
through the first chapter of the book of Job, and wept over
it bitterly; in short, he seemed a true penitent in everything
but in charity to his neighbour.   No business was that day
done in his counting-house.   It is said too, that he was
advised to restitution, but I never heard that he complied
with it, any farther than in giving half-a-crown a-piece to
several crazed and starving creditors, who attended in the
outward room.

Three of the maids of honour sent to countermand their
birth-day clothes; two of them burnt all their collections of
novels and romances, and sent to a bookseller's in Pall-Mall
to buy each of them a Bible, and Taylor's "Holy Living
and Dying."   But I must do all of them the justice to   .
acknowledge, that they shewed a very decent behaviour in
the drawing-room, and restrained themselves from those
innocent freedoms, and little levities, so commonly incident
to young ladies of their profession.   So many birth-day
suits were countermanded the next day, that most of the
tailors and mantuamakers discharged all their journeymen
and women.   A grave elderly lady of great erudition and
modesty, who visits these young ladies, seemed to be extremely shocked by the apprehensions, that she was to
appear naked before the whole world; and no less so, that
all mankind was to appear naked before her; which might
so much divert her thoughts, as to incapacitate her to give
ready and apt answers to the interrogatories that might be
made her.   The maids of honour, who had both modesty
and curiosity, could not imagine the sight so disagreeable
as was represented; nay, one of them went so far as to say,
she perfectly longed to see it; for it could not be so indecent,
when everybody was to be alike; and they had a day or
two to prepare themselves to be seen in that condition.
Upon this reflection, each of them ordered a bathing-tub
to be got ready that evening, and a looking-glass to be set
by it.   So much are these young ladies, both by nature and
custom, addicted to cleanly appearance.

A west-country gentleman told me, he got a church-lease
filled up that morning for the same sum which had been
refused for three years successively.   I must impute this
merely to accident: for I cannot imagine that any divine

could take the advantage of his tenant in so unhandsome a manner, or that the shortness of the life was in the least his consideration; though I have heard the same worthy prelate aspersed and maligned since, upon this very account.

The term being so near, the alarm among the lawyers was inexpressible, though some of them, I was told, were so vain as to promise themselves some advantage in making their defence, by being versed in the practice of our earthly courts. It is said, too, that some of the chief pleaders were heard to express great satisfaction, that there had been but few state trials of late years. Several attorneys demanded the return of fees that had been given the lawyers; but it was answered, the fee was undoubtedly charged to their client, and that they could not connive at such injustice, as to suffer it to be sunk in the attorneys' pockets. Our sage and learned judges had great consolation, insomuch as they had not pleaded at the bar for several years; the barristers rejoiced in that they were not attorneys, and the attorneys felt no less satisfaction, that they were not pettifoggers, scriveners, and other meaner officers of the law.

As to the army, far be it from me to conceal the truth. Every soldier's behaviour was as undismayed, and undaunted, as if nothing was to happen; I impute not this to their want of faith, but to their martial disposition; though I cannot help thinking they commonly accompany their commands with more oaths than are requisite, of which there was no remarkable diminution this morning on the parade in St James's Park. But possibly it was by choice, and on consideration, that they continued this way of expression, not to intimidate the common soldiers, or give occasion to suspect, that even the fear of damnation could make any impression upon their superior officers. A duel was fought the same morning between two colonels, not occasioned (as was reported) because the one was put over the other's head; that being a point, which might, at such a juncture, have been accommodated by the mediation of friends; but as this was upon the account of a lady, it was judged it could not be put off at this time, above all others, but demanded immediate satisfaction. I am apt to believe, that a young officer, who desired his surgeon to defer putting him into a salivation till Saturday, might make this request out of some opinion he had of the truth of the prophecy; for the apprehensions of any danger in the operation could not be his motive, the surgeon himself having assured me, that he had before undergone three severe operations of the like nature with great resignation and fortitude.

There was an order issued, that the chaplains of the several regiments should attend their duty; but as they were dispersed about in several parts of England, it was believed, that most of them could not be found, or so much as heard of, till the great day was over.

Most of the considerable physicians, by their outward demeanour, seemed to be unbelievers; but at the same time, they everywhere insinuated, that there might be a pestilential malignancy in the air, occasioned by the comet, which might be armed against by proper and timely medicines. This caution had but little effect; for as the time approached, the Christian resignation of the people increased, and most of them (which was never before known) had their souls more at heart than their bodies.

If the reverend clergy shewed more concern than others, I charitably impute it to their great charge of souls; and what confirmed me in this opinion was, that the degrees of apprehension and terror could be distinguished to be greater or less, according to their ranks and degrees in the church.

The like might be observed in all sorts of ministers, though not of the Church of England; the higher their rank, the more was their fear.

I speak not of the Court for fear of offence; and I forbear inserting the names of particular persons, to avoid the imputation of slander; so that the reader will allow the narrative must be deficient, and is therefore desired to accept hereof rather as a sketch, than a regular circumstantial history.

I was not informed of any persons, who shewed the least joy; except three malefactors, who were to be executed on the Monday following, and one old man, a constant churchgoer, who being at the point of death, expressed some satisfaction at the news.

On Thursday morning there was little or nothing transacted in 'Change-alley; there were a multitude of sellers,

OF WHAT PASSED IN LONDON 283

but so few buyers, that one cannot affirm the stocks bore
any certain price except among the Jews; who this day
reaped great profit by their infidelity. There were many
who called themselves Christians, who offered to buy for
time; but as these were people of great distinction, I choose
not to mention them, because in effect it would seem to
accuse them both of avarice and infidelity.

The run upon the Bank is too well known to need a particular relation: for it never can be forgotten, that no one
person whatever (except the directors themselves, and some
of their particular friends and associates) could convert a
bill all that day into specie; all hands being employed to
serve them.

In the several churches of the city and suburbs, there
were seven thousand two hundred and forty-five, who publicly and solemnly declared before the congregation, that
they took to wife their several kept-mistresses, which was
allowed as valid marriage, the priest not having time to
pronounce the ceremony in form.

At St Bride's church in Fleet-street, Mr Woolston,[1] (who
writ against the miracles of our Saviour,) in the utmost
terrors of conscience, made a public recantation. Dr Mandeville[2] (who had been groundlessly reported formerly to have
done the same,) did it now in good earnest at St James's
gate; as did also at the Temple Church several gentlemen,
who frequent coffeehouses near the bar. So great was the
faith and fear of two of them, that they dropped dead on
the spot; but I will not record their names, lest I should
be thought invidiously to lay an odium on their families
and posterity.

[1] Thomas Woolston (1669—1733), a deistical writer, born at North-
ampton; became a Fellow of Sidney College, Cambridge. For his
work, "Six Discourses on the Miracles of Christ," he was sentenced to
imprisonment for one year and fined one hundred pounds. [T. S.]

[2] Bernard de Mandeville, M.D., author of the "Fable of the Bees,"
a deistical work, the scope of which was to prove, that private vices
are public benefits. The work was attacked by Bishop Berkeley in his
"Alciphron." De Mandeville was born in Holland about 1670, but
came over to England and settled there about the middle of the eighteenth
century. He also wrote "The Virgin Unmasked," "The Grumbling
Hive," and "Free Thoughts on Religion." He died in 1733.
[T. S.]

Most of the players, who had very little faith before, were now desirous of having as much as they could, and therefore embraced the Roman Catholic religion : the same thing was observed of some bawds, and ladies of pleasure.

An Irish gentleman out of pure friendship came to make me a visit, and advised me to hire a boat for the ensuing day, and told me, that unless I gave earnest for one immediately, he feared it might be too late ; for his countrymen had secured almost every boat upon the river, as judging, that, in the general conflagration, to be upon the water would be the safest place.

There were two lords, and three commoners, who, out of scruple of conscience, very hastily threw up their pensions, as imagining a pension was only an annual retaining bribe. All the other great pensioners, I was told, had their scruples quieted by a clergyman or two of distinction, whom they happily consulted.

It was remarkable, that several of our very richest tradesmen of the city, in common charity, gave away shillings and sixpences to the beggars who plied about the church doors ; and at a particular church in the city, a wealthy churchwarden with his own hands distributed fifty twelve-penny loaves to the poor, by way of restitution for the many great and costly feasts, which he had eaten of at their expense.

Three great ladies, a valet-de-chambre, two lords, a custom-house-officer, five half-pay captains, and a baronet, (all noted gamesters,) came publicly into a church at Westminster, and deposited a very considerable sum of money in the minister's hands; the parties, whom they had defrauded, being either out of town, or not to be found. But so great is the hardness of heart of this fraternity, that among either the noble or vulgar gamesters, (though the profession is so general,) I did not hear of any other restitution of this sort. At the same time I must observe, that (in comparison of these) through all parts of the town, the justice and penitence of the highwaymen, housebreakers, and common pickpockets, was very remarkable.

The directors of our public companies were in such dreadful apprehensions, that one would have thought a parliamentary inquiry was at hand; yet so great was their presence of mind, that all the Thursday morning was taken up in private transfers, which by malicious people was thought to be done with design to conceal their effects.

I forbear mentioning the private confessions of particular ladies to their husbands; for as their children were born in wedlock, and of consequence are legitimate, it would be an invidious task to record them as bastards; and particularly after their several husbands have so charitably forgiven them.

The evening and night through the whole town were spent in devotions both public and private; the churches for this one day were so crowded by the nobility and gentry, that thousands of common people were seen praying in the public streets.   In short, one would have thought the whole town had been really and seriously religious.   But what was very remarkable, all the different persuasions kept by themselves, for as each thought the other would be damned, not one would join in prayer with the other.

At length Friday came, and the people covered all the streets; expecting, watching, and praying.   But as the day wore away, their fears first began to abate, then lessened every hour, at night they were almost extinct, till the total darkness, that hitherto used to terrify, now comforted every freethinker and atheist.   Great numbers went together to the taverns, bespoke suppers, and broke up whole hogsheads for joy.   The subject of all wit and conversation was to ridicule the prophecy, and rally each other.   All the quality and gentry were perfectly ashamed, nay, some utterly disowned that they had manifested any signs of religion.

But the next day even the common people, as well as their betters, appeared in their usual state of indifference. They drank, they whored, they swore, they lied, they cheated, they quarrelled, they murdered.   In short, the world went on in the old channel.

I need not give any instances of what will so easily be credited; but I cannot omit relating, that Mr Woolston advertised in that very Saturday's Evening Post, a new Treatise against the Miracles of our Saviour; and that the few who had given up their pensions the day before, solicited to have them continued: which as they had not been thrown up upon any ministerial point, I am informed was readily granted.

INDEX.

CHISWICK PRESS :—CHARLES WHITTINGHAM AND CO.
TOOKS COURT, CHANCERY LANE, LONDON.

AN

ALPHABETICAL LIST

OF BOOKS CONTAINED IN

BOHN'S LIBRARIES.

Detailed Catalogue, arranged according to the various Libraries, will be sent on application.

ADDISON'S Works. With the Notes of Bishop Hurd, Portrait, and 8 Plates of Medals and Coins. Edited by H. G. Bohn. 6 vols. 3s. 6d. each.

ÆSCHYLUS, The Dramas of. Translated into English Verse by Anna Swanwick. 4th Edition, revised. 5s.

—— **The Tragedies of.** Translated into Prose by T. A. Buckley, B.A. 3s. 6d.

AGASSIZ and GOULD'S Outline of Comparative Physiology. Enlarged by Dr. Wright. With 390 Woodcuts. 5s.

ALFIERI'S Tragedies. Translated into English Verse by Edgar A. Bowring, C.B. 2 vols. 3s. 6d. each.

ALLEN'S (Joseph, R. N.) Battles of the British Navy. Revised Edition, with 57 Steel Engravings. 2 vols. 5s. each.

AMMIANUS MARCELLINUS. History of Rome during the Reigns of Constantius, Julian, Jovianus, Valentinian, and Valens.

Translated by Prof. C. D. Yonge, M.A. 7s. 6d.

ANDERSEN'S Danish Legends and Fairy Tales. Translated by Caroline Peachey. With 120 Wood Engravings. 5s.

ANTONINUS (M. Aurelius), The Thoughts of. Trans. literally, with Notes and Introduction by George Long, M.A. 3s. 6d.

APOLLONIUS RHODIUS. 'The Argonautica.' Translated by E. P. Coleridge, B.A.

APPIAN'S Roman History. Translated by Horace White, M.A., LL.D. With Maps and Illustrations. 2 vols. 6s. each.

APULEIUS, The Works of. Comprising the Golden Ass, God of Socrates, Florida, and Discourse of Magic. 5s.

ARIOSTO'S Orlando Furioso. Translated into English Verse by W. S. Rose. With Portrait, and 24 Steel Engravings. 2 vols. 5s. each

ARISTOPHANES' Comedies. Translated by W. J. Hickie. 2 vols. 5s. each.

ARISTOTLE'S Nicomachean Ethics. Translated, with Introduction and Notes, by the Venerable Archdeacon Browne. 5*s*.

—— **Politics and Economics.** Translated by E. Walford, M A., with Introduction by Dr. Gillies. 5*s*.

—— **Metaphysics.** Translated by the Rev. John H. M'Mahon, M.A. 5*s*.

—— **History of Animals.** Trans. by Richard Cresswell, M.A. 5*s*.

—— **Organon;** or, Logical Treatises, and the Introduction of Porphyry. Translated by the Rev. O. F. Owen, M.A. 2 vols. 3*s*. 6*d*. each.

—— **Rhetoric and Poetics.** Trans. by T. Buckley, B.A. 5*s*.

ARRIAN'S Anabasis of Alexander, together with the Indica. Translated by E. J. Chinnock, M.A., LL.D. With Maps and Plans. 5*s*.

ATHENÆUS. The Deipnosophists; or, the Banquet of the Learned. Trans. by Prof. C. D. Yonge, M.A. 3 vols. 5*s*. each.

BACON'S Moral and Historical Works, including the Essays, Apophthegms, Wisdom of the Ancients, New Atlantis, Henry VII., Henry VIII., Elizabeth, Henry Prince of Wales, History of Great Britain, Julius Cæsar, and Augustus Cæsar. Edited by J. Devey, M.A. 3*s*. 6*d*.

—— **Novum Organum** and Advancement of Learning. Edited by J. Devey, M.A. 5*s*.

BASS'S Lexicon to the Greek Testament. 2*s*.

BAX'S Manual of the History of Philosophy, for the use of Students. By E. Belfort Bax. 5*s*.

BEAUMONT and FLETCHER, their finest Scenes, Lyrics, and other Beauties, selected from the whole of their works, and edited by Leigh Hunt. 3*s*. 6*d*.

BECHSTEIN'S Cage and Chamber Birds, their Natural History, Habits, Food, Diseases, and Modes of Capture. Translated, with considerable additions on Structure, Migration, and Economy, by H. G. Adams. Together with SWEET BRITISH WARBLERS. With 43 coloured Plates and Woodcut Illustrations. 5*s*.

BEDE'S (Venerable) Ecclesiastical History of England. Together with the ANGLO-SAXON CHRONICLE. Edited by J. A. Giles, D.C.L. With Map. 5*s*.

BELL (Sir Charles). The Anatomy and Philosophy of Expression, as connected with the Fine Arts. By Sir Charles Bell, K.H. 7th edition, revised. 5*s*.

BERKELEY (George), Bishop of Cloyne, The Works of. Edited by George Sampson. With Biographical Introduction by the Right Hon. A. J. Balfour, M.P. 3 vols. 5*s*. each.

BION. *See* THEOCRITUS.

BJÖRNSON'S Arne and the Fisher Lassie. Translated by W. H. Low, M.A. 3*s*. 6*d*.

BLAIR'S Chronological Tables Revised and Enlarged. Comprehending the Chronology and History of the World, from the Earliest Times to the Russian Treaty of Peace, April 1856. By J. Willoughby Rosse. Double vol. 10*s*.

BLAIR'S Index of Dates. Comprehending the principal Facts in the Chronology and History of the World, alphabetically arranged; being a complete Index to Blair's Chronological Tables. By J. W. Rosse. 2 vols. 5*s.* each.

BLEEK, Introduction to the Old Testament. By Friedrich Bleek. Edited by Johann Bleek and Adolf Kamphausen. Translated by G. H. Venables, under the supervision of the Rev. Canon Venables. 2 vols. 5*s.* each.

BOETHIUS'S Consolation of Philosophy. King Alfred's Anglo-Saxon Version of. With a literal English Translation on opposite pages, Notes, Introduction, and Glossary, by Rev. S. Fox, M.A. 5*s.*

BOHN'S Dictionary of Poetical Quotations. 4th edition. 6*s.*

—— **Handbooks of Athletic Sports.** In 8 vols., each containing numerous Illustrations. 3*s.* 6*d.* each.

    I.—Cricket, Lawn Tennis, Tennis, Rackets, Fives, Golf.

    II.—Rowing and Sculling, Sailing, Swimming.

    III.—Boxing, Broadsword, Single Stick, &c., Wrestling, Fencing.

    IV.—Rugby Football, Association Football, Baseball, Rounders, Fieldball, Quoits, Skittles, Bowls, Curling.

    V.—Cycling, Athletics, Skating.

    VI.—Practical Horsemanship, including Riding for Ladies.

    VII.—Camping Out, Canoeing.

    VIII.—Gymnastics, Indian Clubs.

BOHN'S Handbooks of Games. New edition. In 2 vols., with numerous Illustrations 3*s.* 6*d.* each.

    Vol. I.—TABLE GAMES :—Billiards, Chess, Draughts, Backgammon, Dominoes, Solitaire, Reversi, Go-Bang, Rouge et Noir, Roulette, E.O., Hazard, Faro.

    Vol. II. — CARD GAMES :— Whist, Solo Whist, Poker, Piquet, Ecarté, Euchre, Bézique, Cribbage, Loo, Vingt-et-un, Napoleon, Newmarket, Pope Joan, Speculation, &c., &c.

BOND'S A Handy Book of Rules and Tables for verifying Dates with the Christian Era, &c. Giving an account of the Chief Eras and Systems used by various Nations; with the easy Methods for determining the Corresponding Dates. By J. J. Bond. 5*s.*

BONOMI'S Nineveh and its Palaces. 7 Plates and 294 Woodcut Illustrations. 5*s.*

BOSWELL'S Life of Johnson, with the TOUR IN THE HEBRIDES and JOHNSONIANA. Edited by the Rev. A. Napier, M.A. With Frontispiece to each vol. 6 vols. 3*s.* 6*d.* each.

BRAND'S Popular Antiquities of England, Scotland, and Ireland. Arranged, revised, and greatly enlarged, by Sir Henry Ellis, K.H., F.R.S., &c., &c. 3 vols. 5*s.* each.

BREMER'S (Frederika) Works. Translated by Mary Howitt. 4 vols. 3*s.* 6*d.* each.

BRIDGWATER TREATISES.

    Bell (Sir Charles) on the Hand. With numerous Woodcuts. 5*s.*

    Kirby on the History, Habits, and Instincts of Animals. Edited by T. Rymer Jones. With upwards of 100 Woodcuts. 2 vols. 5*s.* each.

BRIDGWATER TREATISES *continued.*

Kidd on the Adaptation of External Nature to the Physical Condition of Man. 3*s.* 6*d.*

Chalmers on the Adaptation of External Nature to the Moral and Intellectual Constitution of Man. 5*s.*

BRINK (B. ten) Early English Literature. By Bernhard ten Brink. Vol. I. To Wyclif. Translated by Horace M. Kennedy. 3*s.* 6*d.*

Vol. II. Wyclif, Chaucer, Earliest Drama Renaissance. Translated by W. Clarke Robinson, Ph.D. 3*s.* 6*d.*

Vol. III. From the Fourteenth Century to the Death of Surrey. Edited by Dr. Alois Brandl. Trans. by L. Dora Schmitz. 3*s.* 6*d.*

—— Five Lectures on Shakespeare. Trans. by Julia Franklin. 3*s.* 6*d.*

BROWNE'S (Sir Thomas) Works Edited by Simon Wilkin. 3 vols 3*s.* 6*d.* each.

BURKE'S Works. 8 vols. 3*s.* 6*d.* each.

    I.—Vindication of Natural Society—Essay on the Sublime and Beautiful, and various Political Miscellanies.

    II.—Reflections on the French Revolution — Letters relating to the Bristol Election — Speech on Fox's East India Bill, &c.

    III.—Appeal from the New to the Old Whigs—On the Nabob of Arcot's Debts— The Catholic Claims, &c.

BURKE'S WORKS *continued.*

    IV.—Report on the Affairs of India, and Articles of Charge against Warren Hastings.

    V.—Conclusion of the Articles of Charge against Warren Hastings — Political Letters on the American War, on a Regicide Peace, to the Empress of Russia.

    VI.—Miscellaneous Speeches — Letters and Fragments— Abridgments of English History, &c. With a General Index.

    VII. & VIII.—Speeches on the Impeachment of Warren Hastings ; and Letters. With Index. 2 vols. 3*s.* 6*d.* each.

—— Life. By Sir J. Prior. 3*s.* 6*d.*

BURNEY'S Evelina. By Frances Burney (Mme. D'Arblay). With an Introduction and Notes by A. R. Ellis. 3*s.* 6*d.*

—— Cecilia. With an Introduction and Notes by A. R. Ellis. 2 vols. 3*s.* 6*d.* each.

BURN (R) Ancient Rome and its Neighbourhood. An Illustrated Handbook to the Ruins in the City and the Campagna, for the use of Travellers. By Robert Burn, M.A. With numerous Illustrations, Maps, and Plans. 7*s.* 6*d.*

BURNS (Robert), Life of. By J. G. Lockhart, D.C.L. A new and enlarged Edition. Revised by William Scott Douglas. 3*s.* 6*d.*

BURTON'S (Robert) Anatomy of Melancholy. Edited by the Rev. A. R. Shilleto, M.A. With Introduction by A. H. Bullen, and full Index. 3 vols. 3*s.* 6*d.* each.

BURTON (Sir R. F.) Personal Narrative of a Pilgrimage to Al-Madinah and Meccah. By Captain Sir Richard F. Burton, K.C.M.G. With an Introduction by Stanley Lane-Poole, and all the original Illustrations. 2 vols. 3*s.* 6*d.* each.

⁎⁎ This is the copyright edition, containing the author's latest notes.

BUTLER'S (Bishop) Analogy of Religion, Natural and Revealed, to the Constitution and Course of Nature; together with two Dissertations on Personal Identity and on the Nature of Virtue, and Fifteen Sermons. 3*s.* 6*d.*

BUTLER'S (Samuel) Hudibras. With Variorum Notes, a Biography, Portrait, and 28 Illustrations. 5*s.*
—— or, further Illustrated with 60 Outline Portraits. 2 vols. 5*s.* each.

CÆSAR. Commentaries on the Gallic and Civil Wars, Translated by W. A. McDevitte, B.A. 5*s.*

CAMOENS' Lusiad; or, the Discovery of India. An Epic Poem. Translated by W. J. Mickle. 5th Edition, revised by E. R. Hodges, M.C.P. 3*s.* 6*d.*

CARAFAS (The) of Maddaloni. Naples under Spanish Dominion. Translated from the German of Alfred de Reumont. 3*s.* 6*d.*

CARLYLE'S French Revolution. Edited by J. Holland Rose, Litt.D. Illus. 3 vols. 5*s.* each.
—— Sartor Resartus. With 75 Illustrations by Edmund J. Sullivan. 5*s.*

CARPENTER'S (Dr. W. B.) Zoology. Revised Edition, by W. S. Dallas, F.L.S. With very numerous Woodcuts. Vol. I. 6*s.* [*Vol. II. out of print.*

CARPENTER'S Mechanical Philosophy, Astronomy, and Horology. 181 Woodcuts. 5*s.*

—— Vegetable Physiology and Systematic Botany. Revised Edition, by E. Lankester, M.D., &c. With very numerous Woodcuts. 6*s.*

—— Animal Physiology. Revised Edition. With upwards of 300 Woodcuts. 6*s.*

CASTLE (E.) Schools and Masters of Fence, from the Middle Ages to the End of the Eighteenth Century. By Egerton Castle, M.A., F.S.A. With a Complete Bibliography. Illustrated with 140 Reproductions of Old Engravings and 6 Plates of Swords, showing 114 Examples. 6*s.*

CATTERMOLE'S Evenings at Haddon Hall. With 24 Engravings on Steel from designs by Cattermole, the Letterpress by the Baroness de Carabella. 5*s.*

CATULLUS, Tibullus, and the Vigil of Venus. A Literal Prose Translation. 5*s.*

CELLINI (Benvenuto). Memoirs of, written by Himself. Translated by Thomas Roscoe. 3*s.* 6*d.*

CERVANTES' Don Quixote de la Mancha. Motteux's Translation revised. 2 vols. 3*s.* 6*d.* each.

—— Galatea. A Pastoral Romance. Translated by G. W. J. Gyll. 3*s.* 6*d.*

—— Exemplary Novels. Translated by Walter K. Kelly. 3*s.* 6*d.*

CHAUCER'S Poetical Works. Edited by Robert Bell. Revised Edition, with a Preliminary Essay by Prof. W. W. Skeat, M.A. 4 vols. 3*s.* 6*d.* each.

CHESS CONGRESS of 1862. A Collection of the Games played. Edited by J. Löwenthal. 5*s.*

CHEVREUL on Colour. Translated from the French by Charles Martel. Third Edition, with Plates, 5*s.*; or with an additional series of 16 Plates in Colours, 7*s. 6d.*

CHILLINGWORTH'S Religion of Protestants. A Safe Way to Salvation. 3*s. 6d.*

CHINA, Pictorial, Descriptive, and Historical. With Map and nearly 100 Illustrations. 5*s.*

CHRONICLES OF THE CRUSADES. Contemporary Narratives of the Crusade of Richard Cœur de Lion, by Richard of Devizes and Geoffrey de Vinsauf; and of the Crusade at St. Louis, by Lord John de Joinville. 5*s.*

CICERO'S Orations. Translated by Prof. C. D. Yonge, M.A. 4 vols. 5*s.* each.

—— **Letters.** Translated by Evelyn S. Shuckburgh. 4 vols. 5*s.* each.

—— **On Oratory and Orators.** With Letters to Quintus and Brutus. Translated by the Rev. J. S. Watson, M.A. 5*s.*

—— **On the Nature of the Gods,** Divination, Fate, Laws, a Republic, Consulship. Translated by Prof. C. D. Yonge, M.A., and Francis Barham. 5*s.*

—— **Academics,** De Finibus, and Tusculan Questions. By Prof. C. D. Yonge, M.A. 5*s.*

CICERO'S Offices; or, Moral Duties. Cato Major, an Essay on Old Age; Lælius, an Essay on Friendship; Scipio's Dream; Paradoxes; Letter to Quintus on Magistrates. Translated by C. R. Edmonds. 3*s. 6d.*

CORNELIUS NEPOS.—*See* JUSTIN.

CLARK'S (Hugh) Introduction to Heraldry. 18th Edition, Revised and Enlarged by J. R. Planché, Rouge Croix. With nearly 1000 Illustrations. 5*s.* Or with the Illustrations Coloured, 15*s.*

CLASSIC TALES, containing Rasselas, Vicar of Wakefield, Gulliver's Travels, and The Sentimental Journey. 3*s. 6d.*

COLERIDGE'S (S. T.) Friend. A Series of Essays on Morals, Politics, and Religion. 3*s. 6d.*

—— **Aids to Reflection,** and the CONFESSIONS OF AN INQUIRING SPIRIT, to which are added the ESSAYS ON FAITH and the BOOK OF COMMON PRAYER. 3*s. 6d.*

—— **Lectures and Notes on Shakespeare and other English Poets.** Edited by T. Ashe 3*s. 6d.*

— **Biographia Literaria;** together with Two Lay Sermons. 3*s. 6d.*

—— **Table-Talk and Omniana.** Edited by T. Ashe, B.A. 3*s. 6d.*

—— **Miscellanies, Æsthetic and Literary;** to which is added, THE THEORY OF LIFE. Collected and arranged by T. Ashe, B.A. 3*s. 6d.*

COMTE'S Positive Philosophy. Translated and condensed by Harriet Martineau. With Introduction by Frederic Harrison. 3 vols. 5*s.* each.

COMTE'S Philosophy of the Sciences, being an Exposition of the Principles of the *Cours de Philosophie Positive.* By G. H. Lewes. 5*s.*

CONDÉ'S History of the Dominion of the Arabs in Spain. Translated by Mrs. Foster. 3 vols. 3*s. 6d.* each.

COOPER'S Biographical Dictionary. Containing Concise Notices (upwards of 15,000) of Eminent Persons of all Ages and Countries. By Thompson Cooper, F.S.A. With a Supplement, bringing the work down to 1883. 2 vols. 5s. each.

COXE'S Memoirs of the Duke of Marlborough. With his original Correspondence. By W. Coxe, M.A., F.R.S. Revised edition by John Wade. 3 vols. 3s. 6d. each.

** An Atlas of the plans of Marlborough's campaigns, 4to. 10s. 6d.

—— History of the House of Austria (1218-1792). With a Continuation from the Accession of Francis I. to the Revolution of 1848. 4 vols. 3s. 6d. each.

CRAIK'S (G. L.) Pursuit of Knowledge under Difficulties. Illustrated by Anecdotes and Memoirs. Revised edition, with numerous Woodcut Portraits and Plates. 5s.

CRUIKSHANK'S Punch and Judy. The Dialogue of the Puppet Show; an Account of its Origin, &c. With 24 Illustrations, and Coloured Plates, designed and engraved by G. Cruikshank. 5s.

CUNNINGHAM'S Lives of the Most Eminent British Painters. A New Edition, with Notes and Sixteen fresh Lives. By Mrs. Heaton. 3 vols. 3s. 6d. each.

DANTE. Divine Comedy. Translated by the Rev. H. F. Cary, M.A. 3s. 6d.

—— Translated into English Verse by I. C. Wright, M.A. 3rd Edition, revised. With Portrait, and 34 Illustrations on Steel, after Flaxman.

DANTE. The Inferno. A Literal Prose Translation, with the Text of the Original printed on the same page. By John A. Carlyle, M.D. 5s.

—— The Purgatorio. A Literal Prose Translation, with the Text printed on the same page. By W. S. Dugdale. 5s.

DE COMMINES (Philip), Memoirs of. Containing the Histories of Louis XI. and Charles VIII., Kings of France, and Charles the Bold, Duke of Burgundy. Together with the Scandalous Chronicle, or Secret History of Louis XI., by Jean de Troyes. Translated by Andrew R. Scoble. With Portraits. 2 vols. 3s. 6d. each.

DEFOE'S Novels and Miscellaneous Works. With Prefaces and Notes, including those attributed to Sir W. Scott. 7 vols. 3s. 6d. each.

I.—Captain Singleton, and Colonel Jack.

II.—Memoirs of a Cavalier, Captain Carleton, Dickory Cronke, &c.

III.—Moll Flanders, and the History of the Devil.

IV.—Roxana, and Life of Mrs. Christian Davies.

V.—History of the Great Plague of London, 1665; The Storm (1703); and the True-born Englishman.

VI.—Duncan Campbell, New Voyage round the World, and Political Tracts.

VII.—Robinson Crusoe.

DE LOLME on the Constitution of England. Edited by John Macgregor. 3s. 6d.

DEMMIN'S History of Arms and Armour from the Earliest Period. By Auguste Demmin. Translated by C. C. Black, M.A. With nearly 2000 Illustrations. 7s. 6d.

DEMOSTHENES' Orations. Translated by C. Rann Kennedy. 5 vols. Vol. I., 3s. 6d.; Vols. II.-V., 5s. each.

DE STAËL'S Corinne or Italy. By Madame de Staël. Translated by Emily Baldwin and Paulina Driver. 3s. 6d.

DEVEY'S Logic, or the Science of Inference. A Popular Manual. By J. Devey. 5s.

DICTIONARY of Latin and Greek Quotations; including Proverbs, Maxims, Mottoes, Law Terms and Phrases. With all the Quantities marked, and English Translations. With Index Verborum (622 pages). 5s.

DICTIONARY of Obsolete and Provincial English. Compiled by Thomas Wright, M.A., F.S A., &c. 2 vols. 5s. each.

DIDRON·'S Christian Iconography: a History of Christian Art in the Middle Ages. Translated by E. J. Millington and completed by Margaret Stokes. With 240 Illustrations. 2 vols. 5s. each.

DIOGENES LAERTIUS. Lives and Opinions of the Ancient Philosophers. Translated by Prof. C. D. Yonge, M.A. 5s.

DOBREE'S Adversaria. Edited by the late Prof. Wagner. 2 vols. 5s. each.

DODD'S Epigrammatists. A Selection from the Epigrammatic Literature of Ancient, Mediæval, and Modern Times. By the Rev. Henry Philip Dodd, M.A. Oxford. 2nd Edition, revised and enlarged. 6s.

DONALDSON'S The Theatre of the Greeks. A Treatise on the History and Exhibition of the Greek Drama. With numerous Illustrations and 3 Plans. By John William Donaldson, D.D. 5s.

DRAPER'S History of the Intellectual Development of Europe. By John William Draper, M.D., LL.D. 2 vols. 5s. each.

DUNLOP'S History of Fiction. A new Edition. Revised by Henry Wilson. 2 vols. 5s. each.

DYER (Dr T. H.). Pompeii: its Buildings and Antiquities. By T. H. Dyer, LL.D. With nearly 300 Wood Engravings, a large Map, and a Plan of the Forum. 7s. 6d.

—— **The City of Rome:** its History and Monuments. With Illustrations. 5s.

DYER (T. F. T.) British Popular Customs, Present and Past. An Account of the various Games and Customs associated with Different Days of the Year in the British Isles, arranged according to the Calendar. By the Rev. T. F. Thiselton Dyer, M.A. 5s.

EBERS' Egyptian Princess. An Historical Novel. By George Ebers. Translated by E. S. Buchheim. 3s. 6d.

EDGEWORTH'S Stories for Children. With 8 Illustrations by L. Speed. 3s. 6d.

ELZE'S William Shakespeare. —*See* SHAKESPEARE.

EMERSON'S Works. 3 vols. 3s. 6d. each.

    I.—Essays, Lectures and Poems.

    II.—English Traits, Nature, and Conduct of Life.

EMERSON'S WORKS *continued*.
III.—Society and Solitude—Letters and Social aims — Miscellaneous Papers (hitherto uncollected) — May Day, and other Poems.

ELLIS (G.) Specimens of Early English Metrical Romances. With an Historical Introduction on the Rise and Progress of Romantic Composition in France and England. Revised Edition. By J. O. Halliwell, F.R.S. 5*s*.

ENNEMOSER'S History of Magic. Translated by William Howitt. 2 vols. 5*s*. each.

EPICTETUS, The Discourses of. With the ENCHEIRIDION and Fragments. Translated by George Long, M.A. 5*s*.

EURIPIDES. A New Literal Translation in Prose. By E. P. Coleridge, M.A. 2 vols. 5*s*. each.

EUTROPIUS.—*See* JUSTIN.

EUSEBIUS PAMPHILUS, Ecclesiastical History of. Translated by Rev. C. F. Cruse, M.A. 5*s*.

EVELYN'S Diary and Correspondendence. Edited from the Original MSS. by W. Bray, F.A.S. With 45 engravings. 4 vols. 5*s*. each.

FAIRHOLT'S Costume in England. A History of Dress to the end of the Eighteenth Century. 3rd Edition, revised, by Viscount Dillon, V.P.S.A. Illustrated with above 700 Engravings. 2 vols. 5*s*. each.

FIELDING'S Adventures of Joseph Andrews and his Friend Mr. Abraham Adams. With Cruikshank's Illustrations. 3*s*. 6*d*.

—— History of Tom Jones, a Foundling. With Cruikshank's Illustrations. 2 vols. 3*s*. 6*d*. each.

—— Amelia. With Cruikshank's Illustrations. 5*s*.

FLAXMAN'S Lectures on Sculpture. By John Flaxman, R.A. With Portrait and 53 Plates. 6*s*.

FLORENCE of WORCESTER'S Chronicle, with the Two Continuations: comprising Annals of English History, from the Departure of the Romans to the Reign of Edward I. Translated by Thomas Forester, M.A. 5*s*.

FOSTER'S (John) Life and Correspondence. Edited by J. E. Ryland. 2 vols. 3*s*. 6*d*. each.

—— Critical Essays. Edited by J. E. Ryland. 2 vols. 3*s*. 6*d*. each.

—— Essays: on Decision of Character; on a Man's writing Memoirs of Himself; on the epithet Romantic; on the aversion of Men of Taste to Evangelical Religion. 3*s*. 6*d*.

—— Essays on the Evils of Popular Ignorance; to which is added, a Discourse on the Propagation of Christianity in India. 3*s*. 6*d*.

—— Essays on the Improvement of Time. With NOTES OF SERMONS and other Pieces. 3*s*. 6*d*.

GASPARY'S History of Italian Literature. Translated by Herman Oelsner, M.A., Ph.D. Vol. I. 3*s*. 6*d*.

GEOFFREY OF MONMOUTH, Chronicle of.—*See Old English Chronicles*.

GESTA ROMANORUM, or Entertaining Moral Stories invented by the Monks. Translated by the Rev. Charles Swan Revised Edition, by Wynnard Hooper, B.A. 5*s*.

GILDAS, Chronicles of.—*See Old English Chronicles*.

IBBON'S Decline and Fall of the Roman Empire. Complete and Unabridged, with Variorum Notes. Edited by an English Churchman. With 2 Maps and Portrait. 7 vols. 3s. 6d. each.

GILBART'S History, Principles, and Practice of Banking. By the late J. W. Gilbart, F.R.S. New Edition, revised by A. S. Michie. 2 vols. 10s.

GIL BLAS, The Adventures of. Translated from the French of Lesage by Smollett. With 24 Engravings on Steel, after Smirke, and 10 Etchings by George Cruikshank. 6s.

GIRALDUS CAMBRENSIS' Historical Works. Translated by Th. Forester, M.A., and Sir R. Colt Hoare. Revised Edition, Edited by Thomas Wright, M.A., F.S.A. 5s.

GOETHE'S Faust. Part I. German Text with Hayward's Prose Translation and Notes. Revised by C. A. Buchheim, Ph.D. 5s.

GOETHE'S Works. Translated into English by various hands. 14 vols. 3s. 6d. each.

I. and II.—Autobiography and Annals.

III.—Faust. Two Parts, complete. (Swanwick.)

IV.—Novels and Tales.

V.—Wilhelm Meister's Apprenticeship.

VI.—Conversations with Eckermann and Soret.

VIII.—Dramatic Works.

IX.—Wilhelm Meister's Travels.

X.—Tour in Italy, and Second Residence in Rome.

XI.—Miscellaneous Travels.

XII.—Early and Miscellaneous Letters.

XIII.—Correspondence with Zelter.

XIV.—Reineke Fox, West-Eastern Divan and Achilleid.

GOLDSMITH'S Works. A new Edition, by J. W. M. Gibbs. 5 vols. 3s. 6d. each.

GRAMMONT'S Memoirs of the Court of Charles II Edited by Sir Walter Scott. Together with the BOSCOBEL TRACTS, including two not before published, &c. New Edition. 5s.

GRAY'S Letters. Including the Correspondence of Gray and Mason. Edited by the Rev. D. C. Tovey, M.A. Vols. I. and II. 3s. 6d. each.

GREEK ANTHOLOGY. Translated by George Burges, M.A. 5s.

GREEK ROMANCES of Heliodorus, Longus, and Achilles Tatius—viz., The Adventures of Theagenes & Chariclea ; Amours of Daphnis and Chloe ; and Loves of Clitopho and Leucippe. Translated by Rev. R. Smith, M.A. 5s.

GREGORY'S Letters on the Evidences, Doctrines, & Duties of the Christian Religion. By Dr. Olinthus Gregory. 3s. 6d.

GREENE, MARLOWE, and BEN JONSON. Poems of. Edited by Robert Bell. 3s. 6d.

GRIMM'S TALES. With the Notes of the Original. Translated by Mrs. A. Hunt. With Introduction by Andrew Lang, M.A. 2 vols. 3s. 6d. each.

—— Gammer Grethel; or, German Fairy Tales and Popular Stories. Containing 42 Fairy Tales. Trans. by Edgar Taylor. With numerous Woodcuts after George Cruikshank and Ludwig Grimm. 3s. 6d.

GROSSI'S Marco Visconti. Translated by A. F. D. The Ballads rendered into English Verse by C. M. P. 3s. 6d.

GUIZOT'S History of the English Revolution of 1640. From the Accession of Charles I. to his Death. Translated by William Hazlitt. 3s. 6d.

—— History of Civilisation, from the Fall of the Roman Empire to the French Revolution. Translated by William Hazlitt. 3 vols. 3s. 6d. each.

HALL'S (Rev. Robert) Miscellaneous Works and Remains. 3s. 6d.

HAMPTON COURT: A Short History of the Manor and Palace. By Ernest Law, B.A. With numerous Illustrations. 5s.

HARDWICK'S History of the Articles of Religion. By the late C. Hardwick. Revised by the Rev. Francis Procter, M.A. 5s.

HAUFF'S Tales. The Caravan— The Sheik of Alexandria—The Inn in the Spessart. Trans. from the German by S. Mendel. 3s. 6d.

HAWTHORNE'S Tales. 4 vols. 3s. 6d. each.

    I.—Twice-told Tales, and the Snow Image.
    II.—Scarlet Letter, and the House with the Seven Gables.
    III.—Transformation [The Marble Faun], and Blithedale Romance.
    IV.—Mosses from an Old Manse.

HAZLITT'S Table-talk. Essays on Men and Manners. By W. Hazlitt. 3s. 6d.

—— Lectures on the Literature of the Age of Elizabeth and on Characters of Shakespeare's Plays. 3s. 6d.

—— Lectures on the English Poets, and on the English Comic Writers. 3s. 6d.

—— The Plain Speaker. Opinions on Books, Men, and Things. 3s. 6d.

—— Round Table. 3s. 6d.

HAZLITT'S Sketches and Essays. 3s. 6d.

—— The Spirit of the Age; or, Contemporary Portraits. Edited by W. Carew Hazlitt. 3s. 6d.

—— View of the English Stage. Edited by W. Spencer Jackson. 3s. 6d.

HEATON'S Concise History of Painting. New Edition, revised by Cosmo Monkhouse. 5s.

HEGEL'S Lectures on the Philosophy of History. Translated by J. Sibree, M.A.

HEINE'S Poems, Complete. Translated by Edgar A. Bowring, C.B. 3s. 6d.

—— Travel-Pictures, including the Tour in the Harz, Norderney, and Book of Ideas, together with the Romantic School. Translated by Francis Storr. A New Edition, revised throughout. With Appendices and Maps. 3s. 6d.

HELP'S Life of Christopher Columbus, the Discoverer of America. By Sir Arthur Helps, K.C.B. 3s. 6d.

—— Life of Hernando Cortes, and the Conquest of Mexico. 2 vols. 3s. 6d. each.

—— Life of Pizarro. 3s. 6d.

—— Life of Las Casas the Apostle of the Indies. 3s. 6d.

HENDERSON (E.) Select Historical Documents of the Middle Ages, including the most famous Charters relating to England, the Empire, the Church, &c., from the 6th to the 14th Centuries. Translated from the Latin and edited by Ernest F. Henderson, A.B., A.M., Ph.D. 5s.

HENFREY'S Guide to English Coins, from the Conquest to the present time. New and revised Edition by C. F. Keary, M.A., F.S.A. 6s.

HENRY OF HUNTINGDON'S History of the English. Trans-

HENRY'S (Matthew) Exposition of the Book of the Psalms. 5*s*.

HELIODORUS. Theagenes and Chariclea. — *See* GREEK ROMANCES.

HERODOTUS. Translated by the Rev. Henry Cary, M.A. 3*s*. 6*d*.

—— Notes on. Original and Selected from the best Commentators. By D. W. Turner, M.A. With Coloured Map. 5*s*.

—— Analysis and Summary of By J. T. Wheeler. 5*s*.

HESIOD, CALLIMACHUS, and THEOGNIS. Translated by the Rev. J. Banks, M.A. 5*s*.

HOFFMANN'S (E. T. W.) The Serapion Brethren. Translated from the German by Lt.-Col. Alex. Ewing. 2 vols. 3*s*. 6*d*. each.

HOLBEIN'S Dance of Death and Bible Cuts. Upwards of 150 Subjects, engraved in facsimile, with Introduction and Descriptions by Francis Douce and Dr. Thomas Frognall Dibden. 5*s*.

HOMER'S Iliad. Translated into English Prose by T. A. Buckley, B.A. 5*s*.

—— Odyssey. Hymns, Epigrams, and Battle of the Frogs and Mice. Translated into English Prose by T. A. Buckley, B.A. 5*s*.

—— *See also* POPE.

HOOPER'S (G.) Waterloo: The Downfall of the First Napoleon: a History of the Campaign of 1815. By George Hooper. With Maps and Plans. 3*s*. 6*d*.

—— The Campaign of Sedan: The Downfall of the Second Empire, August – September, 1870. With General Map and Six Plans of Battle. 3*s*. 6*d*.

HORACE. A new literal Prose translation, by A. Hamilton Bryce, LL.D. 3*s*. 6*d*.

HUGO'S (Victor) Dramatic Works. Hernani—Ruy Blas—The King's Diversion. Translated by Mrs. Newton Crosland and F. L. Slous. 3*s*. 6*d*.

—— Poems, chiefly Lyrical. Translated by various Writers, now first collected by J. H. L. Williams. 3*s*. 6*d*.

HUMBOLDT'S Cosmos. Translated by E. C. Otté, B. H. Paul, and W. S. Dallas, F.L.S. 5 vols. 3*s*. 6*d*. each, excepting Vol. V. 5*s*.

—— Personal Narrative of his Travels to the Equinoctial Regions of America during the years 1799–1804. Translated by T. Ross. 3 vols. 5*s*. each.

—— Views of Nature. Translated by E. C. Otté and H. G. Bohn. 5*s*.

HUMPHREYS' Coin Collector's Manual. By H. N. Humphreys. with upwards of 140 Illustrations on Wood and Steel. 2 vols. 5*s*. each.

HUNGARY: its History and Revolution, together with a copious Memoir of Kossuth. 3*s*. 6*d*.

HUTCHINSON (Colonel). Memoirs of the Life of. By his Widow, Lucy: together with her Autobiography, and an Account of the Siege of Lathom House. 3*s*. 6*d*.

HUNT'S Poetry of Science. By Richard Hunt. 3rd Edition, revised and enlarged. 5*s*.

INDIA BEFORE THE SEPOY MUTINY. A Pictorial, Descriptive, and Historical Account, from the Earliest Times to the Annexation of the Punjab. with upwards of 100 Engravings on Wood, and a Map. 5*s*.

INGULPH'H Chronicles of the Abbey of Croyland, with the CONTINUATION by Peter of Blois and other Writers. Translated by H. T. Riley, M.A. 5*s*.

KANT'S Critique of Pure Reason. Translated by J. M. D. Meiklejohn. 5s.
—— Prolegomena and Metaphysical Foundations of Natural Science. Translated by E. Belfort Bax. 5s.

KEIGHTLEY'S (Thomas) Mythology of Ancient Greece and Italy. 4th Edition, revised by Leonard Schmitz, Ph.D., LL.D. With 12 Plates from the Antique. 5s.
—— Fairy Mythology, illustrative of the Romance and Superstition of Various Countries. Revised Edition, with Frontispiece by Cruikshank. 5s.

LA FONTAINE'S Fables. Translated into English Verse by Elizur Wright. New Edition, with Notes by J. W. M. Gibbs. 3s. 6d.

LAMARTINE'S History of the Girondists. Translated by H. T. Ryde. 3 vols. 3s. 6d. each.
—— History of the Restoration of Monarchy in France (a Sequel to the History of the Girondists). 4 vols. 3s. 6d. each.
—— History of the French Revolution of 1848. 3s. 6d.

LAMB'S (Charles) Essays of Elia and Eliana. Complete Edition. 3s. 6d.
—— Specimens of English Dramatic Poets of the Time of Elizabeth. 3s. 6d.
—— Memorials and Letters of Charles Lamb. By Serjeant Talfourd. New Edition, revised, by W. Carew Hazlitt. 2 vols. 3s. 6d. each.
—— Tales from Shakespeare With Illustrations by Byam Shaw. 3s. 6d.

LANZI'S History of Painting in Italy, from the Period of the Revival of the Fine Arts to the End of the Eighteenth Century. Translated by Thomas Roscoe. 3 vols. 3s. 6d. each.

LAPPENBERG'S History of England under the Anglo-Saxon Kings. Translated by B. Thorpe, F.S.A. New edition, revised by E. C. Otté. 2 vols. 3s. 6d. each.

LECTURES ON PAINTING, by Barry, Opie, Fuseli. Edited by R. Wornum. 5s.

LEONARDO DA VINCI'S Treatise on Painting. Translated by J. F. Rigaud, R.A., With a Life of Leonardo by John William Brown. With numerous Plates. 5s.

LEPSIUS'S Letters from Egypt, Ethiopia, and the Peninsula of Sinai Translated by L. and J. B. Horner. With Maps. 5s.

LESSING'S Dramatic Works, Complete. Edited by Ernest Bell, M.A. With Memoir of Lessing by Helen Zimmern. 2 vols. 3s. 6d. each.
—— Laokoon, Dramatic Notes, and the Representation of Death by the Ancients. Translated by E. C. Beasley and Helen Zimmern. Edited by Edward Bell, M.A. With a Frontispiece of the Laokoon group. 3s. 6d.

LILLY'S Introduction to Astrology. With a GRAMMAR OF ASTROLOGY and Tables for Calculating Nativities, by Zadkiel. 5s.

LIVY'S History of Rome. Translated by Dr. Spillan, C. Edmonds, and others. 4 vols. 5s. each.

LOCKE'S Philosophical Works. Edited by J. A. St. John. 2 vols. 3s. 6d. each.
—— Life and Letters: By Lord King. 3s. 6d.

LOCKHART (J. G.)—*See* BURNS.

LODGE'S Portraits of Illustrious Personages of Great Britain, with Biographical and Historical Memoirs. 240 Portraits engraved on Steel, with the respective Biographies unabridged. 8 vols. 5*s.* each.

LONGFELLOW'S Prose Works. With 16 full-page Wood Engravings. 5*s.*

LOUDON'S (Mrs.) Natural History. Revised edition, by W. S. Dallas, F.L.S. With numerous Woodcut Illus. 5*s.*

LOWNDES' Bibliographer's Manual of English Literature. Enlarged Edition. By H. G. Bohn. 6 vols. cloth, 5*s.* each. Or 4 vols. half morocco, 2*l.* 2*s.*

LONGUS. Daphnis and Chloe. —*See* GREEK ROMANCES.

LUCAN'S Pharsalia. Translated by H. T. Riley, M.A. 5*s.*

LUCIAN'S Dialogues of the Gods, of the Sea Gods, and of the Dead. Translated by Howard Williams, M.A. 5*s.*

LUCRETIUS. Translated by the Rev. J. S. Watson, M.A. 5*s.*

LUTHER'S Table-Talk. Translated and Edited by William Hazlitt. 3*s.* 6*d.*

—— Autobiography. — *See* MICHELET.

MACHIAVELLI'S History of Florence, together with the Prince, Savonarola, various Historical Tracts, and a Memoir of Machiavelli. 3*s.* 6*d.*

MALLET'S Northern Antiquities, or an Historical Account of the Manners, Customs, Religions and Laws, Maritime Expeditions and Discoveries, Language and Literature, of the Ancient Scandinavians. Translated by Bishop Percy. Revised and Enlarged Edition, with a Translation of the PROSE EDDA, by J. A. Blackwell. 5*s.*

MANTELL'S (Dr.) Petrifactions and their Teachings. With numerous illustrative Woodcuts. 6*s.*

—— Wonders of Geology. 8th Edition, revised by T. Rupert Jones, F G.S. With a coloured Geological Map of England, Plates, and upwards of 200 Woodcuts. 2 vols. 7*s.* 6*d.* each.

MANZONI. The Betrothed: being a Translation of 'I Promessi Sposi.' By Alessandro Manzoni. With numerous Woodcuts. 5*s.*

MARCO POLO'S Travels; the Translation of Marsden revised by T. Wright, M.A., F.S.A. 5*s.*

MARRYAT'S (Capt. R.N.) Masterman Ready. With 93 Woodcuts. 3*s.* 6*d.*

—— Mission; or, Scenes in Africa. Illustrated by Gilbert and Dalziel. 3*s.* 6*d.*

—— Pirate and Three Cutters. With 8 Steel Engravings, from Drawings by Clarkson Stanfield, R.A. 3*s.* 6*d.*

—— Privateersman. 8 Engravings on Steel. 3*s.* 6*d.*

—— Settlers in Canada. 10 Engravings by Gilbert and Dalziel. 3*s.* 6*d.*

—— Poor Jack. With 16 Illustrations after Clarkson Stansfield, R.A. 3*s.* 6*d.*

—— Peter Simple. With 8 full-page Illustrations. 3*s.* 6*d.*

—— Midshipman Easy. With 8 full-page Illustrations. 3*s.* 6*d.*

MARTIAL'S Epigrams, complete. Translated into Prose, each accompanied by one or more Verse Translations selected from the Works of English Poets, and other sources. 7*s.* 6*d.*

MARTINEAU'S (Harriet) History of England, from 1800–1815. 3s. 6d.

—— History of the Thirty Years' Peace, A.D. 1815-46. 4 vols. 3s. 6d. each.

—— *See Comte's Positive Philosophy.*

MATTHEW PARIS'S English History, from the Year 1235 to 1273. Translated by Rev. J. A. Giles, D.C.L. 3 vols. 5s. each.

MATTHEW OF WESTMINSTER'S Flowers of History, from the beginning of the World to A.D. 1307. Translated by C. D. Yonge, M.A. 2 vols. 5s. each.

MAXWELL'S Victories of Wellington and the British Armies. Frontispiece and 5 Portraits. 5s.

MENZEL'S History of Germany, from the Earliest Period to 1842. 3 vols. 3s. 6d. each.

MICHAEL ANGELO AND RAPHAEL, their Lives and Works. By Duppa and Quatremere de Quincy. With Portraits, and Engravings on Steel. 5s.

MICHELET'S Luther's Autobiography. Trans. by William Hazlitt. With an Appendix (110 pages) of Notes. 3s. 6d.

—— History of the French Revolution from its earliest indications to the flight of the King in 1791. 3s. 6d.

MIGNET'S History of the French Revolution, from 1789 to 1814. 3s. 6d.

MILL (J. S.). Early Essays by John Stuart Mill. Collected from various sources by J. W. M. Gibbs. 3s. 6d.

MILLER (Professor). History Philosophically Illustrated, from the Fall of the Roman Empire to the French Revolution. 4 vols. 3s. 6d. each.

MILTON'S Prose Works. Edited by J. A. St. John. 5 vols. 3s. 6d. each.

—— Poetical Works, with a Memoir and Critical Remarks by James Montgomery, an Index to Paradise Lost, Todd's Verbal Index to all the Poems, and a Selection of Explanatory Notes by Henry G. Bohn. Illustrated with 120 Wood Engravings from Drawings by W. Harvey. 2 vols. 3s. 6d. each.

MITFORD'S (Miss) Our Village Sketches of Rural Character and Scenery. With 2 Engravings on Steel. 2 vols. 3s. 6d. each.

MOLIERE'S Dramatic Works. A new Translation in English Prose, by C. H. Wall. 3 vols. 3s. 6d. each.

MONTAGU. The Letters and Works of Lady Mary Wortley Montagu. Edited by her great-grandson, Lord Wharncliffe's Edition, and revised by W. Moy Thomas. New Edition, revised, with 5 Portraits. 2 vols. 5s. each.

MONTAIGNE'S Essays. Cotton's Translation, revised by W. C. Hazlitt. New Edition. 3 vols. 3s. 6d. each.

MONTESQUIEU'S Spirit of Laws. New Edition, revised and corrected. By J. V. Pritchard, A.M. 2 vols. 3s. 6d. each.

MOTLEY (J. L.). The Rise of the Dutch Republic. A History. By John Lothrop Motley. New Edition, with Biographical Introduction by Moncure D. Conway. 3 vols. 3s. 6d. each.

MORPHY'S Games of Chess. Being the Matches and best Games played by the American Champion, with Explanatory and Analytical Notes by J. Löwenthal. 5s.

MUDIE'S British Birds; or, History of the Feathered Tribes of the British Islands. Revised by W. C. L. Martin. With 52 Figures of Birds and 7 Coloured Plates of Eggs. 2 vols.

NEANDER (Dr. A.). History of the Christian Religion and Church. Trans. from the German by J. Torrey. 10 vols. 3s. 6d. each.

—— Life of Jesus Christ. Translated by J. McClintock and C. Blumenthal. 3s. 6d.

—— History of the Planting and Training of the Christian Church by the Apostles. Translated by J. E. Ryland. 2 vols. 3s. 6d. each.

—— Memorials of Christian Life in the Early and Middle Ages; including Light in Dark Places. Trans. by J. E. Ryland. 3s. 6d.

NIBELUNGEN LIED. The Lay of the Nibelungs, metrically translated from the old German text by Alice Horton, and edited by Edward Bell, M.A. To which is prefixed the Essay on the Nibelungen Lied by Thomas Carlyle. 5s.

NEW TESTAMENT (The) in Greek. Griesbach's Text, with various Readings at the foot of the page, and Parallel References in the margin; also a Critical Introduction and Chronological Tables. By an eminent Scholar, with a Greek and English Lexicon. 3rd Edition, revised and corrected. Two Facsimiles of Greek Manuscripts. 900 pages. 5s.
The Lexicon may be had separately, price 2s.

NICOLINI'S History of the Jesuits: their Origin, Progress, Doctrines, and Designs. With 8 Portraits. 5s.

NORTH (R.) Lives of the Right Hon. Francis North, Baron Guildford, the Hon. Sir Dudley North, and the Hon. and Rev. Dr. John North. By the Hon. Roger North. Together with the Autobiography of the Author. Edited by Augustus Jessopp, D.D. 3 vols. 3s. 6d. each.

NUGENT'S (Lord) Memorials of Hampden, his Party and Times. With a Memoir of the Author, an Autograph Letter, and Portrait. 5s.

OCKLEY (S.) History of the Saracens and their Conquests in Syria, Persia, and Egypt. By Simon Ockley, B.D., Professor of Arabic in the University of Cambridge. 3s. 6d.

OLD ENGLISH CHRONICLES, including Ethelwerd's Chronicle, Asser's Life of Alfred, Geoffrey of Monmouth's British History, Gildas, Nennius, and the spurious chronicle of Richard of Cirencester. Edited by J. A. Giles, D.C.L. 5s.

OMAN (J. C.) The Great Indian Epics: the Stories of the RAMAYANA and the MAHABHARATA. By John Campbell Oman, Principal of Khalsa College, Amritsar. With Notes, Appendices, and Illustrations. 3s. 6d.

ORDERICUS VITALIS' Ecclesiastical History of England and Normandy. Translated by T. Forester, M.A. To which is added the CHRONICLE OF ST. EVROULT. 4 vols. 5s. each.

OVID'S Works, complete. Literally translated into Prose. 3 vols. 5s. each.

PASCAL'S Thoughts. Translated from the Text of M. Auguste Molinier by C. Kegan Paul. 3rd Edition. 3s. 6d.

PAULI'S (Dr. R.) Life of Alfred the Great. Translated from the German. To which is appended Alfred's ANGLO-SAXON VERSION OF OROSIUS. With a literal Translation interpaged, Notes, and an ANGLO-SAXON GRAMMAR and GLOSSARY, by B. Thorpe. 5*s*.

PAUSANIAS' Description of Greece. Newly translated by A. R. Shilleto, M.A. 2 vols. 5*s*. each.

PEARSON'S Exposition of the Creed. Edited by E. Walford, M.A. 5*s*.

PEPYS' Diary and Correspondence. Deciphered by the Rev. J. Smith, M.A., from the original Shorthand MS. in the Pepysian Library. Edited by Lord Braybrooke. 4 vols. With 31 Engravings. 5*s*. each.

PERCY'S Reliques of Ancient English Poetry. With an Essay on Ancient Minstrels and a Glossary. Edited by J. V. Pritchard, A.M. 2 vols. 3*s*. 6*d*. each.

PERSIUS.—*See* JUVENAL.

PETRARCH'S Sonnets, Triumphs, and other Poems. Translated into English Verse by various Hands. With a Life of the Poet by Thomas Campbell. With Portrait and 15 Steel Engravings. 5*s*.

PHILO-JUDÆUS, Works of. Translated by Prof. C. D. Yonge, M.A. 4 vols. 5*s*. each.

PICKERING'S History of the Races of Man, and their Geographical Distribution. With AN ANALYTICAL SYNOPSIS OF THE NATURAL HISTORY OF MAN by Dr. Hall. With a Map of the World and 12 coloured Plates. 5*s*.

PINDAR. Translated into Prose by Dawson W. Turner. To which is added the Metrical Version by Abraham Moore. 5*s*.

PLANCHE. History of British Costume. from the Earliest Time to the Close of the Eighteenth Century. By J. R. Planché, Somerset Herald. With upwards of 400 Illustrations. 5*s*.

PLATO'S Works. Literally translated, with Introduction and Notes. 6 vols. 5*s*. each.

  I.—The Apology of Socrates, Crito, Phædo, Gorgias, Protagoras, Phædrus, Theætetus, Euthyphron, Lysis. Translated by the Rev. H. Carey.

  II.—The Republic, Timæus, and Critias. Translated by Henry Davis.

  III.—Meno, Euthydemus, The Sophist, Statesman, Cratylus, Parmenides, and the Banquet. Translated by G. Burges.

  IV.—Philebus, Charmides, Laches, Menexenus, Hippias, Ion, The Two Alcibiades, Theages, Rivals, Hipparchus, Minos, Clitopho, Epistles. Translated by G. Burges.

  V.—The Laws. Translated by G. Burges.

  VI.—The Doubtful Works. Translated by G. Burges.

  —— Summary and Analysis of the Dialogues. With Analytical Index. By A. Day, LL.D. 5*s*.

PLAUTUS'S Comedies. Translated by H. T. Riley, M.A. 2 vols. 5*s*. each.

PLINY'S Natural History. Translated by the late John Bostock, M.D., F.R.S., and H. T. Riley, M.A. 6 vols. 5*s*. each.

PLINY. The Letters of Pliny the Younger. Melmoth's translation, revised by the Rev. F. C. T. Bosanquet, M.A. 5*s*.

PLOTINUS, Select Works of. Translated by Thomas Taylor. With an Introduction containing the substance of Porphyry's Plotinus. Edited by G. R. S. Mead, B.A., M.R.A.S. 5*s*.

PLUTARCH'S Lives. Translated by A. Stewart, M.A., and George Long, M.A. 4 vols. 3s. 6d. each.

—— Morals. Theosophical Essays. Translated by C. W. King, M.A. 5s.

—— Morals. Ethical Essays. Translated by the Rev. A. R. Shilleto, M.A. 5s.

POETRY OF AMERICA. Selections from One Hundred American Poets, from 1776 to 1876. By W. J. Linton. 3s. 6d.

POLITICAL CYCLOPÆDIA. A Dictionary of Political, Constitutional, Statistical, and Forensic Knowledge; forming a Work of Reference on subjects of Civil Administration, Political Economy, Finance, Commerce, Laws, and Social Relations. 4 vols. 3s. 6d. each.

POPE'S Poetical Works. Edited, with copious Notes, by Robert Carruthers. With numerous Illustrations. 2 vols. 5s. each.

—— Homer's Iliad. Edited by the Rev. J. S. Watson, M.A. Illustrated by the entire Series of Flaxman's Designs. 5s.

—— Homer's Odyssey, with the Battle of Frogs and Mice, Hymns, &c., by other translators. Edited by the Rev. J. S. Watson, M.A. With the entire Series of Flaxman's Designs. 5s.

—— Life, including many of his Letters. By Robert Carruthers. With numerous Illustrations. 5s.

POUSHKIN'S Prose Tales: The Captain's Daughter—Doubrovsky — The Queen of Spades — An Amateur Peasant Girl—The Shot —The Snow Storm—The Postmaster — The Coffin Maker — Kirdjali—The Egyptian Nights— Peter the Great's Negro. Translated by T. Keane. 3s. 6d.

PRESCOTT'S Conquest of. Mexico. Copyright edition, with the notes by John Foster Kirk, and an introduction by G. P. Winship. 3 vols. 3s. 6d. each.

—— Conquest of Peru. Copyright edition, with the notes of John Foster Kirk. 2 vols. 3s. 6d. each.

—— Reign of Ferdinand and Isabella. Copyright edition, with the notes of John Foster Kirk. 3 vols. 3s. 6d. each.

PROPERTIUS. Translated by Rev. P. J. F. Gantillon, M.A., and accompanied by Poetical Versions, from various sources. 3s. 6d.

PROVERBS, Handbook of. Containing an entire Republication of Ray's Collection of English Proverbs, with his additions from Foreign Languages and a complete Alphabetical Index; in which are introduced large additions as well of Proverbs as of Sayings, Sentences, Maxims, and Phrases, collected by H. G. Bohn. 5s.

PROVERBS, A Polyglot of Foreign. Comprising French, Italian, German, Dutch, Spanish, Portuguese, and Danish. With English Translations & a General Index by H. G Bohn. 5s.

POTTERY AND PORCELAIN, and other Objects of Vertu. Comprising an Illustrated Catalogue of the Bernal Collection of Works of Art, with the prices at which they were sold by auction, and names of the possessors. To which are added, an Introductory Lecture on Pottery and Porcelain, and an Engraved List of all the known Marks and Monograms. By Henry G. Bohn. With numerous Wood Engravings, 5s.; or with Coloured Illustrations, 10s. 6d.

PROUT'S (Father) Reliques. Collected and arranged by Rev. F. Mahony. New issue, with 21 Etchings by D. Maclise, R.A. Nearly 600 pages. 5s.

QUINTILIAN'S Institutes of Oratory, or Education of an Orator. Translated by the Rev. J. S. Watson, M.A. 2 vols. 5s. each.

RACINE'S (Jean) Dramatic Works. A metrical English version. By R. Bruce Boswell, M.A. Oxon. 2 vols. 3s. 6d. each.

RANKE'S History of the Popes, their Church and State, and especially of their Conflicts with Protestantism in the 16th and 17th centuries. Translated by E. Foster. 3 vols. 3s. 6d. each.

—— History of Servia and the Servian Revolution. With an Account of the Insurrection in Bosnia. Translated by Mrs. Kerr. 3s. 6d.

RECREATIONS in SHOOTING. By 'Craven.' With 62 Engravings on Wood after Harvey, and 9 Engravings on Steel, chiefly after A. Cooper, R.A. 5s.

RENNIE'S Insect Architecture. Revised and enlarged by Rev. J. G. Wood, M.A. With 186 Woodcut Illustrations. 5s.

REYNOLD'S (Sir J.) Literary Works. Edited by H. W. Beechy. 2 vols. 3s. 6d. each.

RICARDO on the Principles of Political Economy and Taxation. Edited by E. C. K. Gonner, M.A. 5s.

RICHTER (Jean Paul Friedrich). Levana, a Treatise on Education: together with the Autobiography (a Fragment), and a short Prefatory Memoir. 3s. 6d.

—— Flower, Fruit, and Thorn Pieces, or the Wedded Life, Death, and Marriage of Firmian Stanislaus Siebenkaes, Parish Advocate in the Parish of Kuhschnappel. Newly translated by Lt.-Col. Alex. Ewing. 3s. 6d.

ROGER DE HOVEDEN'S Annals of English History, comprising the History of England and of other Countries of Europe from A.D. 732 to A.D. 1201. Translated by H. T. Riley, M.A. 2 vols. 5s. each.

ROGER OF WENDOVER'S Flowers of History, comprising the History of England from the Descent of the Saxons to A.D. 1235, formerly ascribed to Matthew Paris. Translated by J. A. Giles, D.C.L. 2 vols. 5s. each.

ROME in the NINETEENTH CENTURY. Containing a complete Account of the Ruins of the Ancient City, the Remains of the Middle Ages, and the Monuments of Modern Times. By C. A. Eaton. With 34 Steel Engravings. 2 vols. 5s. each.

—— *See* BURN and DYER.

ROSCOE'S (W.) Life and Pontificate of Leo X. Final edition, revised by Thomas Roscoe. 2 vols. 3s. 6d. each.

—— Life of Lorenzo de' Medici, called 'the Magnificent.' With his poems, letters, &c. 10th Edition, revised, with Memoir of Roscoe by his Son. 3s. 6d.

RUSSIA. History of, from the earliest Period, compiled from the most authentic sources by Walter K. Kelly. With Portraits. 2 vols. 3s. 6d. each.

SALLUST, FLORUS, and VELLEIUS PATERCULUS. Translated by J. S. Watson, M.A. 5s.

SCHILLER'S Works. Translated by various hands. 7 vols. 3s. 6d. each :—

I.—History of the Thirty Years' War.

SCHILLER'S WORKS *continued.*

II.—History of the Revolt in the Netherlands, the Trials of Counts Egmont and Horn, the Siege of Antwerp, and the Disturbances in France preceding the Reign of Henry IV.

III.—Don Carlos, Mary Stuart, Maid of Orleans, Bride of Messina, together with the Use of the Chorus in Tragedy (a short Essay).

These Dramas are all translated in metre.

IV.—Robbers (with Schiller's original Preface), Fiesco, Love and Intrigue, Demetrius, Ghost Seer, Sport of Divinity.

The Dramas in this volume are translated into Prose.

V.—Poems.

VI.—Essays, Æstheticaland Philosophical

VII.—Wallenstein's Camp, Piccolomini and Death of Wallenstein, William Tell.

SCHILLER and GOETHE. Correspondence between, from A.D. 1794-1805. Translated by L. Dora Schmitz. 2 vols. 3s. 6d. each.

SCHLEGEL'S (F.) Lectures on the Philosophy of Life and the Philosophy of Language. Translated by the Rev. A. J. W. Morrison, M.A. 3s. 6d.

—— Lectures on the History of Literature, Ancient and Modern. Translated from the German. 3s.6d.

—— Lectures on the Philosophy of History. Translated by J. B. Robertson. 3s. 6d.

SCHLEGEL'S Lectures on Modern History, together with the Lectures entitled Cæsar and Alexander, and The Beginning of our History. Translated by L. Purcell and R. H. Whitetock. 3s. 6d.

—— Æsthetic and Miscellaneous Works. Translated by E. J. Millington. 3s. 6d.

SCHLEGEL (A. W.) Lectures on Dramatic Art and Literature. Translated by J. Black. Revised Edition, by the Rev. A. J. W. Morrison, M.A. 3s. 6d.

SCHOPENHAUER on the Fourfold Root of the Principle of Sufficient Reason, and On the Will in Nature. Translated by Madame Hillebrand. 5s.

—— Essays. Selected and Translated. With a Biographical Introduction and Sketch of his Philosophy, by E. Belfort Bax. 5s.

SCHOUW'S Earth, Plants, and Man. Translated by A. Henfrey. With coloured Map of the Geography of Plants. 5s.

SCHUMANN (Robert). His Life and Works, by August Reissmann. Translated by A. L. Alger. 3s. 6d.

—— Early Letters. Originally published by his Wife. Translated by May Herbert. With a Preface by Sir George Grove, D.C.L. 3s. 6d.

SENECA on Benefits. Newly translated by A. Stewart, M.A. 3s. 6d.

—— Minor Essays and On Clemency. Translated by A. Stewart, M.A. 5s.

SHAKESPEARE DOCUMENTS. Arranged by D. H. Lambert, B.A. 3s. 6d.

SHAKESPEARE'S Dramatic Art. The History and Character of Shakespeare's Plays. By Dr. Hermann Ulrici. Translated by L. Dora Schmitz. 2 vols. 3s. 6d. each.

SHAKESPEARE (William). A Literary Biography by Karl Elze, Ph.D., LL.D. Translated by L. Dora Schmitz. 5s.

SHARPE (S.) The History of Egypt, from the Earliest Times till the Conquest by the Arabs, A.D. 640. By Samuel Sharpe. 2 Maps and upwards of 400 Illustrative Woodcuts. 2 vols. 5s. each.

SHERIDAN'S Dramatic Works, Complete. With Life by G. G. S. 3s. 6d.

SISMONDI'S History of the Literature of the South of Europe. Translated by Thomas Roscoe. 2 vols. 3s. 6d. each.

SMITH'S Synonyms and Antonyms, or Kindred Words and their Opposites. Revised Edition. 5s.

—— Synonyms Discriminated A Dictionary of Synonymous Words in the English Language, showing the Accurate signification of words of similar meaning. Edited by the Rev. H. Percy Smith, M.A. 6s.

SMITH'S (Adam) The Wealth of Nations. Edited by E. Belfort Bax. 2 vols. 3s. 6d. each.

—— Theory of Moral Sentiments. With a Memoir of the Author by Dugald Stewart. 3s. 6d.

SMYTH'S (Professor) Lectures on Modern History. 2 vols. 3s. 6d. each.

SMYTH'S (Professor) Lectures on the French Revolution. 2 vols. 3s. 6d. each.

SMITH'S (Pye) Geology and Scripture. 2nd Edition. 5s.

SMOLLETT'S Adventures of Roderick Random. With short Memoir and Bibliography, and Cruikshank's Illustrations. 3s. 6d.

SMOLLETT'S Adventures of Peregrine Pickle. With Bibliography and Cruikshank's Illustrations. 2 vols. 3s. 6d. each.

—— The Expedition of Humphry Clinker. With Bibliography and Cruikshank's Illustrations. 3s. 6d.

SOCRATES (surnamed 'Scholasticus'). The Ecclesiastical History of (A.D. 305–445). Translated from the Greek. 5s.

SOPHOCLES, The Tragedies of. A New Prose Translation, with Memoir, Notes, &c., by E. P. Coleridge, M.A. 5s.

SOUTHEY'S Life of Nelson. With Portraits, Plans, and upwards of 50 Engravings on Steel and Wood. 5s.

—— Life of Wesley, and the Rise and Progress of Methodism. 5s.

—— Robert Southey. The Story of his Life written in his Letters. Edited by John Dennis. 3s. 6d.

SOZOMEN'S Ecclesiastical History. Translated from the Greek. Together with the ECCLESIASTICAL HISTORY OF PHILOSTORGIUS, as epitomised by Photius. Translated by Rev. E. Walford, M.A. 5s.

SPINOZA'S Chief Works. Translated, with Introduction, by R. H. M. Elwes. 2 vols. 5s. each.

STANLEY'S Classified Synopsis of the Principal Painters of the Dutch and Flemish Schools. By George Stanley. 5s.

STARLING'S (Miss) Noble Deeds of Women. With 14 Steel Engravings. 5s.

STAUNTON'S Chess-Player's Handbook. 5s.

—— Chess Praxis. A Supplement to the Chess-player's Handbook. 5s.

STAUNTON'S Chess - player's Companion. Comprising a Treatise on Odds, Collection of Match Games, and a Selection of Original Problems. 5s.

—— Chess Tournament of 1851. With Introduction and Notes. 5s.

STOCKHARDT'S Experimental Chemistry. Edited by C. W. Heaton, F.C.S. 5s.

STRABO'S Geography. Translated by W. Falconer, M.A., and H. C. Hamilton. 3 vols. 5s. each.

STRICKLAND'S (Agnes) Lives of the Queens of England, from the Norman Conquest. Revised Edition. With 6 Portraits. 6 vols. 5s. each.

—— Life of Mary Queen of Scots. 2 vols. 5s. each.

—— Lives of the Tudor and Stuart Princesses. With Portraits. 5s.

STUART and REVETT'S Antiquities of Athens, and other Monuments of Greece. With 71 Plates engraved on Steel, and numerous Woodcut Capitals. 5s.

SUETONIUS' Lives of the Twelve Cæsars and Lives of the Grammarians. Thomson's translation, revised by T. Forester. 5s.

SWIFT'S Prose Works. Edited by Temple Scott. With a Biographical Introduction by the Right Hon. W. E. H. Lecky, M.P. With Portraits and Facsimiles. 12 vols. 3s. 6d. each.
[*Vols. I.-X. ready.*

I.—A Tale of a Tub, The Battle of the Books, and other early works. Edited by Temple Scott. With a Biographical Introduction by W. E. H. Lecky.

II.—The Journal to Stella. Edited by Frederick Ryland, M.A. With 2 Portraits and Facsimile.

SWIFT'S PROSE WORKS *continued.*

III.& IV.—Writings on Religion and the Church.

V.—Historical and Political Tracts (English).

VI.—The Drapier's Letters. With facsimiles of Wood's Coinage, &c.

VII.—Historical and Political Tracts (Irish).

VIII.—Gulliver's Travels. Edited by G. R. Dennis. With Portrait and Maps.

IX.—Contributions to Periodicals.

X.—Historical Writings.

XI.—Literary Essays.
[*In preparation.*

XII.—Index and Bibliography.
[*In preparation.*

STOWE (Mrs. H. B.) Uncle Tom's Cabin. Illustrated. 3s. 6d.

TACITUS. The Works of. Literally translated. 2 vols. 5s. each.

TALES OF THE GENII. Translated from the Persian by Sir Charles Morell. Numerous Woodcuts and 12 Steel Engravings. 5s.

TASSO'S Jerusalem Delivered. Translated into English Spenserian Verse by J. H. Wiffen. With 8 Engravings on Steel and 24 Woodcuts by Thurston. 5s.

TAYLOR'S (Bishop Jeremy) Holy Living and Dying. 3s. 6d.

TEN BRINK.—*See* BRINK.

TERENCE and PHÆDRUS. Literally translated by H. T. Riley, M.A. To which is added, Smart's Metrical Version of Phædrus. 5s.

THEOCRITUS, BION, MOSCHUS, and TYRTÆUS. Literally translated by the Rev. J. Banks, M.A. To which are appended the Metrical Versions of Chapman. 5s.

THEODORET and **EVAGRIUS.** Histories of the Church from A.D. 332 to A.D. 427; and from A.D. 431 to A.D. 544. Translated. 5s.

THIERRY'S History of the Conquest of England by the Normans. Translated by William Hazlitt. 2 vols. 3s. 6d. each.

THUCYDIDES. The Peloponnesian War. Literally translated by the Rev. H. Dale. 2 vols 3s. 6d. each.
—— An Analysis and Summary of. By J. T. Wheeler. 5s.

THUDICHUM (J. L. W.) A Treatise on Wines. Illustrated. 5s.

URE'S (Dr. A.) Cotton Manufacture of Great Britain. Edited by P. L. Simmonds. 2 vols. 5s. each.
—— Philosophy of Manufactures. Edited by P. L. Simmonds. 7s. 6d.

VASARI'S Lives of the most Eminent Painters, Sculptors, and Architects. Translated by Mrs. J. Foster, with a Commentary by J. P. Richter, Ph.D. 6 vols. 3s. 6d. each.

VIRGIL. A Literal Prose Translation by A. Hamilton Bryce, LL.D. With Portrait. 3s. 6d.

VOLTAIRE'S Tales. Translated by R. B. Boswell. Containing Bebouc, Memnon, Candide, L'Ingénu, and other Tales. 3s. 6d.

WALTON'S Complete Angler. Edited by Edward Jesse. With Portrait and 203 Engravings on Wood and 26 Engravings on Steel. 5s.
—— Lives of Donne, Hooker, &c. New Edition revised by A. H. Bullen, with a Memoir of Izaak Walton by Wm. Dowling. With numerous Illustrations. 5s.

WELLINGTON, Life of. By 'An Old Soldier.' From the materials of Maxwell. With Index and 18 Steel Engravings. 5s.

WELLINGTON, Victories of. *See* MAXWELL.

WERNER'S Templars in Cyprus. Translated by E. A. M. Lewis. 3s. 6d.

WESTROPP (H. M.) A Handbook of Archæology, Egyptian, Greek, Etruscan, Roman. Illustrated. 5s.

WHITE'S Natural History of Selborne. With Notes by Sir William Jardine. Edited by Edward Jesse. With 40 Portraits and coloured Plates. 5s.

WHEATLEY'S A Rational Illustration of the Book of Common Prayer. 3s. 6d.

WHEELER'S Noted Names of Fiction, Dictionary of. 5s.

WIESELER'S Chronological Synopsis of the Four Gospels. Translated by the Rev. Canon Venables. 3s. 6d.

WILLIAM of MALMESBURY'S Chronicle of the Kings of England. Translated by the Rev. J. Sharpe. Edited by J. A. Giles, D.C.L. 5s.

XENOPHON'S Works. Translated by the Rev. J. S. Watson, M.A., and the Rev. H. Dale. In 3 vols. 5s. each.

YOUNG (Arthur). Travels in France during the years 1787, 1788, and 1789. Edited by M. Betham Edwards. 3s. 6d.
—— Tour in Ireland, with General Observations on the state of the country during the years 1776 – 79. Edited by A. W. Hutton. With Complete Bibliography by J. P. Anderson, and Map. 2 vols. 3s. 6d. each.

YULE-TIDE STORIES. A Collection of Scandinavian and North-German Popular Tales and Traditions. Edited by B. Thorpe. 5s.

www.ingramcontent.com/pod-product-compliance
Lightning Source LLC
Chambersburg PA
CBHW020940030726
47496CB00005B/1288